Knutsford
A Cheshire Market Town
c. 1650 -1750

Its Life and People

With a foreword by Dr Alan G. Crosby
Chairman of B.A.L.H.
Editor of the Local Historian

Pam Savage

With best wishes
Pam Savage

First Published 2003
by
Intec Publishing
Cheshire House
164 Main Road, Goostrey
Cheshire CW4 8JP

1st Impression

ISBN 1-899319-21-2

Typesetting and origination by Impressions Print & Design Ltd
Printed by Impressions Print & Design Ltd
Sandbach, Cheshire

Contents

Abbreviations used in references:

CRO   Cheshire Record Office, now CCLAS, Cheshire and Chester Archives
and Local Studies Service.

CCR   Chester City Records, now within the above CCLAS.

JRL   John Rylands Library, Manchester.

PRO   Public Records Office now TNA, The National Archive.

HSLC   Historical Society of Lancashire and Cheshire.

Trans. Hist. Soc. Lancs & Ches   Transactions of the Historical Society of
Lancashire and Cheshire.

Rec. Soc. Lancs & Ches   Record Society of Lancashire and
Cheshire

*Front Cover: Taken from one of the earliest illustrations of Knutsford,
c. 1846 from Adams Hill looking up King Street*

Acknowledgements

A special tribute and my sincere thanks are due to ANN J. KIRK co-originator of this work and research started in the 1970's. We gave then some talks to Local History Societies and wrote some articles on which much of this book is based. Her knowledge eased the understanding of several difficult problems and she has continued from a distance to give invaluable help and suggestions with the writing.

I could not have written this book on my own.

My thanks are due to many who have helped in different ways over the years. Firstly to the late J.Howard Hodson who introduced me to secretary hand and to the seventeenth century, and then to Dr. John H. Smith whose teaching brought that century to life for me. To Kath Goodchild and Joan Leach who have always been available to talk and share their knowledge, who have passed on documents and information, most of which has been used and included. They have read my first drafts and Joan has corrected me on several points and raised queries which I have tried to clarify. They have been generous with photographs and Joan has provided the cover picture and others. Marjorie Cox kindly read the section about schools and gave me constructive advice. For help with Latin translations often difficult to read, David and Sally Walker and Graham Walker. To the National Portrait Gallery for kind permission to print pictures of the Duke of Monmouth and Judge Jefferies. Alan Humphries of the Thackray Museum in Leeds for three photographs from their collection of the late Dr. John F. Wilkinson of Mobberley. Ruth McKew of the Northwich Salt Museum for the aerial view of Booths donated by Brian Curzon. The Warrington Museum for the pictures of James Swinton's trade tokens and the Revd. Canon David Ashworth for permission to print the certificate of burial in woollen found by Barbara Hartley who drew my attention to it. To Mair Strachan for permission to use two of the line drawings of the late Rev. W. R. Strachan. To Donald McLeod for allowing me to photograph the virginals at Tabley House and James Bell who gave helpful suggestions about the maps. To Jonathan Pepler, County Archivist, for permission to use so many and print some of the documents of the Cheshire Record Office, now the Cheshire and Chester Archives and Local Sudies Service and to the staff there, past and present who have been unfailingly helpful and patient. To Tricia Dearden, Olive Wakefield and all kind friends who have shown interest and given help for a long time.

To Dr. Alan Crosby for offering to read this, his subsequent encouragement and valued advice and for so kindly writing the generous foreword.

Finally to my son Martin and his wife Angela without whom this could not have been written, for their time, patient tuition and expertise with the PC and several rescue missions! And not least of all to my husband Harry who encouraged me to write this, little knowing how long it would take.

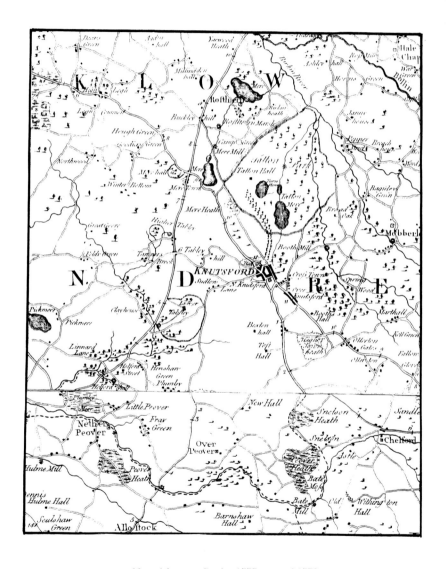

Map of the area - Burdett 1777 surveyed 1772

Foreword

The century after 1650 was a fascinating and exciting time in the history of communities in north-west England, as it was for the nation as a whole. There were, of course, many turbulent and dramatic political and military events. At the start of the period the king had just had his head cut off and England was a republic. During the following hundred years there was the Monmouth Rebellion of 1685, the Glorious Revolution of 1688, two Jacobite Risings in 1715 and 1745, a whole host of foreign wars and celebrated battles (we all remember Blenheim, even if few of us can these days place it in its proper historical context!), changes of dynasty and regime, and endless political upheavals in the high realms of state. Then there are the far-reaching developments in society and economy. The beginnings of industrialisation, the expansion of the empire and the colonies, the growth of towns, the creation of networks of turnpike roads and river navigation, the earliest use of steam, the development of colliery railways, the revolution in the financial world which brought cheques, banks, credit payments and the stock market... all played their vital part in changing the world and all impinged on the lives of ordinary people.

When we study individual communities in this period we cannot fail to be aware that people in 1650-1750 lived in a fast-changing world. Neither could they could fail to be aware of it. But at the same time established and traditional patterns of daily life went on seemingly unaltered by all that was happening. Country market towns continued their usual routines. Kings might lose their heads and wars might be fought and won, but there were still cabbages to sell, ribbons to buy, and shoes to be made. In her book on Knutsford from 1650 to 1750 Pam Savage shows us life in a particular country market town, one which is very special to residents, visitors, and historians alike. The study is the product of long and careful research into the original archive sources, looking at all aspects of how Knutsford fared during this crucial century. We see the innkeepers and their inns, the leading families, the church and chapel and the spiritual life of the community, the school, the market, the crafts and trades and the poor the downtrodden and the victims of plague and impoverishment. Pam has produced a fine account of a delightful place, one which all Knutsford residents will enjoy and appreciate and which will be widely read and equally widely used by others well beyond the town. This was a labour of love which grew from a small project into a full-scale study. Now it is published, and for many years to come Pam Savage's book will be essential reading for the citizens of what is still the most attractive country town in Cheshire.

Alan Crosby

To the memory of my father, Arthur John Gautrey, who shared his love of history and the joy of searching it out.

Chapter One
Knutsford's Origins

Life in Knutsford in the 17th century was still shaped in many ways by a charter drawn up 400 years earlier on its foundation.

The original Knutsford was already established before Doomsday, taking its name from a Danishman and his family who may have lived here earlier even than King Canute who reigned 1017-1035. In this part of Cheshire there is a string of Scandinavian place names quite close together, Rostherne, Knutsford and Toft in a line with a few more stretching southwards, the only others in Cheshire being a far larger group clustered on the Wirral. The 'ford' of Knutsford was more likely to have been across the Birkin to the east of the town on the boundary with Mobberley rather than the small brook which still runs through Knutsford.

In Doomsday, 1086, Knutsford in Bucklow (Bochelau) Hundred was half a hide paying tax, land for two ploughs, waste, and woodland half a league long and two acres wide value 10s. It was held by Egbrand a free man from William FitzNigel Baron of Halton who in turn held it from Hugh Lupus Earl of Chester.

200 years after Doomsday the population in the country had increased and there were many land-owning families well settled in this area descendants of the Doomsday land holders, one of whom William de Tabley, lord of the manor of Over Tabley also held Knutsford which by then had been divided into two manors, Knutsford Booths (later called Over Knutsford) and Knutsford which was a small settlement where Crosstown now is. Each of these hamlets had their own open fields and those for Knutsford covered the land lower down the hill and up the other side over the brook which is where Nether Knutsford the present town came to be built. The open fields were cultivated in strips.

The Charter of 3rd August 1292

King Edward 1st sold and granted a royal charter to William de Tabley, giving him the right to establish a 'new town' in Knutsford. He would give land to men who would call themselves burgesses and be free men with certain rights and duties attached to their burgage plots which was in contrast to the more normal arrangement where inhabitants of a manor were villeins working for the lord, being 'owned' by him, at his command and having his land. The burgesses would be 'chartered freemen', freeholders with unusual independence. De Tabley would benefit from regular rents, dues and tolls from a court, market and fair.

Charters similar to but differing in details from the one granted to Knutsford had already been granted to neighbouring towns, Stockport in

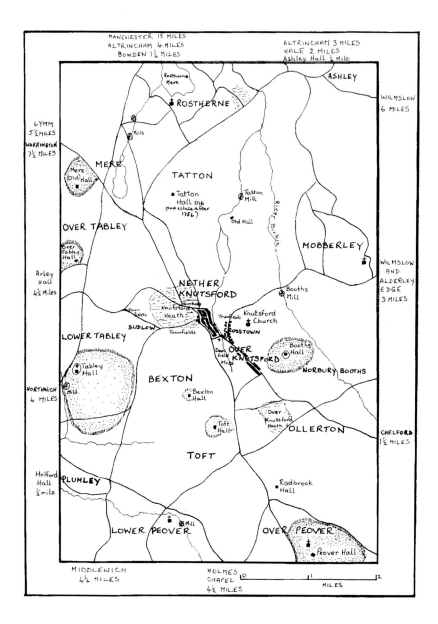

Knutsford Area c1700
Showing Churches, Chapels, mills and approximate local gentry estates

1260, Macclesfield in 1261, Congleton in 1272 and Altrincham in 1290. Knutsford's charter dated 3rd August 1292, contained the following main benefits and conditions for the burgesses, briefly:

38 burgage plots were allocated of 2½ selions or strips of open field to be held 'forever', to live on, mortgage, bequeath or sell, free pasture for cattle, acorns for pigs, wood for building and turf for fuel.

Their obligations were to grind their corn at the lord's mill, bake their bread in the lord's oven in the town and appear twice a year at the lord's court. A weekly market was to be held on Saturdays and a yearly three day fair at the end of June. A second three day fair at the end of October was granted in 1332.

De Tabley soon found that he was obliged to divide his holding with de Massey of Tatton, his feudal superior and in 1300 he sold the manor of Knutsford Booths (Over Knutsford), to John de Legh.

The new town of Knutsford grew up on its present site with burgage plots stretching back each side but fronting onto King Street, called Via Regia after King Edward 1st, the burgesses living by their crafts and trades. More land was cleared to make and cultivate new common fields and a bakehouse was built. The market was held weekly and the inhabitants were under the jurisdiction of the twice yearly manorial court.

The Leghs, living on a moated site in Norbury Booths, began to see the new town as a rival to trade in Over Knutsford and John de Legh obtained a grant in 1335 from the Black Prince, for a market in Over Knutsford on Wednesdays and a fair in Whit week of its own.

Knutsford's soil was similar to the rest of that on the Cheshire plain, clay which could be used for pasture or ploughed for crops, and heath land which gave Knutsford its large open heath, both fields and heath being pocketed by useful sandholes. The area of swampy moss land to the south provided the Knutsford burgesses with their peat turves for fuel. At some point an extra townfield must have been needed for growing numbers in Nether Knutsford and by agreement with the lord of Over Tabley, probably still the de Tableys, Sudlow Townfield was acquired for the town although this was beyond Knutsford's boundary.

The Parish and Church

At the time of the charter both Nether and Over Knutsford were in Rostherne Parish which covered a large area and included among others the townships of High Legh, Mere, Tatton, Tabley Superior as well as Knutsford and Over Peover. The parish church of Rostherne had been built before 1188 about four miles to the north of where the new town of Knutsford was to grow and with its development, Knutsford Chapelry was created out of Rostherne Parish and this comprised the townships of Nether Knutsford, Over Knutsford, Bexton, Toft and Ollerton. In 1313 a Parochial Chapel was built in the fields to the north of Over Knutsford to the east of Knutsford's market place from where a footpath was soon trodden to it. It was a timber building and came to be called Knutsford Church. In 1476 it was referred to in a document as the Church of St. Helena by which name it is still called by local people today even though the church has gone, the site is now level with just some of the seventeenth century gravestones marking its shape and site. All references to the church in that century call it Knutsford's Parochial Chapel but on maps today it is marked as St. John's. This Church was for the use of the parishioners of all the townships within Knutsford Chapelry and very much nearer than the Parish Church at Rostherne but even so was a tiring walk uphill from Nether Knutsford for the old and infirm and unpleasant for all from there in bad weather. In 1398 a Chapel of Ease, St.Mary's, was built in King Street, Nether Knutsford, almost opposite the present Parish Church grave yard.

Development of Knutsford

Knutsford was in a good position in Cheshire fairly central on the eastern plain, a convenient stopping off or resting place for travellers going north-south or east-west, ideal for trade, shops and inns and well centred between other market towns, Congleton, Macclesfield and Stockport to the south and east, and Altrincham and Manchester to the north. It was also on the salt ways from both Middlewich going northwards and nearby Northwich going eastwards. The needs of local people and landowners began to be catered for. The new town grew and was known as a town from the very beginning small though it was and named Nether Knutsford to distinguish it from the higher, Over Knutsford.

The 14th century brought bad harvests and the fearsome Black Death in 1349 when many of the people of Macclesfield are thought to have died and many newly founded towns and villages like Knutsford did not survive. Although Knutsford suffered losses it was able to recover.

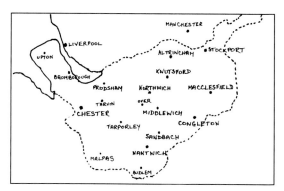

Cheshire market towns in the 17th century - Manchester and Liverpool Fig1.

The two townships, Nether and Over Knutsford grew side by side inevitably having many dealings with each other although each was responsible for its own local matters. For some reason Knutsford failed to develop municipal organisation like the neighbouring chartered towns of Macclesfield, Congleton and Stockport which could run their own affairs by an elected Mayor and corporation. Instead, both Knutsfords had their twice yearly court leet under the auspices of their lords of the manor and their stewards. Nether Knutsford soon grew larger than the earlier Over Knutsford but local memory lasts a long time and even as late as 1667, Over Knutsford was referred to by some as 'the old town'.

Crosstown is within Nether Knutsford township and the place name was in use at the end of the sixteenth century where there was a wayside preaching cross at the top of the hill by the side of the road leading to Mobberley, only the stump of which now survives in Crosstown churchyard. The Crosstown Field was still clearly laid out on the 1847 Tithe Map.

Among the earliest burgesses and settlers in Knutsford was one de Minshull, who may have had one of the open fields named after him, the Minshull town field, the reason for which is not now known. In 1382 and 1396 there was a Nicholas Minshull who was a chaplain to the Parochial Chapel who may have been related to the original inhabitant. By 1430, Minshull Lane had its name according to Peter Leycester, from John Minshull who sold his burgage to his ancestor in 1437, the back side of which ran alongside this lane.

Minshall Street formerly Minshall Lane

The Mill

De Tabley's Charter specified that the burgesses should grind their corn at 'my mill in Knutsford'. The place where this was built was stated as being in the moor of Cresswellcliff now called Sanctuary Moor to the south of

Knutsford, the mill powered by a stream which rises near there. This would seem to have been a rather hopeful venture but a mill dam was built to increase the water head and to give extra power which indeed seems to have worked for about a hundred years but went out of use some time before 1419 by which time it was referred to as, 'the mill between Knutsford Booths and Nether Knutsford' and no longer 'established' or 'suitable'. Failure to keep the waterway clear due to lack of manpower after the Black Death may have been a reason for this. The Dam Field, (mill dam), a town field, was marked on the Tithe Map a reminder of the old mill's existence but today even that reminder has gone for it is called the Dawn Field. There were two other fields near to it in those days, the Middlemost and the Uppermost Dam fields but both of these had gone by 1847.

The Legh's built a replacement mill on the River Birkin near to the road to Mobberley, within Nether Knutsford's boundary, where a mill was still in use into the nineteenth century. The Massey's had a corn mill at Tatton. Both of these were much further away from Nether Knutsford but a horse powered mill was in King Street on the western side towards the Tatton end in the seventeenth century owned by the Leycesters of Toft which could be used by those having no obligation as a tenant to grind at the lord's mill, there being owners and leaseholders of property other than those of the lords of the manor in the town by then.

The continuing predominating trades in Knutsford were in textiles and leather which were common throughout Cheshire and were to remain so into the 18th century. These trades had flourished here and some of the burgesses became prosperous, one of whom, de Oulgreve, sent his son Thomas to London probably initially to serve as an apprentice but he grew to make his fortune as a skinner, rising to become in 1467-8 Lord Mayor of London. When he died in 1473 he left some of his large fortune for a chantry priest to pray daily in Knutsford for two years for his soul and the souls of his parents. He is evidence of trade links with London at that time, working successfully there and still maintaining his Knutsford connections although others may well have gone before. More were to follow.

A large field in King Street now the site of the Parish Church was used as the Tenter Field, where clothworkers stretched their cloth on tenter hooks to weather and where linen and hemp yarn was laid to bleach. Likely to have been in use since medieval times, part of this Tentry Croft was acquired from the lord of the manor in 1741 for building Knutsford's Parish Church.

The Quarter Sessions

The Quarter Sessions began to be held once a year in Knutsford from 1574 in rotation with Chester, Nantwich, Middlewich or Northwich and sometimes Altrincham. This event brought many people to the town which in turn gave Knutsford the opportunity to provide facilities to meet their needs, in particular, inns of a variety to suit all types of customer, legal experts and scriveners, professional services, blacksmiths and many varied shops. There is no doubt that this annual event brought prestige and wealth to the town but Knutsford's position, potential and initial attractions influenced its choice and it was kept as now as a permanent venue for the court. Knutsford was chosen as the only other sessions town outside Chester from 1760, for Midsummer and Michaelmas, meeting in Chester at Epiphany and Easter.

Knutsford was the largest town in Bucklow Hundred which Court also met here frequently.

References:
* ORMEROD, G., *The History of the County Palatine and City of Chester,* 1882, Vol.1. pp.488-498.
* *Knutsford's Charter and references to the mill and fields: Keele University Library, and CRO DLT A25/1. BALLARD and TAIT, British Borough Charters, 1216-1307, 1923.*
* *Legh of Booths Charters Nos. 19 and 163, John Rylands new series 105,1943.*
* *Oulgreve: Cheshire Sheaf 1921, 4250 (PCC 8 Wattys).*
* *Tithe Map of Nether and Over Knutsford, 1848. CRO EDT 316/2.*
* *Old town of Kn., Poll Tax for N.Kn.1677 CRO DLT F/71.*
* *Minshull Lane CRO DLT 83 and Ormerod.*
* *Horse mill: Ormerod p.504.*
* *Place names: DODGSON J. McN. The Place Names of Cheshire, CUP. 1970.*
* *HODSON J.H. Cheshire 1660-1780, Cheshire Community Council 1978.*
* *Rabbit warren, Quarter Sessions Files, CRO QJF 100/3/62 and Legh of Booths Charters.*

Chapter Two
Knutsford in the Seventeenth Century

Nether Knutsford

By the middle of the seventeenth century, Nether Knutsford had grown into a flourishing and prosperous market town. An eye witness account of Knutsford written in 1621 by William Webb on his 'Itinerary of Bucklow Hundred', gives us a good introduction as to what it was like:

... a fine market and pleasantly situate. That where the market is kept is called Nether Knutsford and the other part of the town, situate higher, (which are separated by a brook which they call the Birkin) ... called the Higher Town...

And the nether town having also a chapel in it for divine service, and a town house where the justices and magistrates of the country keep their sessions and other meetings of that nature. The market greatly frequented and the town extraordinarily well traded, which I have been induced to think hath risen from this, that it is on every side beset and environed with gentlemen's houses, who by shortening their own journies to other markets have encouraged the tradesmen there to be furnished with all needful commodities.

Webb commented on the pleasant situation which is something which made it then as it still does today, attractive to residents and visitors alike, gently and more steeply sloping in parts down to the brook from the busy slightly winding main street with narrow passages off to each side. These passages delineate the original burgage plots, the divisions between the 'two and a half selions' of those first building plots.

Perhaps surprisingly, the town was set in open countryside and long uninterrupted views could then be seen to east and west. A description by Peter Leycester in February 1653 gives some idea of this. He was with some friends on the western side of the town on horseback:

upon the little playne or Common at the end of Toft Lane betweene Toft Lane and the little Lane comminge of Knotsford Heath, ... Comminge fromTofte about six of the Clocke in the Evening ... looking on our right hande wee saw Alderley Edge with the Beacon very perfectly and all the rest of the hills ... Turninge towards the left hande we saw Beeston Castle with the hills thereunto adioyninge very plainely.

Neither of these sights is visible today except possibly from the tower of the Parish Church which Henry Green saw and remarked upon in 1859. Alderley Beacon has been shrouded in trees now for over a century.

The location of the Town House where the Quarter Sessions were held which Webb mentions, is not now known. By 1727, 'the old Sessions House' in Knutsford had been converted into a chapel and was registered as a meeting place for Dissenters. A new Sessions House was built on the corner

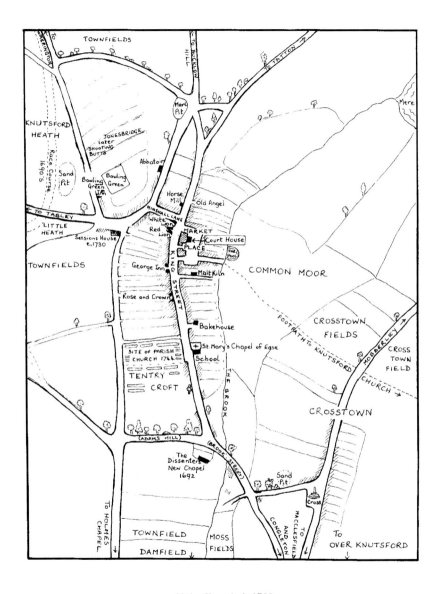

Nether Knutsford c1700

of Canute Square and Princess Street before 1730. This was in turn replaced by the present imposing Georgian building built in 1820.

Nether Knutsford's fairs were still being held in June and October. Fairs were attractive events to which many people were prepared to walk possibly fifteen miles in order to make major purchases or sales and they were an opportunity for shop keepers to replenish their stocks but as roads improved communications became slightly easier and the numbers of shops grew, so the need for fairs gradually diminished. Nevertheless the excitement of a fair's entertainments still held, when the town and inns became filled with people. The fair was also an opportunity for servants and labourers to find jobs, a hiring fair.

Knutsford was comparatively fortunate during the Civil Wars in that no battles were fought here and therefore it escaped battle damage but Northwich only six miles away was occupied by troops on both sides successively which left their mark there but very large numbers of soldiers were encamped on Knutsford Heath at least twice during the War. In 1644 Prince Rupert was here with 10,000 ill disciplined troops who pillaged the town and in 1651 Lambert brought 12,000 Roundhead soldiers here, of which 9,000 were cavalry. These men, often unpaid, and their horses were here in huge numbers.

Knutsford's heath was most useful to the military in times of war and unrest and in peace time the local Militia continued to do their training there. The large open space had for centuries been used for many purposes. It had been gradually encroached upon. In 1629, John Egerton Earl of Bridgwater leased four Cheshire acres 'lately intacked out of Knutsford Heath

The path from Knutsford Market Place to Crosstown and the Old Knutsford Church. 'The Pool' is on the left.

... between the intaken ground of Peter Daniel Esq. (of Over Tabley) on the north side and one Common Field called the Jonathan Bridgefield on the southern side', for three lives. Then as now, it was the venue for many gatherings. It was a place for public, political and religious meetings and debates and also ideal for festivities, fairs, celebrations and bonfires. After Charles 11 popularised horse racing, gentlemen came to race their horses upon it and a racecourse was laid out on the heath where frequent meetings were held, which by the eighteenth century had become such an attraction that stands were built for spectators. One part of the heath was where the cuckstool stood, probably near a pool or an old marl pit.

Webb was mistaken in thinking that the brook which separated Nether and Over Knutsford was called the Birkin. That is the larger stream on the boundary of Over Knutsford and Mobberley which powered the Legh's corn mill. The stream running along the bottom of Nether Knutsford did not have a name 300 years ago, the many references to it just called it 'the brook' which was constantly in need of 'scouring' to keep it flowing. It was referred to in an indenture in 1694 as the rivulet. Local people today call it the River Lily although as it is channelled you can almost step over it. The Moor alongside the brook was common pastureland leading up to the Crosstown Field. There was a pool there, used by the dyers.

The River Lily

Knutsford was still surrounded by its common fields, Crosstown Field, Minshull Townfield, the Moorhead (enclosed in1741), the Damfield Moor (also enclosed in 1741), the Mossfield and Sudlow Townfield which contained Alexanders Ground and the Kitling Field. Jonathan Bridgefield, Jonesbridge and Whitebridge seem to have been remnants of earlier townfields which had already been partly enclosed by the seventeenth century. The 'bridge' part of these names may have arisen from a confusion in times past between 'brych' meaning land cleared of trees, rather than a bridge, these names being another reminder of Knutsford's origins and that language has altered with time. By 1748, Jonesbridge of about an acre, had become the town's Shooting Butts situated on the town side of the present Manchester Road opposite the Heath. Knutsford freeholders were still collecting free peat for fuel from the Mossfield.

A way of fertilising the fields for centuries in Cheshire was to use marl, clay with a lime content. There are still old marl pits, square shaped ponds, in very many fields in the county today and there was one in the seventeenth century in Knutsford where the present Catholic Church now stands on the north west corner of the town but it is not clear whether this was still in use then or had long been a pit full of water and probably rubbish. New marl pits were being dug and marling was still the favoured method of increasing land fertility in Cheshire until the eighteenth century when manuring was used more.

There were many shops selling a great variety of goods representing many trades and crafts in Knutsford, commodities being brought in by mule trains and carts from places near and far which supplied not only basic needs but luxury goods such as fine cloth and silks, books, wine, tobacco and clocks, chemicals and raw materials for dying and tanning and drugs for the medical profession which by this time was well represented.

Over Knutsford

From 1546 the tithes from Rostherne parish went to Christ Church, Oxford but the collection of them was rented out by the early seventeenth century. A tithe barn still stood in Over Knutsford in private ownership in 1680.

Over Knutsford's Wednesday market was no longer in existence by the seventeenth century but its fair was still being held annually on Tuesday and Wednesday of Whit week, it was mentioned in 1700.

The Leghs had an established rabbit warren in Over Knutsford within their estate, supervised and kept securely fenced by a warrener. In 1672, a case was presented at Quarter Sessions about rabbits being killed there.

There was also racing on Over Knutsford's heath.

Population

Several sources give an indication of the population of Knutsford in the seventeenth century. In 1646 Knutsford was reported as having 'above 200 families' which, reckoning at 4.5 per family gives a number of 900 people in the whole of Knutsford chapelry.

In 1664, Charles 11's hearth tax gives sets of lists for Nether and Over Knutsford, for those who were charged on their hearths and for those who were exempt by poverty. Figure 1 illustrates this with 73 households taxed for Nether Knutsford and 63 households exempt, (the poor). In Over Knutsford, 35 were taxed, 23 not. Thus there were 194 households in both townships together which is a remarkably similar number to the 200 families quoted 20 years earlier although the whole chapelry included the extra townships of Toft, Ollerton and Bexton.

Both townships grew slightly in the next ten years when the 1674 lists give only the chargeable figures, Nether Knutsford grew from 73 to 92 taxable households, and Over Knutsford from 35 to 39. They also grew in prosperity judging from the greater number of hearths, see page 175.

The next helpful source is the 1667 Poll Tax taken between the times of two taxes above. It was supposed to name everyone rich and poor, in each township. Nether Knutsford named 340 persons in 126 households and Over Knutsford, c.100 persons in 32 households. Bexton listed 10 households, 45 persons; Toft, 30 households, 114 persons; Ollerton, 31 households, 112 persons illustrated in Figure 3. Thus for the whole chapelry there were 229 households, 711 people, still a similar size to the 1646 reference. With these figures the 4.5 multiplying factor used above for 1646 would seem to be generous, although exactly right for Bexton, but in Nether Knutsford there appear to have been forty three people living alone. However there is no guarantee that any of these lists are completely accurate, both Knutsfords have a few notable omissions in the lists. The Poll Tax is most valuable as a

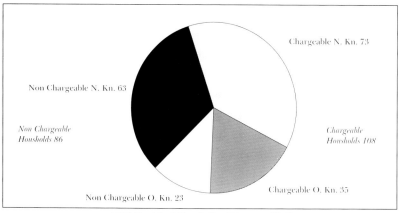

Chargeable N. Kn. 73

Non Chargeable N. Kn. 63

Non Chargeable Housholds 86

Chargeable Housholds 108

Non Chargeable O. Kn. 23

Chargeable O. Kn. 35

1664 Knutsford Hearth Tax Returns - Fig 2

guide nevertheless and will be referred to again. It gives a very good picture of the density of population. Nether Knutsford was the most populated urban area with the other more sparsely inhabited rural townships around it.

The Parish Registers give our next indication of numbers and also show the fluctuations here through the decades of the seventeenth and into the eighteenth century. The overall numbers do not appear to have increased greatly but they were affected from time to time by famine and disease which hit this area particularly badly in 1685/6. Hoskins suggests a way to estimate population is to take the average of 10 years of baptisms multiplied by 30. These are illustrated by the block chart Figure 4 and from it we might assume that Knutsford's population for the whole chapelry, was on average and with fluctuations about 1,000 during the period we are dealing with and before numbers rose in and after the middle eighteenth century.

So Knutsford, the name covering the whole chapelry, was by modern standards tiny, village like and yet it was already an 'ancient market town' serving the surrounding country. Most neighbouring market towns were larger at the end of the 17th century: Nantwich's population was 2,900, Macclesfield, 2,600, Congleton, 1,700, Stockport, 1,400 but Altrincham was no larger than Knutsford. Chester the county town, had a population of 7,500. (Figure 1. p4).

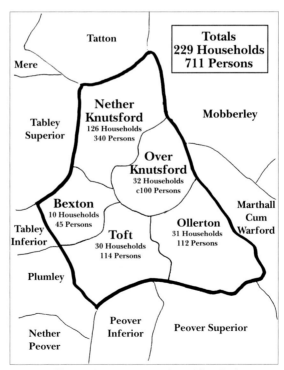

The Population of Knutsford in 1667 - Fig 3

In England country market towns of a size of between 500 to 2,000 inhabitants at this time were the most numerous of all types of town, there being more than 500 like them up and down the country, so in this respect Knutsford was typical.

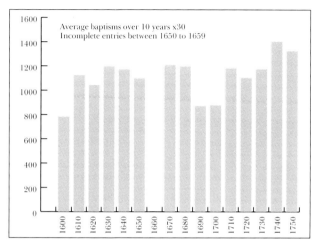

Knutsford Population Estimates 1600 - 1750 - Fig 4

The Gentry

This book set out to be mainly concerned with the ordinary people who lived and worked in Knutsford but before coming to them we need to be mindful of the neighbouring gentry because they were so influential, holding positions of power such as Justices of the Peace, were the major land and property owners who leased out their farms, land and houses, employed many local people, they patronised Knutsford's shops and used the professional services contributing greatly to the town's prosperity. Knutsford thrived on their money and it was the luxury facilities provided ostensibly for the gentry which gave the town its added character and prestige not only in the neighbourhood but in the county. We will see that the lives of the gentry affected life in Knutsford.

There were many ancient gentry families, 'Gentlemen', who lived all around Knutsford: the Leghs of Booths and High Legh, the Leycesters of Tabley and of Toft, the Mainwarings of Peover, the Cholmondleys of Holford Hall in Plumley, the Warburtons of Arley, the Daniels of Over Tabley, the Brooks of Mere and the Booths of Dunham Massey, and more such families within an easy ride of Knutsford. The Egertons of Tatton from the family of the Earls of Bridgewater, became resident in the eighteenth century. Some of these gentlemen had titles but for wealth none of these were in the same league as the rich Stanleys, Earls of Derby who owned vast estates in Lancashire and Cheshire and lived at Knowsley north of the Mersey. A branch of this family

Aerial view of old Booths Hall in August 1973. Trees have grown around the moat surrounding the Legh family's manor house. An archeological 'dig' was in progress and finds included two glass bottles of c. 1690, a child's shoe, a pair of scissors, an 18th century silver shoe buckle and a chamber pot also of that century.
Picture from the Salt Mueseum, Northwich

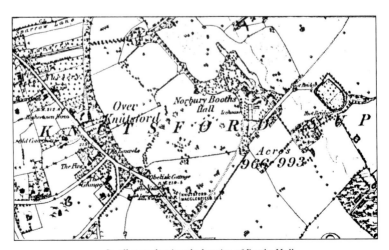

Small map showing the location of Booths Hall

lived at Alderley. The social order and one's place within it was a major part of life at that time and the wealth of even the minor gentry compared with that of the mass of ordinary people bore no comparison.

The gentry lived in large houses. In 1674 within Nether Knutsford the largest houses were three inns which each had eight hearths. There were ten houses which had four hearths, eight with three hearths and the rest had either two hearths, (24 of them), or one hearth, (43 of those) see p.175. In comparison, Sir Peter Leycester living in Tabley, had twenty two hearths. In Over Knutsford, Peter Legh of Norbury (or Knutsford) Booths had thirteen hearths, there was in that township one house with 5, one had 4, four with 2 hearths and thirty two with just 1 hearth. Some of these one hearth homes were the lowliest of cottages or even hovels. This shows the spread of wealth and poverty.

Larger houses needed more servants. Of 126 households in Nether Knutsford in 1667, thirty had servants, 23.8%. One household had five servants, two had three servants, ten had two servants and seventeen kept one servant. Sir Peter Leycester had twenty seven servants. In Over Knutsford the position is not very clear but apart from those in the home of the Leghs of Booths where their number of servants is not known, there were possibly eight servants employed within households in the whole township.

Gentlemen and their ladies were always easily, visibly distinguishable by their fine clothes, their velvets, silks, satins and laces and they were addressed with deference by those 'beneath' them. Local people readily recognised these gentlemen and their families by name whenever they came into Knutsford.

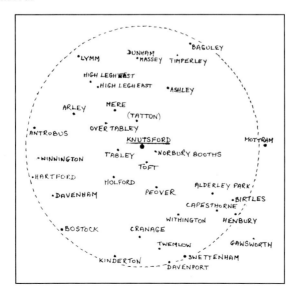

Gentry family seats within 8 miles of Knutsford in the 17th Century - Fig 5

The Lords of the Manor of Nether Knutsford, the Egertons of Tatton

The medieval de Tabley half of the manor of Nether Knutsford had been much divided but all was sold in 1590 to Richard Brereton of Tatton to whom it had come from the Masseys through marriage. On his death in 1598, he left this manor of Nether Knutsford, the manor of Tatton and many others in Cheshire to his brother-in-law Sir Thomas Egerton of Dodleston near Chester who had become Queen Elizabeth's Lord Chancellor in 1596 and was Chancellor, (Lord Keeper) to King James 1. He built a house at Little Gaddesdon in Hertfordshire which was convenient for London. On his death, his son was created Earl of Bridgewater, an hereditary title in his father's honour used by the family thereafter. The family and their descendants continued to live in Hertfordshire throughout the seventeenth century.

It was not until after 1706 that Nether Knutsford came to have a sole, nearby resident lord of the manor for the first time in its established history. This was when John Egerton (1679-1724), the third son, received the manors of Knutsford and of Tatton among others as part of his marriage settlement in 1706, and came to live in Tatton where he started to built a house on the site of the present Hall about 1715. He owned many houses and much land in Knutsford.

The Lords of the Manor of Over Knutsford, the Leghs of Booths

The family of the Leghs or Leighs of Norbury or Knutsford Booths, lords of the manor of Over Knutsford, had lived in a moated, timbered, quadrangular manor house not far from the present Booths Hall since about 1300. John Legh was Cheshire's High Sheriff from 1657 until his death in 1660 aged 59. He had married three times and had had a total of twenty two children in all but at his death only two sons and five daughters were living. His son Peter Legh by his third wife inherited the house and manor while he was still a boy. Peter Legh married in 1680 having come of age some time after 1671 and was to have just one surviving daughter and heiress, Ruth. We will here more of him. He died in 1716. The new and present Booths Hall was built in 1742.

The Leghs of Booths owned houses and the malt mill, kiln, in Nether Knutsford as well as land, houses, farms in Over Knutsford and nearby townships, leased to local inhabitants.

The Leycesters of Tabley

The Leycesters of Nether Tabley had lived adjacent to Knutsford since before the thirteenth century. Peter Leycester, 1613-1678, was Lord of the Manor of Nether Tabley. He lived on an island in a mere originally a moat, within his grounds. This is now a ruin since the new Tabley Hall was built in 1767.

Tabley Old Hall & Chapel

Peter Leycester had a particular interest in the town where he owned some houses. He had many dealings with Knutsford people, meeting friends and doing business in the inns, giving employment, buying household goods, food, drink and services through his steward and knowing rich and poor alike in his capacity of Justice of the Peace which brought him into Knutsford to the Court. He borrowed money at interest from some inhabitants, a seventeenth century form of banking service.

Sir Peter Leicester Bt   1613 - 1678
(The Cheshire Antiquary)

Peter Leycester, trained as a Barrister, had been a very active Royalist during the Civil War, unusual in this part of Cheshire which was mainly Parliamentary. He was Commissioner of Array recruiting troops for King Charles but was taken prisoner in Oxford in 1646, taken to the Tower of London and fined heavily but was eventually released although he had to stay in London for the two years which it took to find the money and it was during this time that he copied old charters and deeds which were in Gray's Inn and other libraries. When the fine was paid he was allowed back to Cheshire, shortly after which his father died and he inherited the Tabley estate.

His activities were curtailed during the Commonwealth and he was watched and arrested once more in 1655 when Royalist spies were found in his house. He had to give a bond for £2,000, 'not to act ... prejudicial to the Lord Protector', but was later re-arrested,  imprisoned in Chester and gave yet another bond for a further transgression. It was during this time that all estates of Royalists were taxed on one tenth of their value. Released but while somewhat housebound then, he studied and translated the charters and documents of Cheshire and Bucklow Hundred in particular, which he called his 'Historical Antiquities' published in 1673, which was incorporated in the nineteenth century within Ormerod's 'History of Cheshire'. This, with his many careful lists and writings, the documents he saved and his own and his steward's accounts continue to be vital information for anyone interested in Cheshire history, Bucklow Hundred and Knutsford in particular.

At the Restoration, Peter Leycester was rewarded for his loyalty to the Crown with a Knighthood, appointed a Justice of the Peace and Custos Rotulorum, in charge of the Bench of the Quarter Sessions in Cheshire and was a frequent visitor to Knutsford for one reason or another and knew many who lived here.

The **Leycesters of Toft**, a branch of this family of old, lived within the Knutsford chapelry at Toft Hall. In 1667 George Leycester lived there with his wife Dorothy, five children and eleven servants. He owned a horse mill in King Street and land and houses in Mobberley at this time.

Toft Hall

The Mainwarings of Peover

The Mainwarings of Peover and Baddiley were another ancient Cheshire family and like the others much inter married with local gentry and called each other 'cozen'. Sir Thomas Mainwaring, first cousin of Sir Peter Leycester, was at the Restoration living mainly at Baddiley near Nantwich but in the 1670's when his wife had died, he came to live mostly at Peover Hall four miles south of Knutsford, his children being then in their twenties. He kept a laconic factual diary which sheds some light onto Knutsford social life at the time. Thomas's father Philip had led troops in the Civil War on the Parliamentary side and his mother had been a devout Puritan.

Peover Hall, home of Sir Thomas Mainwaring

Sir Thomas entertained friends and family among county society from all sides and opinions both Whig and Tory, Nonconformist and High-Church. He died in 1688. His son was elected for Parliament in 1680 one of the only two Knights of the Shire, Members of Parliament, for the whole of the county of Cheshire, (there were also two others for the city of Chester), and again for Chester City later in the century. With members of parliament on their doorstep Knutsford people had a particular interest in politics.

Sir Thomas Mainwaring

Gentlemen living in Knutsford

Within Knutsford were several living at any one time who called themselves gentlemen but not many of these were of 'gentle birth'. A gentleman paid someone to do menial tasks for him and could put on the outward show of status and behaviour whether or not their wealth was recent or acquired, or even lost. We shall see that there were tradesmen, mercers, apothecaries and even a hatter and a tanner who amassed sufficient wealth to aspire to this status and live the lifestyle, some of these having as much or even more money than several of the local gentry.

Knutsford did not have town houses where gentlemen came to live as they did in Chester or even Nantwich and Stockport but some came to live here nevertheless, although at least one was in straightened circumstances in his declining years. The will and inventory of one such elderly gentleman demonstrates that not all gentry were living a life of luxury.

This gentleman was John Venables, previously of Rudheath in the Parish of Budworth, who died in Knutsford in 1684. The Venables of Kinderton family was an old and respected one with members still in the neighbourhood with right of presentment of Rostherne Church but John Venables seems to have had no immediate family and paid people to look after him. He was living sparingly. He was in a room in someone else's house for at his death he left only bedding and 'lumbardie', old furniture, valued at merely a pound and his apparel valued at £1.10s. was worth barely more than some of Knutsford's poorest inhabitants. He made his will in 1681 and possibly did not expect to live as long as three more years and therefore lived frugally, not an unknown trait in old age, in order to have enough money to fulfil all his bequests. He died with bonds and bills to the value of £300 so he could well have afforded some new possessions but this money was carefully apportioned to many recipients, several charitable bequests and for himself a gentleman's funeral. This consisted of a coach to take his body to Rostherne where he wished to be buried in linen two yards or more deep in the earth, the bells to be rung, the minister to preach a funeral sermon, 6d. apiece to be given to all the poor who attended, 50 shillings worth of gloves and ribbons to be distributed, the Minister, the coachman and the ringers to be rewarded for their pains and ale and bread to be provided for refreshment afterwards. He wished to depart with a genteel flourish.

Knutsford was an acceptable place for younger sons and cousins of gentry to come to live as we shall see, those who had to make their living by working and going into trade. One of these was John Legh who made his will in 1662, a relative of the Leghs of Norbury Booths who called himself 'mercer', a cloth merchant and selling ribbons and laces etc. He left bequests of some land leases to his nephew, son of John Legh Esq., and bequests also to another nephew Peter Legh, Clerk, of whom more later, and to other children of gentlemen. Like John Venables above, apart from family he remembered people and wives of friends in the town.

Tradesmen and others who came to acquire gentlemanly status could, as will also be seen within their lifetime lose their fortune with some even leaving their children paupers. Movement in the social scale in Knutsford as elsewhere was never static, some moving up and others moving down.

Property and Land

Because Knutsford was originally a green field site and founded by royal charter there was no copyhold and all property was held either freehold or leasehold.

Holding the freehold was then a form of investment at a time before there were banks. If the freeholder did not want to live in a house himself the owner could then lease out the property either for a term of years or more usually in Knutsford for several lives, the tenant choosing as at least one of the lives someone in the family young and healthy if possible. When one life died, the tenant had to pay a 'fine' in order to add another life.

Individuals bought freehold outright or as today by borrowing the money for a mortgage. A few documents name prices paid, but as the exact property was not described they can only give an indication of some of the Knutsford prices at the time. Henry Antrobus, Knutsford woollen draper and benefactor bought a kiln and barn in 1675 for £50, a house in Knutsford in 1684 for £100 and another in 1687 also for £100, all with mortgages. Similarly in 1679, James and Peter Swinton took over a mortgage from their brother Thomas, Clerk of Wallasey, on a house in Knutsford with eight lands in Sudlow townfield with a mortgage of £66. This money was raised and borrowed from three sources: £33 plus interest came from the charitable bequest of Henry Burgess, £20 was borrowed from Thomas Legh of Alderley, yeoman, and £18 was borrowed from William Ashton (the younger), butcher of Over Knutsford. A Knutsford tanner, Samuel Antrobus, of Over Knutsford, had owing to him on his death in 1684, a mortgage of £103 upon a tenement in Over Tabley.

Several of the leases mention land in a townfield, the two, particularly houses in Minshull Lane had land in Sudlow Townfield which still went together as they had for centuries.

The gentry of course were the principal landowners. In 1642, of the 52 dwellings then in King Street, the Earl of Bridgewater owned thirteen besides those unknown in other parts of the town. In 1671, Peter Legh owned sixteen houses and four cottages in Nether Knutsford besides others elsewhere. In 1656 and in 1671, Peter Leycester named ten different local gentlemen who owned freehold property in Knutsford. The surviving leases from the collections of the three nearest gentry have many similarities, the Leghs and the Egertons both required Knutsford tenants to perform 'suit and service' at their appropriate Manor Court and to grind corn and malt at their manorially held mills. Peter Wood's Leycester lease is quoted elsewhere and contains some requirements not found in the others such as raising trees and planting them in hedges. The annual rent was payable usually in two instalments, on St. John the Baptist's day midsummer and Martinmas, 11th November. These leases contain items which show how the lives of the tenants were bound with certain yearly obligations, the covenants, which

were expected of the tenant. Of the Legh leases, some were lengthy and the
higher the rent presumably for a larger property or acreage, the more the
covenants. For the late seventeenth century some of these sound feudal.

One of these is the lease of John Wainwright the elder of Ollerton,
husbandman, dated 1680. He had to pay a fine for surrendering his old
lease and adding the name of his two sons and his daughter besides those of
himself and his wife. His annual rent was to be 29s.4d. for a 'messuage and
burgage in Over Knutsford known as 'Clark's Tenements' and six closes of
land in Ollerton and Wade Lane, (no acreage mentioned). He was to keep
the property in good repair at his own cost, was not to sub-let, he had the
right to get and dig for marl and clay for manuring, composting or bettering
the land; had the right (obligation) to uproot briars, brambles, gorse, thorns
or underwood, and the right to take timber for repair, 'House Boot, Hedge
Boot, Fire Boot, Plough Boot and Cart Boot'.

There were no less than fifteen covenants. He was to do seven days
work of various sorts during the year for Peter Legh, shearing or ploughing,
harrowing, loading muck and working at Booths Mill, of which three of
these days were to be with an able labourer and three 'with an able and
sufficient team', or pay 13s.6d. He was to provide rent capons at Martinmas
or 2s.6d; a 'sufficient present' was to be brought to the Hall every Mucking
Day or 3s.4d. and bring a quarter of coals every year to the Hall at Booths
or 6s. He was to keep a hound or a hound's whelp and to yield the best
beast or other best goods at the death of every tenant or under tenant as a
heriot. He was to grind all his corn at the Booths Water Mill and his malt
at Legh's Malt Mill in Nether Knutsford 'that they shall use in baking and
brewing upon the premises'; to perform suit and service in the Court Baron
and Court Leet in Over Knutsford; to appear at the Fair in Over Knutsford
with a white coat and halbard at his own proper expense and charges and
wait upon the Steward, 'performing all such duties and services as shall be
required by him'; 'to provide a musket, sword and all other furniture, to
have and keep in readiness therewith to wait and attend upon Peter Legh
... in time of war if it happen that he be thereunto called', and finally he
was to be ready to serve Peter Legh in the office of Bailiff, all these, 'as all
other tenants do of the like yearly rent'.

John Wainwright signed his name competently. He needed to be a good
farmer to bring in an income sufficient to meet all these costs and demands
and to maintain his family. His household in 1667 consisted of himself, his
wife, four children and two servants one of whom John Storker, was probably
the 'able labourer'.

The terms of this lease and those like it were a medieval relic still in use
having remained the same for centuries and illustrate how life at this time
was in transition from the medieval to the modern.

The heriot always seems to be a heartless custom when tenants not only
faced the death of the head of the family but also had to part with their

best prized beast (or best goods), so they were doubly bereft. In 1686, the accounts of the Leycester household state, 'Received for a heriot at the decease of John Carter of Allostock a black mare valued at £6 but kept for Sir Francis for his own use'. Sir Francis was 12 years old at the time. The Egertons also required heriots.

Not all the tenants of the Leghs were farmers. Margaret Birtles, tanner's widow and her daughter of Nether Knutsford leased a house in Minshull Lane in Knutsford with lands in Sudlow Townfield for a lesser rent than John Wainwright, 15s., with fewer covenants to remember but one of these was also for her (or presumably a representative) to attend the Fair at Over Knutsford and attend the steward in a white coat and with a halbard, etc.

The Leghs used the leases as a convenient way of raising income at times of expected expenditure. In the 1640's, one of the covenants in William Legh's leases was for a year's rent at the time of marriage of one of his daughters and two generations later Peter Legh in 1677 required a year's rent, 10s, on the marriage of each of his daughters although he might only just have been married and was only to have just one surviving daughter. One lease with the same covenant was for another house in Minshull Lane for Charles Aldcroft yeoman, his wife and daughter. It was only a modest house with three rooms, the House, the Parlour and the Upper Chamber.

Some leasehold properties were lived in for generations by the same family. In 1678, Richard Aldcroft of Over Knutsford, shoemaker, surrendered a lease where there was yet one life in being which lease had been made by John Legh, great grandfather of Peter Legh dated 30th January, 1612. Richard Aldcroft renewed the lease with more lives, those of himself, his wife and his son.

Even the most hopeful of lives could die and sometimes there was no other family member to replace the last life of a lease. This and non payment of rent within ten or twelve days meant repossession as often stated in the deed. It is not known how often this happened but the Quarter Sessions reported two particularly unpleasant instances of this for non payment of rent.

In March, 1670, Ellen Grange of Nether Knutsford spinster, gave evidence that

on Friday last in the afternoon she being at the house of Thomas Alcock of N. Kn., who was then very sick and like to be dead there came to the house John Woolmer and Peter Antrobus the younger of Nether Knutsford. John Woolmer - took out a paper and arrested Thomas Alcock then sitting sick in his chair and said he must have ready money or plate or his body to prison. He was carried forth in his chair and set without in the wind and rain. John Woolmer and one Samuel Bartington of N.Knutsford went into the house and took possession and shut the door after them and then came forth and suffered the sick man (who was then almost starved), to be carried into his house again and went their ways. Samuel Bartington took the key of the house door with him and keeps it still. On Saturday they came again, and the door being shut and not opened at their request ... prized the door open. They went into the house again and John (Woolmer) continued there in the house till Monday morning the sick man Thomas being dead in the house the night before. John Bartington went away and left but (others) came in his room to keep possession.

Another said that the sick man was kept in the street, 'very neare an hour' and a further witness said that Bartington took possession of the house by ' bringing forth some clay in his hand and took some thatch in his hand from the evesing' before taking the key.

On another occasion in 1696, very early on a May morning, Peter Lowndes of Higher Knutsford, Bailiff and John Swann silkweaver, of the same town, came to Robert Taylor, butcher's house when he and his family were in bed and they came 'in a very rude and riotous manner' to his house in Over Knutsford, and broke down the door.

Peter Lowndes immediately came into the house with a drawn sword in his hand and swore 'damme him if he ... would not deliver them possession of his house, he would have his blood, or words to this effect'. (One of the constables of Higher Knutsford) said that about one or two o'clock on Sunday morning last as near as he could guess the time being then in bed, Robert Taylor came to his house and desired him to come and assist him telling him what had happened and that his life had been threatened. (The constable) got up and they immediately went to Robert Taylor's house where they found the door locked again and Taylor's wife and children in bed as they believed. Taylor desired the constable to go to Peter Lowndes' and ask him for the key of his house door. Lowndes told him that the key was in the entry belonging to his house but on looking they could not find it but Lowndes then gave them the key out of his own house and (followed them into) the street with a drawn sword in his hand.

These violent scenes show how little protection tenants had. Most Knutsford people would be mindful of their leases to a greater or lesser extent throughout the year for the ability to pay the rent and fulfil their covenant obligations was vital for the roof over their head, their home and their livelihood.

It is not surprising that those who could afford to used property ownership as an investment by letting or sub-letting.

William Ashton was a successful butcher of Over Knutsford whose goods totalled over £600 at his death in 1686. He had four houses, two freehold and two leased. One he had erected himself, another had freehold lands in Over Knutsford and two were leased from local gentry. One of these which he leased from Peter Legh Esq., with the shop and stable was where he lived. He had bought parcels of land from Thomas Swinton, clerk, near Boothsmills in Nether Knutsford and more from Peter Antrobus, gent. of Nether Knutsford, 'which said parcels of land are now joined into one messuage and tenement and upon the same I have erected a dwelling

house and outbuildings' from which he expected to raise £20 p.a. on the
lease and profits of it. When his son William Ashton died in 1694, these
properties were mentioned again and one which had only one life left in
being, was later valued in his inventory, a rare occurrence, at £32, and the
Over Knutsford property with 'three lives yet in being which - lease value
of fifty shillings' was valued on his death at £25. Few freehold properties,
strangely, were valued to be included in an estate although some mortgages
were included. Some had terms on a property valued as, 'for a term of 11
years' or for so many lives.

Joseph Harrison hatter, died 1703, had six shops in Knutsford, a house
and land in Cranage, more houses in Allostock and Knutsford, the Chapel
Croft and ground in Sudlow.

John Swinton grocer, ironmonger and gentleman of Knutsford, died 1684,
owned property at Radbrook (the Hall) and also in Withington, Ollerton
and Pickmere, he leased three houses in Nether Knutsford including the
property he lived in which was owned by Peter Legh, three leased in Over
Knutsford, he held land in Pickmere and terms of 8 years in Sudlow tithes, 2
years in 'Bowers intack', one term in Warburton's shop and one in Antrobus'
warehouse. A man of property.

With the eighteenth century came the first signs of improvement in
standards of living for some.

Margaret Furness 1718, the benefactress, had five adjoining houses on
King Street which can still be identified, two were lately built by her late
brother Henry Antrobus, one with a shop and at the back, a yard, a barn,
garden, orchard, fuel house, a pump and a House of Ease. Two of these
houses were leased from Mr. Legh of High Leigh. She held land on or near
Knutsford Heath and a barn, and a house and land in Toft leased from Mr.
Leicester of Toft. Having her own House of Ease and access to her own
pump were rare luxuries then. Living opposite to her in a newly built 1701
very large house, John Bostock, gent. of Knutsford, only had 'liberty to the
pump' of the house south of the one in which he lived. He also owned
several properties in Congleton and Mobberley and lands in Davenham
and Leftwich.

There were also land or property owners who were lesser yeomen and
husbandmen. In 1662, Richard Brownfield, plasterer, left two houses and
two shops including the one in which he lived and land in the Damfields,
leased for a term of 16 years. In the same year John Stubbs blacksmith, had
already given four cottages with their sitting tenants to his daughter for her
natural life before he died.

In 1680, Thomas Gallimore, husbandman, had a cottage or tenement in
Knutsford lately purchased from Joseph Hobson with all edifices, buildings,
yards, orchards, backsides and one land belonging to the same.

In 1684, Richard Aldcroft, shoemaker, the same who renewed the lease
of 1612 with Peter Legh, had lands lately purchased from Mr. Swettenham

being two closes in Over Knutsford, 'free and clear without any manner of charge'. In 1685, all John Gandy's worldly goods were valued at only £13. 6s, in which was included as assets: 'for crops on two crofts in the bigger town of Knutsford, £4, and rent of two crofts called the Leprous crofts, £1.10s.'.

The new brick buildings with slate roofs in Knutsford built towards the end of the seventeenth century and into the eighteenth, replacing timber and thatch, were beginning to change the appearance of the town, many of which still remain but timber framed properties were still being built like The Rose and Crown, rebuilt again in the early twentieth century, The White Lion, which still stands and possibly the building of The White Bear, as well as some cottages.

Having mentioned property costs and prices, only those with property worth 40s. a year or more were entitled to vote. In 1714, 42 men from Knutsford recorded their vote at the parliamentary election.

References:
- *Peter Leycester's description of Kn. 1653 Chester City Recs (now CRO) ZCR 60/26/32*
- *Tithes: Manchester Central Library, Letters & Papers of Henry VIII 1546 p333 648 no.25, and Ormerod.*
- *GREEN, Henry, Knutsford its Traditions and History, Smith Elder & Co., 1859 p.11.*
- *Heath Indenture CRO DET 154.*
- *O.Kn.'s Tithebarn: Inv. Dr. Bentley of Northwich CRO WS 1691.*
- *Market tolls: JRL Egerton Papers 2/2/12 (1727, June & Oct).*
- *Population: Plundered Ministers A/cs, Trans. Hist. Soc. Lancs. & Ches. 1886, Harl. Ms. 2074. Plundered Minister's A/cs. Rec. Soc. Lancs. & Ches. Vol.28 Pt.1 p.173 1647. Poll Tax, (see above). Hearth Tax returns, PRO E197/86/155, RP/1337 and E179/86/145, RP/1337.*
- *Knutsford St. John's Parish registers CRO p7.*
- *Ormerod Vol. 1. 1882 for inf. for Legh of Booths, Egerton, Leycester and Mainwaring.*
- *GAUTREY, A.J., Sir Peter Leycester of Tabley, Journal Knutsford Hist. and Arch. Asscn., Autumn 1979.*
- *Diary of Sir Thomas Mainwaring, CRO. DDX 384/2. DORE R. N., Cheshire, B.T. Batsford 1977.*
- *Wills of J. Venables, 1684 and J. Legh, 1662, WS at CRO. Over Knutsford fair 1700 CRO QJF 128/2/50*

Property and Land
- *Houses in King Street, list of owners: 1642 Randle Holmes Collection, Harl. Mss. 2137 no.2 p527 CRO Mf20*
- *Freeholders in Knutsford in 1656 and 1671, Tabley Papers CRO DLT B27. Legh of Booths Charters, Keele University. Manchester Local History Archives, Leases. Egerton of Tatton Records, CRO DET.*
- *Wills and Inventories, CRO WS or WI*
- *John Wainwright's family, Poll Tax. Ellen Grange 1670 CRO QJF 99/1/87*
- *Peter Lowndes 1696 CRO QJF 124/2/11. Voters, 1714 CRO QDV 1/-2*

Chaper Three
The Manor Court

Nether Knutsford and Over Knutsford each held their own Manor Court or Court Leet which were in effect the town councils dealing with every aspect of the townships' daily affairs. Freeholders of the manor formed the 'jury of the grand inquest', and the lords' tenants were required to attend the court to perform 'suit and service', one of the first conditions of a lease of land and /or property.

The Leghs' Over Knutsford court was held in the court building in Chelford Road which still stands, now a private house but no records for this have been found. The Egerton's Nether Knutsford court was held in the Court House in Knutsford Market Place which building remained until 1740 when it had became ruinous. The Courthouse which replaced it stood until the 1970's when it was demolished, a block of flats being built in its place.

The Court House in the Market Place built 1740 - the right hand building
The square window, barred, was the lock-up

Nether Knutsford

Despite various changes and divisions of the lordship of the manor of Nether Knutsford over the centuries, the Court in the 17th century was being held regularly twice a year in April and October 'as of old' and opened each time with some ceremony with halberds. The town was in effect running itself, the Egerton's steward coming from time to time to collect monies and tolls due on a regular basis. The presence of a steward representing the lord was noted for the first time since 1643, once in October 1676 and

then from October 1696 when the Rt. Hon. John Egerton the prospective
heir of the lordship was 20 years old, and at each meeting of the 'Court
Leet and Court Baron' thereafter. The entry of October 1696 says, 'by and
with the consent of the Steward of this Leet', and 'consented unto in Court
by Thomas Hunt, Steward', he made sure his presence and position of
authority was recorded. We can almost hear them standing to attention but
the records of the Court proceedings continued exactly as they had done
since 1643 except for some missing and sketchy years during the Civil War
and Commonwealth period.

The business of the court covered many diverse things: the daily and
seasonal running of the town and its common fields, the upkeep of pavements,
clearance of ditches, the fabric and running of the school and the bakehouse,
the pinfold, the organisation of the market, the town's finances and anything
which impinged upon the well being of the town. To oversee all these things
and to uphold the town's by-laws, the town's officials, its many 'lookers',
were elected each year.

The Jury was first elected of named freeholders, between eleven and
fifteen of them, the town's 'principal inhabitants'. In 1701, 3rd October, of
the thirteen elected, four called themselves gentlemen. They were to hear
any contraventions of the by-laws and impose fines appropriately and were
also responsible for the finances of the town which business could have been
very time consuming throughout the year. All those who owed appearance
at court and had not come were, on this 1701 date, each fined 12d. apiece.
This was roughly the amount a labourer could earn in a day. Presentments
were made of three women and fourteen men for various faults: breach
of assize of bread, selling butter in the market being short of weight, for
suffering a horse to go in the common moor and such like.

The officers of the year were appointed with a job for most of the able
bodied men. In 1701, two men were appointed for each of these positions:
Constable, Chapel Reeve and well looker (these two combined) and two
lookers each for the Townfield, for Crosstown, overseers for Jonesbridge
and Whitebridge, market lookers for flesh, market lookers for weights and
measures and bread, pavement lookers, ale tasters, bakehouse lookers,
Damfield Moor lookers, Moss lookers, barleymen and afferators. Three
men were appointed market lookers for green hydes, searchers and sealers of
leather and three common moor lookers. There was one market looker for
swine but four fire lookers and four assessors. All these jobs were of course,
unpaid. With the jurors, some of whom held one of these posts there were
50-60 of these positions for Knutsford men to be involved with running the
town, some of the lookers needing to be vigilant just once a week on market
day but others needed nearly every day. They were elected yearly and while
some were rotated others required special knowledge of the trade such as
those dealing with leather and possibly the ale tasters and here the choice
was limited. All positions would be undertaken with varying degrees of

enthusiasm but however well carried out, belonging and working together bonded them, for people from other towns near or far were 'forreners'.

Some of these positions covered a variety of responsibilities. The pinfold for stray animals came to the court's attention in 1643, the constables being required to, 'appoint someone to look to the pinfold and to be ready to keep the key in lieu of receiving from every Townsman a half penny and from every forrener, one penny for every several trespass'. In 1681, the constables were to raise the height of the pinfold. Some places charged four times as much where pigs were involved as they were notoriously difficult to control or catch and loose pigs were and had been for centuries, a menace particularly on market days. 'Those whose swine soever shall any market day hereafter breake any man's sac of corne to the spilling of his corne, that for each such defect the damage shall be by the owner of the swine 6d. for the benefit of the town' (1643). Despite these by-laws and increasingly high fines for trespass of them, pigs continued to cause problems for centuries although there was only one market looker for swine in 1701, not an enviable job.

The offences of causing an affray and assault and that of selling bad meat (for which the fines were 3s. 4d.) were considered the most serious cases. Presentments were made to the jurors by the two 'market lookers for flesh' who were ordered in future to, 'burn what flesh they find not marketable' and the lookers would be fined 'upon every neglect thereof'.

Fifty years earlier it had been agreed that, 'no butcher within the manor of Nether Knutsford or others shall empty any beasts, cows, sheep, veal's bellies and cast them in any part of the streets or market place of Knutsford upon pain of 5s.' In 1661, 'no person shall dress any calves tandril or beasts entrails at the Town Well, but only by that one stock which stands near to John Long's ditch'. At this same court, 'any person that put into the well any fowle, dirty or unsweet paile, piggin bowl or other vessel, forfeit 6d.' In 1674, 'no person to bring or lead down any horse, cow or other beast to the Town Well there to water them nor at the hole near the well commonly called the Little Well, 4s. to the lord of the manor'. In 1696, 'Upon complaint by several inhabitants that are concerned with the water that runs under the town, it is this day ordered that some of those that slop the water for the concern of their trade, shall not do so to the prejudice of those that receive it below'.

There is no mention of where beasts were slaughtered. An abattoir was built in Tatton Street towards the end of the century which hopefully saved the well from some contamination but this is not mentioned in the Court records. The City of Chester however in 1671 decreed that butchers should not slaughter at their shops but at their slaughter houses, certainly some years ahead of Knutsford.

The pavement lookers also had a thankless task. As early as 1643, they were charged to 'Look that the pavement shall be kept whole at all times and made clean and the dust thereof carried away' every fortnight in the

The Slaughter House in Tatton Street now demolished

winter and every week in the summer, 'by whom they belong unto'. It is
very unlikely that this could have been enforced especially as the entries
concerning pavements continue regularly right up to 1827, the end of
this Court book. Before drains, running water ran in runnels and ditches
around the town, across the footpaths along the street, you would certainly
watch your steps at the best of times but blockages and rubbish caused extra
constant problems. Old inhabitants were asked what they could remember
of ancient water courses to give them precedents and orders were given to
build 'platts', bridges and constantly to scour ditches but the rubbish heaps,
'midingsteads', middens and dung heaps continued to accumulate on the
pavements and in the streets despite persistent offenders being charged to
remove them throughout the years. Horses and mule trains through the
streets constantly left their traces.

Many of the court orders give us an all too vivid picture of what had been
going on unquestioned for centuries. In 1703, W. Woolmer a pavement
looker, was to 'dillygently observe any person or persons above the age of 6
years that shall ease himselfe of his excrements within the compass of the
Shambles', (where meat was sold below the George Inn on King Street). They
were to be fined 1s. half to the Lord of the Manor and half to the informant.
An incentive was required for this. By inference, we note this practice was
quite acceptable for all age groups in all other parts of town.

Pavements and streets were a problem everywhere. In 1686 in Chester
after yet another order that no person was to cast dust or ashes into the
street, (a euphemism, in Knutsford by then they were calling it 'muck and
manure'), they decided to engage two scavengers to take away dirt in a cart
and clean the streets at least twice a week for which service the inhabitants

were to pay. This might have helped but in little Knutsford there was no such solution and even in the 19th.century Mrs.Gaskell ensured that her Cranford ladies were wearing pattens to raise them above the mire.

Another unpleasant hazard in the streets all the year round was winnowing, with chaff blowing in the wind into one's eyes. We would not think of this happening within a town but rural practices like this were common in Knutsford until 1737 when the court decreed that, 'No person shall for the future winnow any corn in any of the streets or public highways within the town of Nether Knutsford on pain of 3s.4d. each offence'.

Venturing out at night must have been difficult except in moonlight for even with 'lanthorns', the light was feeble and Knutsford court did not suggest improvements until as late as 1810, when, 'It is ordered that a Town's meeting be called (in November) to take into consideration the expediency of lighting the town with lamps'.

After Saturday market days the mess underfoot must have been a great deal worse. In 1689, 'such person and persons as doe receive toll for stallidge in Nether Knutsford shall from time to time cleanse such parts of the pavement as are dirted by reason of the said standings'.

Market days were always busy with people thronging the streets from the country around. They even had parking problems as early as 1657: 'Noe market folk shall tye up their horses upon market day under the Court House upon pain of 6d. apeece'.

The market tolls of the Saturday market were being leased out by the absent lord of the manor in 1622 if not before, in a somewhat similar manner to a house or land lease. At that time the rent was 20s. a year for 99 years with a best beast for heriot, two days reaping and to give to the Earl of Bridgewater an account yearly on the profits and not to exact any unjust tolls. In 1626 this seems to have been forgotten and their value was negligible for they were leased to a linen draper in Salford for 10 years for a peppercorn rent but by 1646 their value had increased to £10 p.a. when they were leased to another Salford linen draper for 10 years.

The types, places and times of the markets were specified and modified by the court, as follows:

YARNE MARKET (HALL)   Lady Day to Michaelmas.

1653   Bell to be rung at 7am. in summer, 9am. in winter.
1657   No bell to be rung but all people to have liberty to sell as they come to market.

CORN MARKET

1657   Bell to be rung at 1pm.
1672   Bell to be rung at 1pm. in winter 25th March 29th.September.
                     2pm. in summer (Lady Day to Michaelmas)
1693   (the same again)

LEATHER ("LEDDER") MARKET

1661   To be kept in the old accustomed place, i.e. in the open street
        near the Cross. (In Crosstown)

THE SHAMBLES

1703   Mentioned as where butcher's meat was sold, in the Lower
        Street leading from the George Inn.

SWINE MARKET

1764   Shall be kept in that part of the Market Street between the
        Bakehouse and Edward Fairbrother's gate stump and the
        South East corner of the Court House.

Knutsford market was traditionally opened and closed by the bell as it was in Stockport and other places. This was performed by the **Bellman** a familiar figure and character of the time. This ancient office sometimes called the Crier or later the Town Crier, belonged for some years to John Hunt of Crosstown until he died in 1687. He lived in a small basic cottage with one or at the most two rooms, with probably an earth floor with a hearth, untaxed, so it was worth less than 20s. a year, with his wife Jane and family. She bore him 7 children of which 5 died. The Bellman carried a bell, a staff and at night a lantern, for his job was very varied, being town crier, a night watchman at times, ringing the bell on time for markets and courts, collecting and being allowed to keep some manor court fines and keeping an eye open for vagrants and any untoward happenings. The Leycester family paid the Bellman 4d on court days, 'for warning the Court'.

One memorable day for him was when he was called before Sir Peter Leycester and Sir Peter Brook at the great house in Mere in June, 1662, to give a statement about a poor Knutsford woman of rather dubious character. He said that,

'On Wednesday in Whitsun week last between the hours of six and seven of the clock in the evening, I saw Margaret Meares and one Nathaniel Lloyd's son being a fiddler, going into a field of Peter Antrobus being about 2 roods from the highway, and were together on a hedge back and going to see what they were doing and coming near them, Margaret Meares slipped away and the said fiddler also tyed up his breeches, took up his fiddle which lay on the hedge back and put it under his cloak and went away'... - .

The City Treasurers in Chester in 1686, were ordered to buy a coat and a badge for their Common Bellman but no such item is in the Knutsford Court book. William Woolmer was Bellman or Under Bailiff in 1695. He was market looker for swine in 1701.

The common moor was of importance either for hay or for grazing sheep and geese as other animals were excluded specifically in 1703, and the inhabitants urged again to keep the trenches and gutters well scoured so that it drained better. In 1676 the Moor Lookers complained that Ellen Shaw of The Cock had forcibly broken open the common moor gate so that she might 'fetch and deliver cattle at her pleasure to and from the Cock Meadow contrary to custom to the great prejudice of a way both to the Church and market with several other inconveniences'. Upon consideration of this, the jury ordered 'that neither the said Ellen Shaw or any other person occupying the said close shall have admittance as aforesaid'.

A few Manor Court entries refer to the common fields and common moor but give few hints of agricultural practices. In 1717 no one was to tether horses or cows in Crosstown field in the night time until all the corn was carried out and in 1719, the Townfield Lookers for Crosstown field, Jonesbridge and Whitebridge were to make sure that no cattle or swine were let loose in the townfields after the winter corn had been sown.

The Court also had jurisdiction over the waste land and the cottages built upon it.

The Town's Money

The town's money was a considerable responsibility. It came from two sources, rates and charitable bequests.

Any one entering into the porch of Knutsford's Parish Church today will immediately be struck by the five huge boards on the walls with lists of names and details of those who left money for charitable purposes in their wills. The money was left either for the poor, for the school or for the use of a preaching minister.

One of the charity boards in the porch of Knutsford Parish Church

The seventeenth century was notable for people's benevolence and in Knutsford this certainly applied, their charity filling a great need and lack of 'official' funds. Church boards proclaim similar lists up and down the country in town and village alike and Knutsford's lists are unusually long but even so incomplete.

The money from charities became the responsibility of the Jury of the Manor Court, the freeholders. From 1697 a body of about eleven men were appointed annually 'to receive all officers' accounts and to manage affairs of the town'. It is not sure how this came about in Knutsford for traditionally looking after charities especially, belonged to the Vestry. Possibly the onerous nature of administering the charities was more than the Vestry could undertake and the task was better shared by the larger Jury, after all the inhabitants were the same and they all took on these jobs of Vestry and Manor in rotation. Overseers of the Poor and Constables were elected for each township, Over and Nether Knutsford etc., each having their own. It was traditional for Vestry records to be kept in the Parish Chest within the Parish Church but in Knutsford there was the problem that the Parish Church was in Rostherne about four miles away and the Parochial Chapel was not centrally situated especially for Nether Knutsford inhabitants. In St. Mary's Chapel of Ease on King Street space may have been at a premium.

Wherever it had been kept before and however it came about, by mutual agreement the Nether Knutsford Town Chest came to the Court House in the sloping Market Place in October 1665 and two locks were put upon it, one for the Constables and one for one of the trustees of the charities. The Parish Registers were traditionally kept in the Parish Chest.

Knutsford's Town, Parish Chest

Trustees, feoffees, were appointed yearly from the Jury to be responsible for the charities; they were to lend the money at interest, collect the interest in due course and eventually reclaim the capital to lend to someone else. Dated bonds were drawn up between the parties concerned and a copy of these as well as the list of the donors and their bequests were kept in the chest. Bonds were inspected annually by members of the Jury. In 1720 something very serious must have occurred for, for reasons now unknown, the Squires themselves of both Tatton and Over Knutsford, The Hon. John Egerton Esq. and Richard Leigh Esq. were just for that year, the first named on the list of the eleven men managing the affairs of the town, a most irregular and unusual occurrence.

Mr. William Mann's Bequest

One of the charities had unusual terms of administration and occupied a great deal of their time. It came from an Elizabethan benefactor, Mr. William Mann of London who came originally from Northwich and was 'one of the servants of the Queene's Majestie's Chamber' of Queen Elizabeth. How he came to this position and what his connections were with Knutsford, we do not yet know. His deed of 1573 left £100 to be lent without interest, to 'young beginners and decayed tradesmen within the township of Nether Knutsford in the County Palatine of Chester', not more than £5 per person and to be paid back after 5 years. 'Decayed', could mean a decline in prosperity or fortune as well as aged. £5 may seem to us to be a small sum but it was similar to the annual wages of the Minister and the Schoolmaster then who received officially £5.6.8d a year, a very useful amount. The bequest embodied an Elizabethan idea that sometimes a seasonal loan without interest might stimulate industry in the recipient more than would a gift. Although there was no interest to collect, five feoffees were appointed yearly of which three were changed one year and two the next to give some continuity. The two groups of recipients of this charity the young beginners, inexperienced and the decayed, having already suffered some misfortune were both vulnerable and in order to keep the charity going the feoffees needed to be vigilant to make sure that the money was being used wisely to ensure that the £5 would be there to be returned at the end of the 5 years. The names of these feoffees were recorded faithfully each year throughout this Court Book until 1827 and in terms of benefiting recipients this charity must surely rank highly. Over the 250 years that this charity ran, it is possible that over 1,000 recipients could have benefited from Mr. Mann's bequest.

A testimonial to this charity was given by Mrs. Margaret Furness (Furnace), a wealthy Knutsford widow who when making her will in 1719 asked that the £100 which she was leaving to the poor should be administered 'as near as the manner and method of Mr. Mann's legacy'. This implies that what she had seen in her lifetime of the workings of it had impressed her enough to think it worthwhile for her money to be used similarly. Mr. Mann's bequest had then already been in operation for 150 years.

Before her, in 1649 Squire Thomas Legh of Booths in his will, thought it appropriate to bequeath £50 to, 'young beginners and the rest of the tradesmen of Over Knutsford' but they were to pay interest of 6p. in the pound which was to maintain a preacher. Squire Legh's widow Elizabeth married again fairly soon after her husband's death and did not hand over this money so Robert Griffiths, gent., sued the executors in 1666 and the money was eventually paid with interest on past years for the benefit of the preacher.

The other large Knutsford charity was from **Henry Burgess**, draper of Knutsford, who died in 1612. He left £200 to the Church the interest forever for the use of a preaching Minister and £10 for the poor.

Henry Burgis or Burgess, a bachelor, was a wealthy wholesale cloth merchant with a shop or warehouse here with huge stocks of cloth, over 1,000 yards of many wondrous types including French russet and greenes, 'Spanish deroy', more mundane kersies, baise, fustians and serge and over 150 pairs of men's and women's hose, ribbons, lace and buttons by the gross, felts, bands and garters and much more. He had book debts of over £1,100 which was an enormous sum at that time. He also left, 'towards paving of the market place of Nether Knutsford £5, the said paving to be done at the nearer end of the said market stidde towards my house'. He was generous with his money in his own lifetime and was still remembered in the next century when his gravestone in the churchyard was cleaned in July 1708.

The trustees originally appointed to this bequest decided to lend Mr. Burgess's money in six amounts of £33.6.8d. It seems that those who were in a position to borrow this amount of money and pay the interest were themselves made feoffees of the charity. In 1676, 'John Cowpes one of the feoffees for a legacy by Henry Burgess ... doth willingly resign the feoffeship and pay in the £33.6.8d which was the sum intrusted in his hand'. In 1678, James and Peter Swinton took out a mortgage on a property, using £33 from this bequest to cover part of the required money. In 1653, eight bequests were recorded for the use of a preaching Minister in Knutsford amounting to £336 and five bequests for the poor amounting to £171.3.4d including Mr. Mann's money. More charities came with the years, some for the use of a schoolmaster or to pay for poor children to be taught to read in the Bible. In some places when a large sum of money was donated to charity, land or property was bought and rents collected yearly but this does not seem to have been the practise in Knutsford until the 1740's.

Some of the contents of the Town Chest in 1665 included nineteen bonds for money lent out, of amounts ranging from £4 to £33.6.8d. and some other very assorted papers amongst which was a letter from the Bishop about putting in a schoolmaster, a poll deed, several writings about Mr. Mann's gift, a bond to discharge the town from a bastard child and another to indemnify the town from one William Walker. The Overseers of the Poor put in a few accounts. By 1674 they decided to write no more bonds in the book but to write them upon more loose papers and they decreed that the old book of orders was 'to be bound up in Calves Ledder and clasps at the town's charge'. In 1688 a third lock was to be fixed to the Chest, one key to be kept by the constables, one by the Chapel Warden and one by the Overseers who all needed to be present in order to open the chest. As this order was repeated in 1694 it had obviously not been done by then but from that year it was decided that the Chest was to be kept in the house of Robert Thornley, no reason given. Robert Thornley, barber surgeon, was the parish clerk and had previously been a chapel warden.

The main source of the town's income came from the rates decided by a meeting of the Church Wardens, Overseers of the Poor and of the Highways, the Constables and the freeholders. These rates, approved by the Justices of the Peace, were charged to householders to pay for the upkeep of the poor within its township and rates for the constables and those for the upkeep of the roads were levied yearly, the accounts submitted to 'those appointed to manage the affairs of the town'.

Knutsford's Town Chest was taken to the new Parish Church when it was completed in 1744 where it can still be seen today, appropriately beneath those charity boards in the porch. A rather sad postscript is that much of this charity money was invested in the nineteenth century in Stock and Annuities which later went bankrupt.

The Constables deserve a special mention, two elected each year to do many tasks, being responsible for law and order and directly responsible to and under the orders of the Justices of the Peace. Both the Overseers of the Poor and the Constables attended the Quarter Sessions wherever they were held. In 1654 in Knutsford the Manor Court ordered new equipment for their constables: one bridle, one crowe net, two 'holdbeards', four muskets, four pairs of bandoleers and two black staves. The staves were kept outside the constables' homes and carried by them as a badge of office, forerunners of the truncheon and to be passed on each year to successive constables. The crow net was for boys or men who were paid to catch crows which ate the grain newly sown in the fields. The muskets were for town practice at the shooting butts having moved on in time from the days of bows and arrows. Bandoleers were broad belts worn over the shoulder upon which wallets could be attached in which they collected the rates, (leys), any other taxes levied and interest from the bonds. The bridle must have replaced an old one for riding journeys.

A Constable

In 1694 the Constables were instructed to 'take care of the cleansing and layding of the well and to perform that office which formerly only belonged to the well lookers' for that present year so they needed to be prepared to turn their hands to anything. The jobs of Constable, Chappell Reeve and Well Looker were amalgamated at about this time. It was often almost a full time job remembering that they all had their own businesses to attend to, trades or shops to run, crops to grow and stock to rear. We will meet the constables again in the course of their duties.

The School and the Schoolmasters.

The first we hear of a school in Knutsford is in 1537 when the schoolmaster here had a son at Oriel College, Oxford but of this school or its origins we now know no more. It may have been in existence from the chantry of Thomas Oulgreve in 1473. In 1549 Sir John Legh of Booths purchased land and houses from King Edward V1 which had come to the King upon the dissolution of the Chantries. Of the income from these, Sir John Legh was bound to the King for 200 Marks upon condition that he and his heirs would, 'from time to time for ever, find one able schoolmaster well and sufficiently learned for the teaching and bringing up of youth' and to pay the rent of the land, £5.6.8d. a year in two instalments for a schoolmaster to teach the children of the township and for a priest to sing Divine Service in the (Parochial) Chapel and to administer Holy Communion there and to 'pray for all Christian souls'. The small grammar school was then built next to the Chapel of Ease in King Street. The number of pupils is not known but there seem to have been places for six poor scholars to be taught free from an early date, despite the meagre endowment.

The school's link with the Church from its foundation continued with all schoolmasters licensed by the Bishop and checked at each Visitation. It features in the earliest entries of the court book but no records of the school itself have been found. The Knutsford grammar schoolmaster was still being appointed by the Leghs of Norbury Booths and paid as above, the same rent from the land as at the foundation was recorded in 1653 plus a bequest of £10 for the schoolmaster from John Wright of Over Knutsford, a chapman.

Before 1660, Knutsford school was one of seven grammar schools in the county but more were founded before the end of the century. This was a time of growing interest in education when parish schools were established and more schools of various sorts were founded and being set up throughout the eighteenth century. The school building had become the town's responsibility which in 1643 the Court agreed to, 'cause the schoolhouse to be put in sufficient repair at the charge of the Town'. A picture is conjured by the remembrance of William Highfield of Bexton in 1697 then an elderly man

An ABC horn book, horn covered paper on an oak slab. A reading aid. Peter Swinton (p118) sold ABC's in his bookshop.

of 86, who recalled that when he was a schoolboy at Knutsford school, 'he hath frequently gone to the Clerk's house for the keys of the Chapel that he might go into the same to ring a bell to call in the scholars to the school'. Knutsford's morning bell.

This was likely to have been quite early in the morning, 6 or 7 a.m. in the summer, the school day often until 6pm. with a lunch break from 11 - 12.30, giving boys time to walk possibly some distance home and back. In winter with less daylight hours, 7.30am. or 8am.- 4pm. School was on Saturday mornings as well but some schools allowed pupils home on Thursday afternoons after 2pm. They had holidays of course, the Church festivals and a month in the summer at harvest time.

The salary of the master in Knutsford was the lowest in the county and towards the end of the seventeenth century this caused recruitment problems. Most of the other schools in Cheshire received more than twice that of Knutsford with Macclesfield the most richly endowed and here they paid an usher as well whose salary alone was £30 p.a. Not unnaturally this was an attraction and several Knutsford masters moved on to teach there. More charitable bequests raised Knutsford's pay slightly higher but this was only the basic salary. The master was paid for the six free boys and above that by the other boys' parents for the subjects he taught them. The Manor Court book gives the details in 1653:

Agreed by the Great Jury for the maintenance of the schoolmaster that such persons that send their child or children to be taught at the school of Knutsford shall pay for every child,

> That shall read Greek   5s. the quarter.
>
> That shall read in the Grammar   2s.6d. the quarter.
>
> That shall read in the Accedence   2s. the quarter.
>
> (These two items refer to Latin grammar).
>
> And   18d. a quarter for all English scholars.

There is no mention of maths. The above subjects formed the basis of the standard classical education which was expected by the Universities of Oxford and Cambridge. Schools for these universities were mainly concerned that pupils learned Latin grammar, (requiring many exercises), to speak Latin and read classical Latin literature and for older boys, learning Greek to read classics. Some schools taught Hebrew. English was taught to the younger boys with often the Bible as the chief reading book starting with the New Testament and then proceeding to the Old. All the professions had the same basic education at school and university and having qualified in theology they could then be ordained in the Church or go on to study law or study medicine with practising Doctors or in Hospitals. There was strict discipline, often beatings and much learning by heart. New teachers learned with practising teachers in schools.

We can compare Knutsford's school charges with those of grammar schools elsewhere. In 1676, in Ormskirk School, Lancashire, the master's salary could be augmented by charging 16d. a quarter for English scholars, 2s. for Latin scholars and 3s. for Greek. In Frodsham in Cheshire in 1678, the school governors authorised charges of 2s. a quarter for the Latin accedence and 5s. a quarter for Greek. At Lymm school which was founded in 1698 they were to charge 4s. a quarter for writing lessons and 6s. a quarter for writing and accounts combined.

Writing was a separate subject. In 1703 Knutsford had a writing master, Joseph Clough, whose son was born here that year. In 1706 he had moved to Northwich and was teaching under an agreement in the free grammar school in Northwich, for writing was commonly looked on as an extra subject to be paid for by a special fee. Clough was in Lymm in 1719 where he taught writing and accounts. It is likely that unknown numbers could read but not write.

Pupils entered grammar school between the ages of 6 and 9 having learned to read, some possibly to write, and do some arithmetic at a Dame, or Petty school. There were no official records of these mixed primary schools which sprang up and in time closed as women took them on who had some education themselves and as circumstances prevailed. There was such a school in Knutsford for some years run by Elizabeth Antrobus (died 1694), whose schoolroom was in her house in King Street, of whom more later. Others probably existed of which we now know nothing. Peter Swinton, Knutsford's bookseller who died in 1698 sold ABC books in his shop and also left a legacy for the use and benefit of a public schoolmaster.

Girls were only allowed to attend the primary, petty or dame schools where they were taught to read and then to write and to learn such useful skills as knitting, sewing, spinning etc. Some children were taught by private tutor.

There were inevitably times when there was no petty school in Knutsford and this added to the teaching problem in the grammar school in Knutsford as well as elsewhere, for teaching small children to read was time consuming and not always considered to be the responsibility of grammar schools although several charities were left for the express purpose of teaching children to read in the Bible.

Knutsford School was obviously an all age school with boys from ages about 7 up to 18 but not all boys would stay until that age. There were 30 boys in 1778 and 50 - 60 plus the six free boys in 1818, some boarding by then but at both these dates the school was in different premises.

Pupils were sons of gentry and professional men as well as those of the wealthier tradesmen from the town and surrounding area, the middle classes. The free boys would be those who were spotted from a young age as being quick to learn and showing interest and aptitude to benefit from schooling but free tuition did not necessarily mean free everything, for it would be a sacrifice to lose a son's help and labour at home and often students were required to bring their own candles for winter time or even books and writing materials and sometimes a contribution was needed for 'firing', for heating in the winter. It is slightly worrying that no hearth for the school was mentioned in the hearth tax returns in either 1664 or 1674, as there must have been a fire in the school. William Antrobus in fact was listed as being charged on one hearth, he was schoolmaster at the time but there was also a maltster in the town of the same name at the same time and there is no way of knowing to which of them it referred. Some boys were given schooling by their father paying for them instead of, or as part of their 'portion', a share of the family fortune to help a son set up in business or for a son or daughter to get married.

It is difficult to know what proportion of people could read and write. Some of the very poorest in Knutsford possessed a Bible. Certainly some of those, some of them women, living alone in a house with only one hearth, were able to write their names very clearly, so poverty was no indication of illiteracy. Many could read but not write.

There was much criticism nationally about the limited traditional curriculum especially in the second half of the century at a time when interests were widening in many fields and focusing on navigation with trade increasing almost world wide and growing colonisation abroad. Maths and accounting were essential for business life. There were schools that taught maths and science but changes did not come to some grammar schools until the eighteenth century and some not even then. Parish and independent private schools taught these subjects and often had a much wider curriculum. Maths was taught at the parish school at Rostherne founded to be free for poor boys, held in a room beneath the steeple of the Church (until the steeple fell in 1744) and it gained a high reputation for maths throughout the county. The Vicar the Rev. Adam Martindale taught maths after he was ejected from his Rostherne living because he would not conform to the Church of England at the Restoration and he went to Manchester to teach in 1666 for a time. He was proud of his pupils there who, he said, became skilful in logarithms and, 'could in an houre answer such a question as professours could not solve in a month, as for example such as this: What is 5d.3qs. a day, to continue 300 years, worth in readie monie at £6 12s 6d. per cent?'. The controversy over the classical curriculum continued and intensified in the late eighteenth century and into the nineteenth century when the Endowed Grammar Schools Act of 1840 empowered trustees to broaden curricula.

After detailing the charges for the various subjects in 1643, Knutsford court book goes on to say, 'And if any person ... refuse to pay, ... the said schoolmaster to send for such wages ... in the Town Court of Knutsford ... to recover the same'. Bad payers were obviously a problem from time to time. A Knutsford schoolmaster, Caleb Pott, here from c.1670(?)-1677 went on to become Macclesfield's head schoolmaster who when he died in 1690 had debts owing to him of £62, a considerable sum out of his total estate of £157 despite his high salary. He had books worth £61 including two Dictionaries, Cooper's and Minshall's and two folios of Mercator's Atlas, pictures, maps and two wall maps of universal history, a pair of globes and some compasses in his possession then. He was certainly teaching more than English, Latin and Greek.

Knutsford could not have afforded to have a paid usher which some schools had, to help with the teaching although the master could have delegated an older boy to teach younger ones English, but there was more than one teacher recorded as being at the school on several occasions. On looking at the dates of graduation of Knutsford's Masters it is clear that some were appointed before going to University like Ralph Malbon and Randle Hazelhurst. These were taken on to gain classroom skills and experience. Ralph Malbon was appointed by Peter Legh on 23rd.March 1691. He went on to Jesus College, Cambridge as a sizar in December 1693, (he carried out certain menial duties for tuition at a reduced fee) and then went as usher to Macclesfield in 1694 before graduating in 1697-8 and becoming Master of Congleton from 1709 to 1721. It seems to have become the pattern for Knutsford to have had young masters who did not stay long before moving on to another, better paid position.

Tombstone of Alice Crosedale

William Antrobus was a young schoolmaster of Knutsford from 1662 and in 1666 when he was 25 he was sent for from the school one afternoon to write a will for a Knutsford inhabitant, Henry Antrobus. Because this will was later contested the circumstances of its writing were recorded. He wrote with a very readable, clear hand and later signed, not suprisingly, a statement for the Probate Court containing Latin phrases and expressions. He probably moved on to another school or might have become a clergyman somewhere.

Henry Crosedale was Master in Knutsford before 1645 when he went a nonconformist, on to Macclesfield where he was very well liked and treated handsomely. Apart from his far greater salary he was given grants to keep his son at Cambridge in the 1650's and at the Restoration because he would not conform to the Act of Uniformity he had to leave his position but was given £100 by the Governors as compensation. This may have enabled him to retire and he bought a lease on a property in Goostrey, 'in consideration of the love and affection I have for my wife Alice, my son Habor and daughter Hannah'. At some point his widow came back to live in Knutsford, possibly after the death of both her children as she mentioned neither of them in her will. She was a cousin of Henry Antrobus and his sister Margaret Furnace, both of whom were generous benefactors to Knutsford. Alice Crosedale was buried in St.Helena's Churchyard where her gravestone can still be seen inscribed, 'relict of Henry Crosedale late of Macclesfield Schoolemaster who died the 13th day of September AD 1690'. She, knowing the schoolmaster's salary, left £10 for the use of Knutsford's master.

Another benefactor of the school was an unmarried blacksmith, John Allen, who died in 1682. He left,

'£20 for the use of a schoolmaster at Knutsford to be imployed yearly for that use at interest for ever with this condition that every schoolmaster shall teach six poor children every year without wages until every one read well in the bible which said children shall be chosen by the feoffees for Mr. Man's money, whereof ... one shall be taken out of Bexton (if there be any such children there) and the other five children out of Nether Knutsford.'

These free children do not seem to be recorded as extra to those of the original foundation in either Bishop Gastrell's notes in 1718 or in Carlisle in 1818, which is something of a mystery. Perhaps being taught to read was thought too basic a skill to be included in the classical education given in the Grammar School which Gastrell and Carlisle were dealing with.

Yet another mystery is that of other charitable bequests for the school. On the Parish Church charity boards drawn up by the Churchwardens in 1719, four donors' names of bequests for the school are given, John Wright,

Over Knutsford Chapman, £10, John Aldcroft,
Nether Knutsford Mercer, £6, Robert Ridgway,
Rector of Davenham, £10 and John Allen, the
above blacksmith. Yet there exists a list dated 1718
signed by four Churchwardens containing thirteen
names of benefactors for the school but even this
does not mention either Alice Crosedale or Peter
Swinton. It is possible that some of the money
from bequests was lost to men who went bankrupt
or could not repay the loan.

Copy of certificate issued by
Peter Legh (of Booths)
to Ralph Malbon,
appointed Schoolmaster
of Knutsford
23rd March 1690

The only insight we have of the doings
of Knutsford school comes from Sir Thomas
Mainwaring who on two successive years, 1686 and
1687, was with his 'two little grandsons my coz Leigh
of Booths and others to see and heare the exercise
of the school boys there at their breaking up for Christmas'. In 1686 it was
to 'see the boys performe their exercise'.

Official records of schoolmasters' names only begin in Knutsford in the
1670's with the Clergy Call Books which were the records, although not all
survive, of the Archdeacon's Visitation.

In 1700 and 1701, John Spencer was recorded as a Master in Knutsford at
the Visitation. There had been a difficulty in filling the position permanently
and John Spencer may have been another young man not yet gone to University
and Mr. Thomas Spencer (a relative ?) seems to have been here also, prior
to official appointment but was reluctant to take on the post because of the
low salary and after much discussion, in 1700 whether voluntarily offered
or not, on 18th October the Court Leet ordered,

that there shall be paid to Mr.Thomas Spencer now schoolmaster of Nether
Knutsford by the constables of the said township for an augmentacion of his
sallery and for his Incuridgement to continue in the place, the sum of 40/-
quarterly for one whole year... .

This does not sound over generous especially as the offer here seems to
be for one year only nor was it mentioned again but according to Bishop
Gastrell, the charitable bequests had risen to £106 by the early eighteenth
century from which he would have had the interest. The town wanted
Thomas Spencer as schoolmaster and six prominant townsmen including
the parson signed a letter to the Bishop saying,

Mr.Thomas Spencer had (has?) waited on you sooner for a licence to keep a
Grammar School in Knutsford but that he had no encouragement to continue
with us till the inhabitants did lately voluntarily offer an augmentation of the
salary by way of contribution; which being done he now applies himself to you
for a licence to the said school and we whose names are underwritten, being
convinced both by the Character which hath been given of him by those that

are acquainted with him before he came among us and also by his behaviour since, of his Sobriety, Loyalty and entire conformity to the Church of England, do hereby attest the same and express our unanimous and earnest desire that he may be admitted. Witness our hand this 29th October" 1700 ... .

To authenticate this plea was another letter to the Bishop from Peter Legh Esq. of Booths dated 8th December 1700, both letters carried in person by Mr. Spencer, 'the bearer hereof':

A Gentleman we have had some tryall of in order to supply our vacancy as Schoolmaster of Knutsford ... we find him in every way very well qualified for the employ and hope that he will give your Lordship such satisfaction of your Licence which I shall acknowledge as a very great favour to your Lordship's humble servant.

Thomas Spencer was granted the licence and was still master here at the Visitation in 1705 but not long afterwards he went on to Lymm grammar school where he stayed for the rest of his career until 1753.

John Robinson was master in Knutsford from 1733 until his death in 1742.

A dispute was reported around the middle of the eighteenth century respecting the duties which ought to be performed by the schoolmaster. Mr. Legh insisted that the matter rested entirely in his discretion and that he was at liberty to appoint a master who might not be able to teach the learned languages, while others maintained that Greek and Latin had always been taught in the school and therefore ought to be taught in future. The Knutsford schoolmasters, Oxford or mostly Cambridge graduates or undergraduates until 1746, gave the school a good reputation and sent boys to university throughout the seventeenth and eighteenth centuries but following this dispute, in 1746, Joseph Foden, a non-graduate, was appointed and contrary to the many previous masters who did not stay long, he stayed, a valued and respected teacher for 48 years. He was 82 when he died and was buried in the Parish Church graveyard.

One of Knutsford's bright students sadly lies buried in St.Helena's graveyard which still records the reminder of a life of promise brought to an untimely end:

'Here lyeth interred the body of John Birtles son of Edward Birtles A Student of Trinity College Cambridge who departed this life July the 19th 1717 aged 21 years'. He had entered the college in 1714 but had not been to Knutsford school but to Sir John Deane's Grammar School in Northwich which was a free school to all pupils but soon after 1717 the school's feoffees limited free entrance there to boys from Northwich and Witton parishes only. One of their schoolmasters in the 1670's claimed that, 'Most of the gentry of Cheshire have been brought up at Northwich School'. It was a good school of high reputation and as tuition was free and it was only about

7 miles away it must have attracted other pupils from Knutsford ever since its foundation in 1558.

Tombstone of Edward Birtles, student of Trinity College, Cambridge, in St Helena's graveyard

The Knutsford Grammar School building and the Chapel of Ease next to it were demolished in 1741 when Knutsford became a Parish. A new school was built in 1744.

Some Schoolmasters of Knutsford Grammar School

- 1549 Richard Oldfield. Retained for life.
- 1563 John Brook.

***

- 1645 Henry Crosedale. Master at Macclesfield 1645 - 1662.
- 1649 William Long, schoolmaster died, (Kn. Parish register).
- 1653 Mr. Sanchy of Toft. Peter Leycester's account: CCR 60/26/32.
- 1662-67(?) William Antrobus (Mentioned in will of William Antrobus and other docs.)
- 1670 (?) - 77 Caleb Pott. Vist.Bk. 1674 & 77. Master at Macclesfield after 1677 - 1690.
- 1683 - 86 - John Boydell. Vist. Bk. 1686. Master at Nantwich 1693.
- 1686 - ? John Percival. Named as a dissenter in Church Court case.

- 1691 - 94 Ralph Malbon. Sizar Jesus Cambs. 1693. Usher at Macclesfield 1694. Matric. 1695. BA. 1697-8. Master at Congleton 1709 -21.
- 1700 - 01 John Spencer. Appt. 1700. Licence 1700. Vist.Bk. 1701.
- 1700-05 Thomas Spencer. Court Leet Kn. 1700. Vist.Bk 1705. Sizar age 20 Jesus Cambs. 1696. Matric 1696. BA. 1699-1700. Master at Lymm 1706 - 53.
- 1707 - 09 Charles Aldcroft. Licence 1707. Vist.Bk. 1709.
- 1712 William Lockett. Vist.Bk. 1712. Sizar Jesus Cambs. 1707.Matric 1707. BA.1710-11. Curate in Derbyshire, then usher at Derby School 1716 -22, Vicar in Derby, 1722- 51.
- 1712 John Beckett. Vist.Bk. 1712 and 1716.
- 1716 Edward Cartwright. Vist.Bk. 1716. From Rostherne Vist.Bk. 1712.
- 1721 Randle Hazlehurst. Appt. 1721. Matric Brasenose Oxford age 17, 1717. BA. 1722-3. In Sandbach 1718 (Ralph ?) and again in Kn.1725 (Vist.Bk.) then as Curate and Master, in Sandbach.
- 1724 John Swinton. Appt. 1724. Vist.Bk. 1725. Wadham Oxford 1719 age 16. BA. 1723. MA. 1726. On to be Rector in Oxford then in Middlewich 1731-7, then in Herefordshire.
- 1733 - 42. John Robinson Vist.Bk. 1733. Appt. 1733. Sizar St. Johns Cambs. 1725-6 Matric 1726. BA. 1729-30. Died 1742.
- 1742 Thomas Barlow Appt. 1742, resigned 1743. Curate of Ringway. Wadham Oxford BA. 1751
- 1746-94 Joseph Foden Appt. Peter Legh, testimonial as to ability for past 3 years as Schoolmaster at Over Peover. Vist.Bk. 1747, 66, 70.

Churchwardens' list of those who left charities for the school, 1718.

£10   Mrs. Margaret Furness gave £10 for the use and benefit of a lawful licensed public schoolmaster in Nether Knutsford from time to time for ever.

£10   John Wright late of Over Knutsford Chapman.

£6   John Aldcroft late of Nether Knutsford.

£10   Robert Ridgway late Rector of Davenham.

£20   John Allen late of Nether Knutsford Blacksmith, the interest to make the said school fees for six poor children till they read well in the Bible and to be chosen by the feoffees of Mr. William Mann.

£10   Mr. Joseph Harrison of Nether Knutsford, poor children to be chosen by the Minister of Knutsford.

£10   Thomas Baguley schoolmaster of Ollerton.

£100 Mr. Samuel Leigh, Ollerton, schoolmaster.

£10   to buy books for children of Ollerton.

£10   Elizabeth Swinton spinster of Nether Knutsford, to the school till
       they can read well in the Bible.

£5   Elizabeth Swinton of Nether Knutsford widow, for the schoolmaster
       of Knutsford.

£5   Mrs. Rowley of Nether Knutsford widow.

£10   Henry Antrobus of Nether Knutsford Mercer.

£10   Thomas Baguley of Sandbach.

    To which must be added £10 from Alice Crosedale, widow, and £10 from
Peter Swinton, bookseller if not others.

The Bakehouse and Bakers

The bakehouse was still used by the majority of the townspeople and was
situated on Bakehouse Brow, now the entrance to the car park opposite
the graveyard of Knutsford Parish Church, off King Street. Knutsford's
thirteenth century Charter had included a clause about the bakers and
the oven: 'whoever ... desires bread from the oven ... will pay to my baker a
halfpenny for each bushel' (of flour ground at the lord's mill) 'and none ...
will build an oven within the ... town'. By the seventeenth century this was
long forgotten and no longer applied although the Bakehouse was still a
vital necessity to the many people who took their dough to be baked there
and still under the authority of the Lord of the Manor and therefore the
Court Leet. The baker was renting the Bakehouse from the Egertons as it
had been in 1621 when a lease of that year was drawn up between the Earl of
Bridgewater and Arthur Bentley 'for a cottage and a quarter of an acre, one

Bakehouse Brow, site of Knutsford's bakehouse

Common Bakehouse in Nether Knutsford late in tenure of Jeffrey Bentley of Nether Knutsford, Innholder'.

Private ovens were built into some properties and are sometimes to be seen in houses and cottages of this age built into the wall near to a fireplace, of brick or stone, heated by placing hot coals inside which when raked out left an oven hot enough to bake the bread first and when that was removed, cakes, pies etc. Some people had bakestones on their fires which enabled them to bake scones, biscuits etc. The Court though, might still have been mindful of its previous monopoly and even in 1688 wanted to propose that, 'noe inhabitant in Nether Knutsford shall bake bread to sell in any private oven nor offer to bake anything for others therein', but this was not agreed to. This is rather strange because several Knutsford men and women were presented at the court at intervals for breaking the assize of bread which must have meant that they were baking for themselves and others. Sarah Hough was selling bread in the 1690's. Not all Knutsford's inhabitants were tenants of the lord of the manor and therefore did not have an obligation to bake at the lord's bakehouse as was the situation with the flour mill.

The large town Bakehouse was heated with wood which the baker needed to have in great quantities ready to hand. In 1643: 'Touching the Bakehouse. It is ordered and agreed that those that tend the Bakehouse shall not have above 2 loads of fewell lying neare unto the Bakehouse at one time'. It was a fire risk and wood took up too much space, dangerous for pedestrians.

Two bakers were reported in the court for overcharging.

1682: 'Robert Hall, baker, was complained of for exacting the price of white bread and was pained in 6s.8d. if he shall continue to doe so againe'. He probably took care not to do so despite trying to increase his profits for a baker's living was not very easy. A few years later Robert Hall fell victim to Knutsford's epidemic and died in April 1686, leaving his 'deare wife Shusannah' and his 'lovinge daughter Mary' in their 3 roomed cottage with the apprentice Henry Beane who still had some time to serve. Hall must have felt confidant that his apprentice could carry on the Bakehouse until his term was finished because he requested that he 'bee provided for and found with meate and drink and lodging untill Candlemass Day come Twelve Month which shall be in the yeare of our Lord God 1687 And all his weareing apparell but shoes during the whole terme of his said prenteshipe'.

Robert Hall's possessions show the importance of fuel and how much spare time was spent in its gathering with the 'one frameing saw, 2 mattocks and a hacke, five wagges, 3 billes, one ax and other working toules' which he kept in his buttery. He had fuel on the Heath and on Bakehouse Brow, firewood and other fuel in the Bakehouse, wood lying on Mr.Daniel's demesne and another load in the hands of Nathan Cooper, all reckoned as being worth £4 10s. He also had 'backhouse scoves' worth £2.2s. sometimes called scovels or bakers' malkins, types of broom used to rake the fire from the oven. There were 'Bakers Armes' in his Chamber, worth very little.

In his 'house', open to the rafters, he had cooking utensils, vessels, spoons, two knives and a flesh fork with the hanging brundritt, pot hooks, racks and hanging irons for cooking on the fire and even a smoothing iron with heaters box, although Hall's own apparel was worth only £1.10s. All the family slept in the Chamber, Robert and Shusannah with red curtains and vallance round their bed, Mary also had curtains around hers and Henry Beane the apprentice slept on the truckle bed on the chaff and feather mattresses under '3 old blankets and a coverlid'. All Hall's worldly goods including the fuel and 'dubeous debts' were valued at £29.10s.6d. Because he had goods worth more than £10 he was taxed on his one hearth, 2s. a year. Robert Hall could not write his name but that was no bar to his being a sidesman at church and was one of those who felt strongly about the Church and broke open the locks of the Chapel of Ease in 1685.

A previous baker had been Hugh Pritchard from Wales who died in 1662. Pritchard, Breadbaker, had kept in touch with his friends and relations in 'the Dominion of Wales', Wrexham, Welshpool and the parishes of Llandicilia and Eberrua, leaving them small sums of money and £2 and £3 for the poor of two of those parishes. Pritchard could not write either but he could easily have asked someone who could, to write for him and to read any letter which he may have received for a small fee or a flagon of ale in the ale house. Some of these people may have travelled to Knutsford from time to time on business or trade. He left bequests to eight recipients in Wales but to fourteen in Knutsford, gloves to some of them, and £2 for Knutsford's poor. He had kept a few sheep and left a ewe and a lamb, to two of Knutsford's good wives and a lamb each to '2 of Randle Woolmer's children' and one 'to Alice Rutter's boy'. He left 8s. to the Minister Mr. Hunter and 8s. to the ringers, and he dated his will '30th March 1662 according to the computation of the Church of England'.

By 1698 the baker was Henry Jewel who also displeased the Court: 'Whereas Henery Jewill, Baker, hath formerly exacted from the inhabitants of this Town one piece of dough at every Household and likewise doth extremely advance his prices more than the usual custom, therefore it is ordered that upon every just complaynt of any inhabitant for any such offence to the persons appoynted to manage the Town's afayrs the said Henery Jewill shall forfett 12d. for every offence to the Lord of the Manor. And the said Henery Jewill to be ready at 9 o'clock in the morning upon customary Bakeing days to sett in the Household bread'. Henry Jewel died in 1705. His son was apprenticed to a goldsmith in Chester.

This was the last reference to the Bakehouse in the Court Book except when it was mentioned as a place, in 1764.

The baker was baking dough made by inhabitants, (kneading turnells were in several Knutsford homes), and baking his own dough for sale. Knutsford people could collect their own bread from the baker but bakers were subject to regulations nationally and bread could only be sold in public market not in a baker's shop 'before his oven'. It was brought to market in panniers by townspeople, often women who carried the bread for sale from house to house having bought it or obtained it on credit from the baker. They made a profit on every thirteenth loaf.

In 1701, five people were presented to the Court for the breach of the assize of bread: Mary Toft, Sarah Hough, Elizabeth Toft, Ralph Culcheth and John Fisher were amerced 6d. apiece. Were these people baking bread at home and selling underweight or overcharging on the baker's bread? The assize was often invoked for selling substandard products, weights and measures of many commodities were of constant concern to the market and bakehouse lookers.

The price of bread was again regulated nationally in 1709 making the size of the loaf conform to the price of wheat by sliding scale but an Assize of Bread (and Ale) regulating the weight and price of bread, had been brought in going back as far as the time of Henry 111 before Knutsford was founded. There was a Cann Office in Knutsford by the side of the Heath, mentioned in 1691, where it is thought that standard weights and measures were kept.

The Town Clock

There were a few private clocks in Knutsford. Knowing the time was necessary for Church services, starting the markets, ringing the school bell, 'for setting in the town bread' and for the various Court sittings. Most people could judge the time of day quite well, one local witness in a Sessions Court stated that 'the sun was two hours high', but for more accuracy Knutsford had its town clock probably on the Court House, with only one hand which showed the hour like the one on the Over Knutsford Court House. It could well have been here since Elizabethan times. Wilmslow Parish Church Wardens met their clockman in 1599 and later spent a day collecting it from the smithie and putting it up on the Church.

How reliable and what the quality of Knutsford's town clock was, can only be surmised but in 1680 it had been giving some trouble and the Court was only too delighted to have a willing and able volunteer to undertake to attend to it and to put it into working order. The Court records:

Robert Thornley shall put the Town Clock in good repair and keep it in good repair dureing his life for which he shall have 5s. p.a. from the constables'.

Robert Thornley as already mentioned, barber surgeon, was the parish Clerk. The constables were responsible for Over Knutsford's Court clock and later, Peter Lowndes was paid 2s.6d for a quarter year for tending their clock in 1711, twice the rate of that in Nether Knutsford 30 years earlier.

There was a watchmaker George Leicester in Knutsford in 1685, and there may well have been watch and clock makers here earlier than that.

Many fine clocks and watches were made in the seventeenth century of highly skilled workmanship and after the invention of the balance spring in 1675 watches became accurate to well within a minute a day, becoming useful items which were not just ostentatious jewellery.

When Knutsford's Parish Church was built in 1744, a clock was put on its tower. When the old Court House was demolished no clock was placed on the new building as far as we know.

Officers elected at Nether Knutsford Court Leet, 3rd October 1701

3 8br 1701   We returne for officers for this yeare as follows:
Constables, Chappell Reeves
and well Lookers: .... Wm. Mundall and Henricus Long.
Townfield Lookers for
Crosse Town: .... John Chorley, Abell Kinsey
                                         Richard Toft Jun.
                                         Jno. Bostock currier
Assessors: .... Edward Jackson, Wm. Delves
                                         Jno. Swinton, Thos. Baguleigh
Common moore Lookers: .... Rich. Shaw feltmaker, Jno. Yarwood Sen.
                                         Wm. Woolmer
Market Lookers for Flesh: .... Wm. Skellorne, Jno. Leech
Overseers for Jones Bridge
& Whitebridge: .... Jno. Jones, Tho. Rutter
Market Lookers for weights
& measures & bred: .... Ralph Toft & Jno. Tompson
Moss Lookers: .... Thos. Dore, Ralph Gee
Market Lookers for green
hydes searchers &
sealers of leather: .... Edward Birtles, Abram Blackshaw
                                         Josiah Birtles
Pavement Lookers: .... Tho. Morton, Ralph Darlington
Damfield moore Lookers: .... Wm. Drinkwater, Richd. Hely
Fyre Lookers: .... Jno. Chorley, Jno. Jones,
                                         Tho. Dickynson, George Hurst
Aletasters: .... Jno. Moores sen. Jno. Moores Jun.
Bakehouse Lookers: .... Jno. Acton, Richd. Wrench
Market Looker for swine: .... Wm. Woolmer
Barleymen: .... Randle Read & Phillip Antrobus
Afferator: .... Willelmus Delves, Johes. Bostock

(Barleymen: haywards who were overseers for the common lands, their fences and hedges.
Afferator: one who judges the fines or amercements according to the offence.)
JRL Egerton Papers 2/2/1

References:

- *A brown calf skin volume recording Nether Knutsford's Court Leet from 1643-1827, was deposited in Chester as recently as 1983 by a firm of solicitors in London, trustees of Lord Egerton of Tatton. It reveals much of Knutsford life which could not be found from any other source. There are more loose Court papers in Manchester's John Rylands Library.*
- *Nether Knutsford Court Book 1643-1827: CRO DET/3244/14.*
- *1701 List of Officers & Lookers : JRL Egerton Papers 2/2/1.*
- *Will of William Mann. PRO : PROB 11/56.*
- *Hearth Tax Returns: CRO Mf 13 or PRO 1673/4 E/179/86/155 RP 1337.*
- *Knutsford St. John's Parish Registers CRO p.7 Wills and Inventories: CRO WS.*
- *McKENNA and NUNN, ed. Stockport in the Seventeenth Century, Stockport Hist. Soc.1992.*
- *The Bellman at Mere: CRO Quarter Sessions QJF/90/3 162.*
- *References to Chester City from index of Chester Assembly Records CRO City records 1686*
- *Much information re Schools and Schoolmasters in this section gathered from ROBSON Derek: Some Aspects of Education in Cheshire in the 18th Century. Mcr. Chetham Soc. 1966 and COX Marjorie, A History of Sir John Deane's Grammar School, Witton, Northwich, 1557- 1908, Mcr. Univ. Press 1975.*
- *Wm. Highfield's account as a schoolboy: CRO Incumbents Misc. 1697 P/7/7/1-10.*
- *Rev. Adam Martindale's Diary: Chetham Soc.Vol.1V, p 187.*
- *Charity Commissioners' Report for Cheshire, 1810. Clergy Call Books CRO EDV/2/7-17.*
- *GREEN Henry: Knutsford its Traditions and History. Mcr. Simms 1859 & 1887.*
- *Caleb Pott: 1690 CRO WS and for Macc. Gr. Sch VCH Vol. 3 p 234-5.*
- *Henry Crosedale: VCH Vol 3 p 237-8 and for Kn. Gr. Sch. John Rylands Handlist, Egerton deed no. 795.*
- *Isaac Antrobus and Nonconformist Schools: VCH Vol 3 p 221-7.*
- *Letters re Thomas Spencer and licence of Ralph Malbon, letters re Rev. John Robinson, nomination of Mr. Randle Hazelhurst, John Swinton Thos. Barlow and his resignation, nomination of Joseph Foden: CRO Parish Bundles EDP 164/9. William Woolmer: Qu. Sess. CRO QJF/124/2/113.*
- *Not.Cest. (Bishop Gastrell) Chet. Soc. Vol. 8 p 343. Carlisle: 1818. List of charities : C.R.O. QDL 2/3, 2/4.*
- *Baking: Middlemen in English Business, particularly between 1660-1760, WESTERFIELD R.B. Yale Univ. Press 1915 reprint David and Charles 1968, p174. Cann Office: CRO QJF 119/2/80 and GREEN (above).*
- *Wilmslow St. Bartholomew's Parish Church Wardens' Accounts 1591-1633 (now in CRO)*
- *Clock maker : PRO Chester Assizes 1685.*
- *Legh of Booths Charters. Keele Univ. L / 163.*
- *Egerton Leases, Manchester archives.*
- *Henry Jewill's son's apprenticeship, Chester Marriage Bonds, Part 1, Rec. Soc. of Lancs & Ches. 1933*

Chapter 4
Church and Chapel
Man shall not live by bread alone. Matt. 4: 4.
'Knutsford was a place of (as) much Sobriety and Religion as any in those parts'
William Tong : A Life of Matthew Henry

Newcomers to Knutsford are surprised to find that for a place with such an early foundation, the Brook Street Unitarian Chapel is the town's oldest place of worship, fifty years older in fact than its Parish Church. The Chapel was built in the 1690's so we will follow the turbulent events which led to its building and then how the Parish Church came to be built and meet some of the personalities involved with them both.

The 17th century was one of persecution, change and turmoil because of religious beliefs, their effect on politics and swings with each change of monarch. It was extremely difficult for anyone who had strong views on religion then to be honest and safe, he was bound to find himself on the wrong side of the law at one time or another. The Civil War and the Commonwealth were a culmination of this upheaval but between the Restoration and the Glorious Revolution in 1688 life was certainly no easier for those with firm and outspoken faiths. Even on into the 18th century in a small place like Knutsford, religious arguments affected many lives.

The seeds of the situation here which developed after 1660 had already been sown at the end of the previous century. Ecclesiastical authorities favoured puritan teaching which they saw as a way of winning people from the greater evil of popery. There came to be many clergy and parishioners who were won over in this staunchly Presbyterian north eastern part of Cheshire where there were very large parishes with scattered settlements which meant that ecclesiastical discipline was weak when national edicts demanded change. Despite a few bishops in Chester lenient towards them, government decrees c. 1620-30 increasingly required the presentment at Visitations of those not conforming to current episcopal practises. Clergy in Knutsford were prosecuted, among 60% of places in Cheshire, for not wearing a surplice (thought to be 'popish') and parishioners for not kneeling for Communion. Services had been neglected for the emphasis on the sermon.

The sermon was valued highly by the congregation especially by Presbyterians for whom preaching and education were their marks. Sermons were a free teaching and learning medium for everyone and a bridge and a propaganda vehicle for the illiterate into the educated and political world, stimulating thought and discussion. As early as 1612 Knutsford's benevolent mercer Henry Burgess, specified that the interest on his bequest of £200 was to be 'for a preaching minister' in Knutsford hoping to attract such a one by the incremented salary. This was not always successful for not all the appointed Knutsford clergy were graduates and the Bishop of Chester appointed a lecturer in Knutsford in 1622, 'to supply the want of a non-preaching incumbent'. Books of Homilies were available with printed sermons to be read aloud.

That life was not easy and growing more difficult for local puritans is evident in that it resulted in the emigration to America of Jeffrey Massey, cordwainer (shoemaker), of Over Knutsford in 1629/30. He had been presented by the Churchwardens for not kneeling while receiving the sacrament, which was not the first occasion that he had upset the Church authorities but this could have been the last straw for him. He paid £50 for the promise of land in Massachusetts and sailed from Bristol with his wife and family to become one of the first families to settle and found the port of Salem, Massachusetts. There were others from this area who emigrated to America for similar reasons. A conventicle, an illegal assembly of nonconformists, was reported in Knutsford among other places in the 1630's.

During the Civil War most of the High Church and the Roman Catholics were on the side of the King, and Puritans, Independents and Presbyterians, on the side of Parliament. After the Parliamentary victory in 1645 Bishops were imprisoned and High Church clergy hounded. Presbyterians in particular wished to reform national church organisation so that none among them held higher rank other than lay 'elder'. They considered every man to be equal in the sight of God and hoped to install educated Presbyterian ministers in the Churches. All services were to be conducted using the Presbyterian Directory and say extempore prayers instead of using the C of E Prayer Book which was declared illegal. All ministers, from High Church Anglican through to Low Church Presbyterian nevertheless considered themselves to be within the Church of England. Many churches in the country were without a minister then but there was no difficulty in finding Presbyterian ministers in Cheshire. The Rev. Edward Bold MA was retained in Knutsford during the Commonwealth having been incumbent since 1635 and after his death in 1656 the Rev. Robert Hunter was appointed to succeed him.

The salary of Knutsford clergy was meagre like many others nationally which was something which the Civil War administration tried to improve and in 1646/7, both Houses of Parliament ordered that the yearly sum of £40 should be paid to the minister in Knutsford,

out of the impropriate tythe corn of the Rectory of Frodsham ... sequestered from John, Earl Rivers, delinquent, ... the present maintenance belonging to the said chappell, (Knutsford), being but a stipend of £5.6.8d. per annum the towne of Knutsford being an ancient markett towne and the said chappellry consisting of above two hundred families.

Whether or not this sum was ever paid is not known, nor even whether the authorities were aware of this order ten years later for in 1657 a yearly sum of £25 was approved 'by His Highness and Council', (Oliver Cromwell), for Robert Hunter minister of Knutsford, but was this sum ever paid?

With the Restoration all was changed back again when Bishops and deposed ministers were reinstated and by 1662 all clergy were required to take the oath of allegiance and supremacy of the Crown, to subscribe to the 39 articles of faith, to use the revised Book of Common Prayer and to be re-ordained in the Church of England. Presbyterian Ministers would be ejected if they would not conform to these requirements.

A great many Ministers would not so conform some 2,000 of them throughout the country, thirteen initially in Cheshire soon to be followed by twenty nine more, who were ejected from their livings. In this area these included Robert Hunter in Knutsford, Adam Martindale of Rostherne, Hugh Henshaw of Chelford and the ministers of Over Peover, Nether Peover, Mobberley, Gawsworth, Wilmslow, Macclesfield, Goostrey, Congleton, Holmes Chapel, Alderley and Great Budworth etc. 'Thus we see how deeply, widely and conscientiously in this part of Cheshire the principals of nonconformity, of the sufficiency of the Scriptures and of the private judgement pervaded the minds of the clergy' one said at the time. Most of these continued to preach and pray publicly and locally despite the new legislation with threatening prosecution, large fines, imprisonment and increasing pressures to suppress them. Many members of the Commonwealth Presbyterian congregations felt loyal to their ex-ministers even after 1665 when the Five Mile Act forbade ministers to live or preach within five miles of their former Parish. They were prepared to walk miles to go to hear them. They held secret meetings and services with prayers and Bible readings in private houses, they repeated sermons they had heard in barns or out of doors in fields and clearings in woods sometimes very early in the morning. This was even though on Sundays everyone was required by law to attend the Parish Church or chapel and partake in the C of E services three times a day with the afternoon for catechism for the young, questions and answers on the reinstated Prayer book. Any absence from Church without good cause was to be noted by the Church or Chapel wardens, (there were five Chapel wardens in Knutsford after the Restoration) and culprits were liable to be reported at the next Visitation. Many people were generally familiar with the Bible and well instructed on most facets of their faith because of their many attendances in Church and for those who could read, the Bible was often the only book they ever came to possess or to which they had access. Throughout the period religion was important to many ordinary people, it was the topic of the age, they enjoyed debating and discussing the tenets and nuances of their faith and forms of worship.

People did not need reminding by the church that life was fragile. In their will preambles they wrote often, 'knowing the certainty of death and the uncertainty of the time thereof' and sometimes 'calling to remembrance the uncertain estate of this transitory life and that all flesh must yield unto death when it shall please God to call', for sickness and death were commonplace, medical skills were rudimentary and life was hard. Some barely mention their faith, 'in perfect memory blessed be God I do dispose of my estate after my decease as followeth'- but others wrote more like Philip Hewitt, tanner in 1702: ' I commend my soul into the hands of Almighty God fully trusting that in and through my Saviour Jesus Christ I shall have free remission of all my sins and to inherit eternal life'. Some wrote at much greater length. The church and religious faith provided comfort and strength to many.

The Church was also a disciplinary body responsible for maintenance of public morals and its court, the Consistory Court, was still effective although its powers were beginning to diminish and the institution was and had been controversial since before the Civil War. People were not only fined for failing to attend church but also for failing to pay church lays, taxes for maintaining church property and for the poor, and public penance was demanded for adultery, fornication and libel which required the offender to confess his sin publicly in church, barefoot, wrapped in a white sheet with a wand in his hand. Later in the century this was in some cases changed to a fine. This system offended the Presbyterians who thought that each man was answerable before God and his conscience and that each parish should be responsible for its own discipline.

In 1662 apart from Presbyterians there were Quakers meeting in Knutsford. They would have remembered the confrontation on Knutsford Heath between Rev. Adam Martindale of Rostherne and the Quaker Mr. Hubberthorn who both expressed their differences 'fiercely but on a high plain'. Quakers believed that the individual's soul could be in immediate contact with its maker without the necessity of church or priest. In 1669 in Knutsford, there was 'an unlawful assembly of Quakers to a considerable number in the house of Richard Yarwood'. Quakers evoked strong passions against them by many including Presbyterians and Thomas Yarwood of Knutsford, 'declaring the truth in his birthplace had violent hands laid upon him and was afterwards pursued into a private house by a man with a weapon'. There were also over twenty Quakers in Mobberley where they had their own graveyard for a considerable area but any caught attending a Quaker burial were presented to Quarter Sessions for punishment. Their newly founded meeting house was in Morley near Wilmslow near where they set up their own school about 1698. Quakers were a caring society looking after their own from an area as far as Wildboarclough and were liable to be fined by JPs if they did not go to church but had to confess with penitence to their own brethren if they did attend the 'steeple house'.

It is remarkable that no records of Roman Catholics have been found in Knutsford. These, called recusants with others and Quakers were all named and noted by the authorities in Quarter Sessions if they failed to attend church or made anti-Anglican views known. Sir Peter Leycester quoted 25 Quakers, 9 Sectaries and 2 Papists in Mobberley in 1677.

Rostherne Church

Knutsford was a chapelry within the large parish of Rostherne of which church Adam Martindale was vicar from 1648-1662, and during the Commonwealth in 1653 he formed a 'Voluntary Association' of like-minded ministers in Cheshire, (Presbyterian and Independents), later called a Classis, which met to discuss theology, approve elders and to ordain ministers for congregations locally. This Classis dissolved with the Restoration, but it was to be revived again in 1690 with new members as we shall hear.

Rostherne Parish Church - Cheshire Image Bank

Martindale's diary is a colourful account of the impact of national policies upon his life and the locality and illustrates contemporary attitudes, problems and some of the very strong feelings aroused. With the Restoration in 1660, Martindale at the age of 37 was imprisoned in 'The Feathers' in Chester (at his own expense) on a charge of 'disaffection to the King's Majesty' but a petition was sent from his parish which included Knutsford, signed by 'six score hands of gentlemen of quality, freeholders and other householders' certifying,

we verily believe in our consciences that Adam Martindale, Minister there, is a very faithful friend to his Majesty's person and government and a real enemy to all plotters against the same as his frequent and finest prayers in public for these many months past, besides other evidences thereof so abundantly manifest.

This helped and speeded his release.

Although most members of the Church supported or at least did not object to Presbyterianism some did resent the killjoy aspect of Puritan doctrine and when Martindale came home again he found that a maypole had been set up so that he would have to pass it to get to the church. With the Restoration, maypoles were allowed again. Martindale was very put out by this, knowing it was put there with the express purpose of annoying him, 'but he would not gratify their spiteful humour by taking notice of it'. He preached a sermon from Proverbs about simple people loving simple things and referred to the maypole as a shameful relic of the worship of the Strumpet Flora in Rome. He said that although it was harmless in itself it was sinful to have put it up on purpose to affront him, their spiritual father and pastor.

This nettled some of the parishioners who then asked a previous minister to come and preach one Sunday morning hoping that he would be on their side. This vicar was the Rev. Brooke, then minister of Congleton aged 68, (who was called 'Bawling Brooke' by his enemies) who came, but Martindale said that when he saw the maypole in his way 'and understood by whom and to what end it was set up, he did most smartly reprove their sin and follie, calling them the most approbrious names as scumme, rabble, rife rafe (or such like) of the parish; insomuch that my words were smooth like oyle in comparison of his, so full of salt and vinegar'.

Not long after this, Martindale's wife and three young women cut it down in the night with a framing saw.

His troubles were just starting. He was ejected from his Rostherne living in 1662 because he would not use the Book of Common Prayer or declare unfeigned assent and consent to all things contained in it and prescribed by it by the deadline date of 24th August, protesting that his ejection had been arranged (but as Martindale never afterwards conformed as some others did, it did not alter the situation).

The newly restored Bishop of Chester lost no time and sent out an order on 29th August to the Churchwardens of Rostherne, strictly charging that Martindale, 'late Vicar', was to

forbear preaching, lecturing or officiating in the said church or elsewhere in the Diocese, and they were to secure and preserve the said parish church from any invasion or intrusion of the said Adam Martindale, disabled and deprived as aforesaid ... the churchwardens to show this order to the said Martindale and cause the same to be published the next Sunday after in the parish church before the congregation.

So he had to remove himself from the Vicarage to make way for his soon to be appointed successor. After his ejection he stayed in Rostherne until the Five Mile Act in 1665 and regularly attended the services of his successor. He sadly missed the income of £60 per annum living but he was never at a loss. To support his family he studied mathematics and took in pupils, some boarders and began teaching again as he had at the start of his career. He also 'had an abundance of French wheat and rye out of my ground at Tatton amounting to 12 pounds or 20 marks a year and what I got by schooling and tabling of young gentlemen and others for two of the first years and teacher of mathematics afterwards (in Manchester), which was far more considerable, brought me sometimes 15 and sometimes 20 shillings a week or more, besides my own diet and keeping of my horse'. He later became chaplain to Lord Delamere, (Sir George Booth of Civil War fame) and after the 1672 Toleration Act he preached again in the district. He died in 1686 and was buried in the chancel of Rostherne church aged 63, without stone or epitaph.

Of his ordained successor the Rev. Benjamin Crosse, Adam Martindale as well as criticising his sermons had some rather tart comments to make.

'His voice being so weak and lisping, that multitudes could not at all understand him (that had understood me plainly) and those that could, generally thought him a very mean preacher. People declined his company and he being young and sociable, always either tippling in an alehouse or very near one, was laid open to the temptation of wild company and got such an habit of loving strong ale and brandy that it prejudiced his studies and at last killed him'.

Benjamin Crosse was vicar at Rostherne for less than 10 years and Martindale commented on his death that Mr. Delves, the apothecary in Knutsford who was the Rev. Crosse's apothecary, told Martindale that gills of brandy which he got elsewhere when Mr.Delves refused to sell Mr. Crosse any, had been his death by making his liver as hard as horn.

Knutsford Chapelry

For most of the century and possibly before, Knutsford's timber-framed, Parochial Chapel was only used for services in the summer season because of its distance from the town and the lane or footpath leading to it known as Bache Lane became very muddy in the winter. The lane was presented to Quarter Sessions for this reason on one occasion although there were frequent visits up there to the graveyard for burials and for bell ringing. Standing unused each winter could not have been good for its fabric and the windows were regularly broken. There was also a hazard getting in and out of the building. In 1670 the chapel wardens petitioned the Chancellor and the Rural Dean for collection of a lay in order to build a loft in which to ring the bells as the four ropes from them

Ringing the bells at Lower Peover church, a timber framed building with a stone tower and no ringing loft, just as at Knutsford's old church

hung dangerously in the west passage by the widest door where people came and went. The bells were in the stone tower which was built in the reign of Henry Vl11th. This Church was then called by local people Knutsford Church (now called locally, St. Helena's) and they called the Chapel of Ease, St. Mary's in King Street, the Chapel in the Town where the winter season services were held. Services were not taken in both places at the same time, they were either at one or the other.   Here in the town, pews had been installed earlier in the century possibly with some money towards the cost from Henry Burgess but the rest were paid for by the inhabitants.

The site of Knutsford's Parochial Chapel, the old Knutsford Church called locally, St. Helena's.
Some of the seventeenth century gravestones mark its shape.
The adjoining stone tower was built in the sixteenth century

In Knutsford the Rev. Robert Hunter did afterwards conform and although no longer the appointed minister continued to live in Knutsford where three of his children were baptised. He removed to Macclesfield after about 1670 but died later in Liverpool. After Hunter's ejection in 1662 the Rev. John Small was appointed, but he died intestate a few months later having barely had time to make his mark on the town. From his letters of administration it seems that he came from London, but he was such a stranger that no one here even knew his Christian name at the time.

After his death of in 1664, the Rev. Samuel Hanmer came from Weaverham and may have been the choice or a family friend of the Leghs of Booths for Peter Legh's eldest half sister Dorothy later married Hanmer who was minister here for only three years. (Peter was still a youth at this time). They too continued to live on in Knutsford after his succession probably on his wife's marriage allowance. It seems unlikely that he was the choice of the inhabitants for whether or not he was High Church or his preaching was not to their liking he soon provoked and so upset many in the congregation that many families began to meet and talk together for the first time with a view to breaking away from the established church and building their own chapel. This was a very serious step to consider and one that was at that time not legally possible to do but when the Rev. Kettelby Turner BA came in 1667, chosen by the inhabitants, these dissenters, Presbyterians, 'found him so godly that they gave up the idea of a new chapel and followed him'. Rev. Turner was Knutsford's minister for almost 20 years during which time the national scene saw more religious fluctuations.

There were more prosecutions of illegal gatherings although in this area it was chiefly Quakers who were brought before the magistrates. When caught at these illegal meetings, Quakers were repeatedly gaoled or sent to the House of Correction in Middlewich and for non payment of tithes were fined and goods and cattle distrained. In 1682, a young Quaker Knutsford couple, George and Ann Clave (nee Duncalfe), sailed for a new life free of persecution, to Pennsylvania. They bought land through William Penn on the Delaware River, the minimum holding was 250 acres for £5, and settled there with other Quakers from this area. They sailed on the 'Friends Adventure', a sixty day passage from Liverpool.

That chiefly Quakers were prosecuted was probably because the constables as well as some local Justices turned a blind eye to illegal meetings of nonconformists as they were themselves somewhat sympathetic to their activities but Sir Peter Leycester JP was not at all sympathetic to nonconformists. He was fiercely determined to uphold the laws to suppress them and try and help to stamp out heresy and sedition as he saw it. As not many culprits were brought before him he urged juries to seek out and present those who did not conform. He gave very long speeches to the juries of the Quarter Sessions quoting the law,

Every person obstinately refusinge to come to church every Sunday not having any lawful excuse: Fine for every Sunday X11 pence ... Every seditious sectary not hearinge Divine Service ... for a moneth together obstinately, or shall joyne in Private Conventicles of their owne, being above 16 yeares old ... shall be committed without baile till they conforme and make open submission ... which if they refuse they shall be abjured the Realme.

Constables and church wardens who failed to report absences from church of all 'Popish recusants' were to be fined 40 shillings, but in vain. The fines soon increased to £s and imprisonment and after a third offence if found guilty, 'to be transported beyond the sea'. The Presbyterians were still meeting together in places apart from the church and in 1672 came the first Act of Toleration which eased matters briefly for many of them. Rev. Hugh Henshall, a previously ejected minister from Chelford who had come to live in Crosstown, applied for a license to preach in his own house or cottage so that dissenters could go there for sermons and Bible study. His house called

'Chapel House' stood near to where Crosstown Church now is until 1905. Another minister was also then living with his family in Knutsford, Rev. Peter Leigh or Legh, a relative of the Leghs of Booths who had been ejected from St. John's Church in Chester also obtained a license. Although not in good health for many years he lived until 1693. These two ministers came to be regarded as the first leaders of the dissenters in Knutsford.

The third cottage on the right, where Dissenters met before 1689
(Photograph presented by Mrs Cooper)
Hugh Henshaw's 'Chapel House'

The liberty which the 1672 licences gave was short lived as they were soon withdrawn, once more driving dissenters' meetings underground. They later rioted outside the Chapel in the town.

Squire Peter Legh having come of age and married in the 1670's seems to have had a difficult and stormy relationship with the inhabitants of the parish with regard to the church. In the 1680's the Anglican church was strong and Charles 11 began to lean towards Catholicism. In 1682, 'the excellent Godly Minister' Rev. Turner was fined for not giving due notice of Saints' Days. There was evidently mounting friction between parishioners who were happy with Rev. Turner and Squire Peter Legh who wanted High Church services with more emphasis on ritual, ceremony and the sacraments. Since the Restoration, as Communion services were only held in Knutsford Church this may have been the reason why Peter Legh preferred services to be held there. It was also slightly nearer to his Hall of Booths although he and his family would not have had to walk there in bad weather. He was also insisting that he had the advowson which the freeholders disputed, but whatever his quarrel was, he was suddenly triggered to anger on 20th December 1684, just before a Christmas time service. He obtained the Town Chapel keys and had the doors locked. Despite several requests for the keys for the doors to be opened so that they could hold their service he refused and 'this caused outrage, an uproar and a great commotion', a large crowd of the congregation milling outside the Chapel.

Some men armed themselves with whatever they could find and led by William Birtles tanner, Thomas Harper shoemaker, both of Nether Knutsford and John Rylands of Over Knutsford tanner, with others who wielded staves, swords, hammers, axes and other arms and implements, with an iron bar riotously broke open the lock of the door of the chapel where they had been 'prevented from attending common prayer and divine service, a grievous loss to all the inhabitants'. Henry Long, webster, Chapel warden, Edward Legh, tailor and Robert Hall, labourer, a sidesman, all of Nether Knutsford, were arrested and charged that they, 'armed with staves, swords, knives and other offensive weapons riotously broke into the Knutsford Chapel in possession of Peter Legh knight and destroyed ('turned over') the chapel and took away one bar of iron priced at 6d. and one iron bolt worth three times as much, both the goods of the said Peter Legh'.

The constables were obliged to arrest these men and also had the difficult task of reporting the Squire for his part in the matter. The case was heard at Quarter Sessions six months later and the first three Knutsford men were acquitted but this could not have improved relations with the Squire.

In 1686 the Rev. Kettelby Turner died and was buried in the Knutsford Church graveyard. His death brought matters to a crunch. Now with a new minister needed, at least twenty dissenters decided to oppose Peter Legh and claim that they, the Nether Knutsford freeholders, the owners of the burgage plots, had the advowson, the right to choose the next minister, one congenial to their point of view. The dispute was fierce and continued for months but Peter Legh held his ground. The Church Court became involved to settle the matter and an Interrogatory was ordered, an inquiry before a Court case could be heard. This was the very worst possible time for a sympathetic hearing of the dissenters with Catholic King James on the throne and it was therefore no surprise that they lost, but a grave and bitter disappointment.

The verdict was that Peter Legh, the Egertons, (the two Lords of the manors), the Bishop of Chester and Christ Church, Oxford, had the right to chose the minister in turns. The freeholders maintained that they usually appointed ministers and that the parish clerk usually held the keys of the Chapel but that Peter Legh had obtained the key upon demand. This gave the Bishop's court reason to find against the freeholders. One of the many questions asked at the Interrogatory was whether the town Chapel had ever been locked before and William Highfield of Bexton was called as a witness. He told of the time when he was a school boy in about 1617 when

one Thomas Bateman did cause a Bear to be brought into the chapel and into the pulpit there his paws or foremost feet were laid on the Desk of the said pulpit whereupon much trouble ensued and preaching and other public exercise of religion was by the Bishop prohibited for about a twelve month until the same was consecrated anew.

He said that he was there at the time, (during service), and that his father had told him it had cost the inhabitants £5 or more for the reconsecration. The freeholders were aggrieved that they had spent money over the years to repair and beautify the chapel. The floor had been 'new layd with clay' in about 1677, and a new form or seat was erected for the constables or chapel reeves, the four or five chapel wardens and the sidesmen, which was later moved to a more convenient position and at that time a new window was put in. This was all to no avail in the outcome of the dispute. Presbyterians felt the right to choose their own minister was centrally important but Chester's Bishop Cartwright being very High Church and anxious to please King James was keen to suppress all signs of nonconformity.

After the case the Rev. Samuel Hulme was appointed to be the new incumbent, Bishop Gastrell, said later that Knutsford's patronage lay with Christ Church, Oxford that year and that their Dean and Chapter nominated him which then he, the Bishop licensed. Christ Church, tithe owners and holders of the glebe land were taking their turn to appoint, first. This could have been why it proved to be such an unpopular appointment in Knutsford. Samuel Hulme, though, was the son of dissenting parents and had succeeded Adam Martindale as chaplain to Lord Delamere, the Booth family, the local JP with known nonconformist leanings who had lavishly entertained the Protestant Duke of Monmouth in 1682. But Samuel Hulme may have turned his coat like the proverbial Vicar of Bray for he proved to be so  High Church that he drove many members of the Knutsford congregation who had not previously been dissenters to join their ranks in protest. James 11 was coming to a critical stage in his reign and there were hopes of religious toleration again, even if ostensibly for Catholics. The freeholders had lost the right to chose the minister and with this unpopular appointment then the dissenters felt more strongly that they must now become a separate congregation. Among these men were Isaac Antrobus skinner, Peter Wood ironworker and scrivener, William Leftwich shopkeeper, John Bostock

A Non Conformist Minister

gent., John Percivall, schoolmaster and Dr. William Smith, physician.

While the Rev. Samuel Hulme was parson in Knutsford, unpopular, Peter Legh was blamed for his appointment. After James II's Declaration of Indulgence in 1687, the dissenters including the new 'recruits' from the church took matters into their own hands and appointed their own preacher, young Rev.William Tong (p70). It was his first appointment and he came to Knutsford in November 1687 despite his misgivings about the 'great contentions' here at the time, the long standing arguments with the Squire. Tong also feared that the new members 'would not prove so steady or so regular as those that had been instructed in the principals of nonconformity'. He need not have worried for their numbers grew and with William and Mary on the throne in 1689 there came the Act of Toleration when 'leave was given for all to meet and serve God in their own manner, peaceably and publicly' (except for Catholics). Dissenters were now no longer obliged to attend the C of E services which most had been doing dutifully each Sunday and could now lawfully hold their own services. Even so for a person to stand outside the established church and be prepared to declare himself as different took some courage, for no-one was a dissenter by accident or default.

The Act of Toleration marked the beginning of the official break up of the old community. No longer did the whole town attend services together under one roof. The cracks beneath the surface, different religious preferences of old, were now in the open and separate.

The next minister appointed only a few years later by Peter Legh and the new Bishop was quite acceptable to them all.

The Dissenters' Chapel

In 1689 the dissenters had the freedom to worship separately but had no building in which to do so. The chief family involved in the foundation and building of the new chapel was the Antrobus family who had been dissenters for many years.

After the accession of James II in 1685, Isaac Antrobus was one of about twenty men in the County who was brought before the notorious Chief Justice, Judge Jeffries in Chester at the General Assize for not attending Church for a month, his protest at a Catholic King. Jeffries told the Court sternly on this occasion that 'these dissenters are dangerous enemies to the public peace and their conventicles are nurseries of faction and ought by all lawful means to be suppressed'.

Isaac Antrobus born 1627, was an educated man, a skinner, who was very much to the fore in the town's activities, had taken on many responsibilities in the Court Leet and the church (see Chapter 5). He lived in a modest home with only one hearth even in 1674 in what is now Holford Crescent where Brook House, built later, stood until the second World War. This was the home of Lady Jane Stanley from 1780 until 1803.

At the same time as the dissenters grew in number, he and his two eldest sons decided to give the land adjoining their house on Brook Street, just round the corner from them facing Adam's Hill, for the building of the chapel. This freehold land was part of these sons' inheritance so their joint gift was a generous one, the size of the plot large enough not only for the chapel itself but for a burial ground at the front and at the side.

In 1689/90, William Tong their first preacher moved on to Coventry but kept up his contact with the town and visited it on many occasions afterwards. His place was taken by another young man, Rev. Thomas Kynaston. who was to join with others to found the revived Cheshire Classis which was led chiefly

Brook Street Chapel

*Interior of Brook Street Dissenters' Chapel with central pulpit and lectern
Picture - Kath Goodchild*

by Matthew Henry of Chester. This Classis was an association of Presbyterian ministers covering a wide area, Shropshire, Derbyshire and Lancashire some coming even from London. The Classis met regularly in Ministers' homes in the locality. Firstly they decided on their forms of service and then they undertook to ordain men for the Presbyterian church in Cheshire. Candidates were questioned in Latin on languages, philosophy, physics and Divinity and after presenting a Latin thesis if they were approved in this examination, they were eligible to be ordained. The ordination services were held the next day in public. Records

The Reverend Mr William Tong

of the minutes of these meetings still exist from its inception in 1691. These ministers were academics capable of delivering good sermons expounding the Word of God valued so highly by their congregations.

After 1689 plans were mooted to build almost identical chapels in Knutsford, Macclesfield and Dean Row, Wilmslow for the large congregations which were gathering weekly from well beyond their own parishes. Chapel building was not the province of the ministers of the Classis but for the congregations who had their own committees for raising funds for building and furnishing the Chapels and also for paying their ministers a salary. Some of the local gentry and high standing families who helped with contributions for Knutsford were Mrs. Ward of Capesthorne, Mr. Holland of Mobberley, Col. Venables' widow of Wincham, Mr. Lowe of Chelford and Mr. Robert Kell of Marthall. No records remain of the costs of Knutsford's Chapel but in Macclesfield the money paid to workmen and for building materials between February and July 1690 when their Chapel was completed came to £85.17s.5d. At about this time sixteen dissenters' chapels were built in Cheshire.

Knutsford's Brook Street Chapel is a simple cottage style building with a door in the west end with an upstairs gallery having two separate outside staircase entrances. Inside, it is plain with wooden pews surrounding a central large pulpit and lectern in the middle of its north wall, emphasising the Presbyterian emphasis on the Word of God.

Knutsford's chapel building was certainly completed by January 1694 when Brook Street Chapel was officially licensed. The 'Settlement Indenture' of the New Chapel or Meeting Place dated 7th March 1694 names some of the persons closely involved.

Isaac Antrobus and sons John and Walter, leased the land for 1,000 years for a yearly rent of 20 shillings as well as donating £25 towards the cost of the building. The Chapel with its furniture was in the hands of six Trustees: Peter Coulthurst, John Leadbetter, John Bostocke, John Dean, Peter Wood and Robert Kell.

Brook Street Chapel, W.R. Strachan

Peter Coulthurst was a gentleman of Sandlebridge (1669-1741). He was one of those who encouraged Knutsford parishioners to join the dissenters after Samuel Hulme's appointment, 'a most substantial leading person of Nether Knutsford'. His son became a doctor in Nether Knutsford and one of his daughters married John Holland of Mobberley, one of whose great grand daughters was to be Elizabeth Gaskell. Thomas Holland was ordained by the Classis.

John Leadbeater was Attorney at Law of Knutsford (died 1704) and must have helped to draw up the documentation of the new chapel. He may have been related to Thomas Leadbeater of the Hermitage in Holmes Chapel, an ejected dissenting minister.

John Bostocke, ironmonger and gentleman, formerly of Crosstown but later of King Street, Knutsford. Actively involved in town and county, a considerable property holder, a juryman of the Court Leet he became head Constable for Bucklow Hundred in 1697. His large house with his initials and that of his wife Mary still stands in King Street Knutsford with the ground floor now converted into shops. He died in 1707.

John Deane was a tallow chandler from Over Peover.

Peter Wood 1638-1706, originally from Lower Peover was Knutsford's respected scribe, later a freeholder and a prominent inhabitant who appeared at the Church Court as a spokesman and witness for them in the advowson dispute.

The initials and date on John and Mary Bostock's house, King Street

Robert Kell 1654-1722, was a yeoman of Marthall whose daughter married Isaac Antrobus's youngest son Isaac the schoolmaster.

These were the Trustees. Of the rest of the congregation the Settlement mentions but does not name, eighty members heads of households, by whose efforts enough money was raised to build the chapel. Like the Trustees they came from surrounding places so it is not easy to calculate the proportion who were Knutsford people. The Knutsford population was about 1,000 but just recovering from the severe epidemic and famine in 1685-6. Taking an average of 4.5 per family could it be that nearly a quarter were dissenters? Over the next two decades and by 1715, the Rev. Thomas Lea then minister, had '500 hearers', of whom '18 were gentlemen, 64 yeomen, 5 tradesmen and 47 labourers, amongst whom were 77 voters'. This shows the wide cross section of society who were dissenters. There were similar numbers in Macclesfield but more than twice this number in Dean Row, Wilmslow. 1715 was probably the peak time of dissenting popularity. Numbers like these would have had difficulty in squeezing into the almost cottage like buildings of the new chapels.

Among these members were many of the town's successful professional, business and tradesmen including the medical men, for the protestant work ethic was part of their beliefs, if they worked hard and gave of their best God would prosper them. Having survived danger and persecution since the Commonwealth who could foretell how certain or safe the future would be? Not unnaturally a clause was included in the Settlement to cover the event of toleration being withdrawn, Isaac Antrobus and his heirs were then to enjoy the chapel premises either as a dwelling house or an outbuilding. Building the chapel was a visual concrete achievement, a step of determined confidence made in faith in their new right to religious freedom.

Before, during and after the building of the Chapel, private houses continued to be licensed as meeting places for the dissenters where they read, prayed, repeated sermons, enjoying the company of like minded friends, sharing, discussing and exchanging thoughts and ideas.

The first minister of the new chapel building, Thomas Kynaston died early in 1696 aged only 29. After the founding of the Classis, his home was often its venue and his wife Hannah must have become used to catering for a house full of reverend gentlemen arriving on horseback travel weary from far flung places. When he died she was expecting their fifth child. She was supported by the chapel community who paid for the education of their children. His tombstone in the Chapel calls him 'Pastour for 6 years of this Congregation, who was the first that ministred ...'.

In the summer of 1696 Mr. Samuel Lowe (1669-1709) replaced him from his position in Chorlton, Manchester. He had hesitated before accepting the appointment because he already had a ministry and he wanted to be sure that he had received God's call to come. After being here a year, in June 1697 he married Katherine, the only daughter of Isaac Antrobus. Where

they lived is not clear because a 'new erected house in possession of Samuel
Lowe' was licensed in the name of Dr. William Smith as a dissenters' Meeting
Place in July 1697 only a month after the wedding. A
daughter Mary was born to them in 1698 but Katherine
nee Antrobus died the following year. Samuel Lowe's
family may have come from Chelford.

In October 1698, one of this congregation, Robert Blacklocke, Nether
Knutsford chapman (tradesman), formerly from Dumfries, Scotland, left a
legacy of one gold guinea to 'Samuel Lowe now minister of the New Chapel',
20s. to be given to the poor of Nether Knutsford to be disposed by Peter
Wood and John Bostock and '£5 for the use of a preaching minister of the
new chapel whilst the dissenting liberty is continued', with provisions in case
it should be restrained. No one was totally confident in this new liberty.

When Samuel Lowe died in 1709 having been secretary to the Classis, 'a
faithful and beloved Minister', he was buried under the floor of the Chapel
having been living in a room (in Isaac Antrobus's house) with his collection
of over £23 worth of books. The Classis minutes recorded his death after
thirteen years by saying among other things that 'some that were acquainted
with him said they never knew him to be angry'.

The Rev. Thomas Lea (1656-1733), was a Minister at Upton in the Wirral
before coming to Knutsford where he had been many times to the Classis.
His popularity must be evident by the numbers quoted above who came to
hear him preach. His record is of 'a diligent and conscientious Minister of
great humility and tenderness'. He lived to the age of 77 and was still 'in
harness' when he died.

One of the disabilities faced by non-conformists not being within the
Church of England was not being eligible to take degrees from the Universities
of Oxford or Cambridge so some went to Scotland to graduate. As they valued
education their remedy was to establish schools and Academies, teaching
universities of their own. These first Ministers who came to Knutsford had been
pupils of Franklands Academy which was the first nonconformist Academy.
Based near to or in the Lake District, they often moved to escape detection.
Some entered legal and medical professions some went to commercial and
country life but the greater number became ministers of religion.

Isaac Antrobus's youngest son Isaac had been to Franklands Academy
and was a schoolmaster at first in Stand Grammar School, near Prestwich,
north Manchester and then opened his own private non-conformist school
in Knutsford and he took in boarders. Schools such as this often had a
high reputation. He taught here from 1716 until he died in 1734 aged 57.
He is known to have taught two brothers from Bury, John and Samuel Kay,
Samuel later becoming one of the first physicians of Manchester Infirmary.
Their father paid £4 a quarter for the two boys for boarding and teaching
in 1724. There is a long Latin eulogy inscribed in praise of Isaac Antrobus,
schoolmaster, within the New Chapel built on his father's land.

Despite having their own Chapel and minister the dissenters still had strong links with the established Church which was the only place where people could be legally married. Even Elizabeth Gaskell in the 19th century when marrying a Unitarian Minister had to be married in Knutsford Parish Church. Many still wished to be buried in the old Knutsford churchyard with their families. The town was small, they were neighbours and friends, they lived and worked together and despite arguments and disagreements, respected each other and still remembered their roots in the Church. John Bostock one of the Chapel trustees, when writing the codicil to his will in October 1708, left £5 to the poor of Nether Knutsford, £3 to the poor of Mobberley and £5 to be employed at interest for the maintenance of a pious preaching minister of the new chapel in Knutsford 'where Mr. Samuel Lowe now preaches' and 20s. to Mr. Samuel Lowe. He appointed John Lowe his loving brother in law from Chelford to be one of his executors. A surprise comes in the instructions for his funeral: '- my body on the day of my funeral to be carried out of my house at Knutsford exactly at one of the clock and from thence to the Chapel at Chelford there to be decently interred in such place as my executors shall think fit, Mr. James Robinson, Minister of Knutsford to preach my funeral sermon'. He did not have a Presbyterian burial in Knutsford.

Knutsford Church and the Chapel of Ease

In Knutsford's established church in 1690, the Rev. James Robinson MA was appointed. He was to be Knutsford's parson for 54 years. While here he married and had a daughter and a son. The Rev. James Robinson was a Glasgow graduate, which could signify dissenting beginnings or training. He became known and was referred to as Parson Robinson, a well loved and respected parson who helped to heal some of the earlier breaches in the community. He watched the new dissenters' Chapel being built and completed and experienced part of his congregation defecting to it. He also witnessed the further lengthy dispute with Peter Legh which he must have tried to help resolve.

During the 1690's Sir Samuel Daniel, Lt. Col. of the militia, son and heir of the Daniels of Over Tabley, built Bexton Hall, a 'fair capital house or messuage' with a considerable estate said to be worth £100 p.a. within the Chapelry of Nether Knutsford where he had come to live. He came to the Chapel in the town to worship on Sundays and sat on the front pew. The social structure of the parish was traditionally seated with the gentry at the front, yeomen and husbandmen in the middle and the cottagers at the back, the town's officials in their own pew near to the front. Whether or not Peter Legh had a pew of his own in the town Chapel is not known, he certainly sat at the front and had his own pew in Knutsford Church. Col.

Daniel wanted his own pew to be built in the town Chapel but his approach towards this end was hardly straightforward.

Early in February 1697 when Thomas Hall a young clothworker was on business with him at the Bexton house he explained to Hall his request for a pew and entrusted him with £50, the interest of which was to be for the Knutsford Minister for ever, on the condition that Daniel might have leave to erect this pew.

The proposition was received by the parishioners very favourably and especially the news of possible extra money for the Minister's salary. On 29th March a petition for a pew next to the Clerk's reading desk was submitted to the Bishop signed by 50 of Knutsford's chief freeholders including leading dissenters, Isaac Antrobus, Peter Wood and John Leadbeater. They were still involved with the Church. Perhaps they saw this as a chance to review and settle the advowson dispute that had been started and decided so unsatisfactorily to them eleven years earlier.

When Peter Legh learned of this petition his reaction was fury. He was affronted. In anger once more he obtained the keys of the town Chapel and this time had the door locked and nailed closed. Jealousy could have come into it this time but he alleged that the townsmen must have been forced to sign the petition as not all the names were signed by the men themselves. He said that not all the Sacraments were held in the Town Chapel and that anyway it was used by the market people to set their horses there (quite untrue). Would he have reacted better to the proposition of a pew being built in the Parochial Chapel? This we do not know for nowhere is Peter Legh's point of view stated.

Parson Robinson had a difficult task to keep the situation calm, but he must have succeeded to some extent because there were at least no arrests made but the Consistory Court was once more involved.

On 17th June 1697 the Church Court interviewed Peter Wood and Thomas Hall who both affirmed Samuel Daniel's right to a seat as he had come to live within the parish. Peter Wood said he had known Samuel Daniel since Samuel's childhood. They acknowledged his kind and generous offer to the Minister but denied any pressure on them to sign their names which they had done cheerfully and freely and Thomas Hall said he had written his father's name by his direction or consent. They also denied that the market people ever used the Chapel for their horses. They said that the sacrament of Baptism was frequently held there, but that the Lord's Supper was these days only held at the Higher Parochial Chapel. All the old questions were raised again, who kept the keys, the right to choose the Minister, how much the inhabitants had spent on the Chapel and had the Chapel doors been locked before.

The Church decided to hold another Interrogatory, and this was called on 2nd November at the George Inn with ten witnesses several of whom had appeared at the hearing eleven years before, including William Highfield then aged 86 who again told the story of the bear, Isaac Antrobus then 70 and Peter Wood aged 57.

The political and religious climate was in 1697 in the reign of William and Mary very different from that of 1686 but the outcome of the case was no different. The now Bishop although with different leanings, would not lightly relinquish his patronage of this Chapelry shared with Peter Legh, the Egertons and Christ Church and as for Col. Daniel's pew, the long very faint, faded Latin document about it is listed as 'prohibition'. Col. Daniel wished in his will, to be buried in his chapel in Rostherne Church so after this episode he retrieved his £50 and took the longer ride to Rostherne for his Church attendance. He served in Ireland with King William and was knighted by him.

The Parish Church

In the 18th century the old Knutsford Church became increasingly unsafe, its 14th century timber structure in imminent danger of collapse and in 1713, it was so decayed that it was 'not capable of being repaired but must be pulled down' and the Chapel in the town not a great deal better.

Permission was granted from the JPs at Quarter Sessions for 'Knutsford Chapelry which is very numerous' to become a parish in its own right that year and a Brief was circulated nation-wide to raise the money for the new Parish Church. Estimates were obtained from workmen for building the new Church including the mason, the carpenter, the painter for plastering and for 'ornamenting the Church with ... the Queen's Armes, the Commandments, Lord's Prayer and Creed', the 'plumer' for lead for the roof and glazier (the same man). Estimates begin with the words, 'Suppose the Church to be 30 yards long and 18 yards broad and the tower to be 84 feet high'... with pillars, 14 arches, 3 doors and 30 windows and pews, but no drawing or plan among them. The total estimated cost was for more than £4,000 but the Brief was given a license for £2,700. Briefs were read in churches countrywide hoping for donations towards the causes in them.

The money raising took thirty long years and the Brief did not raise an eighth of its hoped- for amount. £200 was vested from Queen Anne's Bounty and legacies for the minister then amounted to £300. The inhabitants had to pay for the shortfall who were to raise £225 a year for four years. Plots of common land were sold including Moorhead and Damhead Moor and glebe land was enclosed to raise more money. The Church was to be built on the Tentry Croft belonging to Samuel Egerton Esq., who was to be compensated for it. The tower of the ancient Chapel was to be taken down and some of the stone removed to the Tentry croft. The four old bells were to be recast into a peal of five if the tower of the new church was thought to be strong enough to bear them. Abell Redhall of Gloucester was the bellfounder chosen, in June 1748. Bricks were to be drawn from the kiln on the Heath next to Tatton. A plan for the church was drawn by John Garlive. The Act of Parliament stated that Knutsford parochial chapelry should become a distinct parish and vicarage, independent of the mother church of Rostherne from 25th March 1741. The advowson was not changed, the Lords of the Manor of Over Knutsford should present alternately and Col. Egerton being Lord of the Manor of Nether Knutsford had one presentation in four.

James Robinson lived to become the first Vicar of Knutsford in 1741, thirty years of his ministry spent waiting for and raising sufficient funds. He died just six months before the Church was consecrated on 24th June 1744.

Knutsford Parish Church, St John's built 1744

Evidence of the practical extent to which religious belief was part of daily life is reflected in the inventory of Henry Long in 1715, where his 'holy day pewter dishes' and 'workday pewter dishes' were valued separately.

Into the 18th century other sects grew up, split off and met elsewhere. In 1727 Knutsford's old Sessions House was converted into a Chapel and licensed for the use of nonconformists. Knutsford already had its Presbyterian Chapel so this was for an another group. Methodists were on the scene soon after Wesley preached in the town in King Street in March 1738. There were Baptists in Warford and Independents also in the area.

Brook Street Chapel became Unitarian some time during the 1760's like many other early Presbyterian Chapels in the country.

Ministers in Knutsford and Rostherne c. 1640 - 1750

Knutsford

Church of England	Non-conformist	Rostherne
1640 Edward Bold MA		1648 Adam Martindale
1657 Robert Hunter		
1663 John Small	(Hugh Henshall d.1686)	1663 Benjamin Crosse
1664 Samuel Hanmer	(Peter Leigh d.1693)	
1667 Kettleby Turner MA		1673 John Wall MA
1687 Samuel Hulme	1687 William Tong	
1691 James Robinson MA	1690 Thomas Kynaston	
	1696 Samuel Lowe	
	1709 Thomas Lea	
	1733 Robert Lord MA	1732 Robert Frodsham
1741 (Apptd. First Vicar of Knutsford)		
1744 Samuel Saunders BA		1758 Ellis Farnworth MA

References:
- *Victoria County History Vol. 111.p102-8, 111, 114.*
- *'Massey of Salem Mass. USA.' (Family of Raymond Massey, actor, and his brother, Governor of Canada).*
- *Plundered Ministers Accounts Rec. Soc. Lanc. And Ches. 1646-7 Part 1 Vol. 28 p173 and Part 11 Vol. 34 p180*
- *Quaker Records, Morley 1677-1753 CRO EFC 2/9. (also re Quakers): GROSE Polly, Thomas Janney 1638-1697 Publisher of Truth.*
- *Sir P. Leycester's charges to the Grand Jury, Chetham Soc.Vol V 1953 and his list of sectaries, etc. in Mobberley 1677 CRO DLT B/56.*
- *G. Ormerod, Hist. of Ches. Revised by G. Helsby 1882 Vol. 1 1 xvii.*
- *Squandered Ministers a/cs. Adam Martindale autobiography, Chetham Soc. Vol. 1V.*
- *Wills and inventories, WS at CRO except for Admon. of John Small which is WI.*
- *Appeal for bell loft: CRO EDV/1 37 p9 40/1 Bache Lane: CRO QJF 109/1/13.*
- *Knutsford Classis Minutes 1691, Knutsford Brook St. Chapel Records.*
- *Tong W, Life of Matthew Henry, Calamy's Nonconformitist Memorials, Henry Newcome's Diary quoted by the late Rev. W.R. Strachan.*
- *Historical Sketches in Nonconformity in the Co. Pal. of Ches. By various ministers and laymen in the Co. 1864 p14-15 and 443-7.*
- *Lady Jane Stanley, LEACH J., Kn. Hist. and Arch. Asscn. Vol 2 No. 2 Autumn 1984.*
- *Chester Consistory Court recs., Citation Books CRO EDC 3 and Penances and excommunications EDC 6.*
- *Riot outside Chapel 1685 CRO QJF 112/4/25-28.*
- *Register of Dissenting Meeting Places CRO QDR 7 Mf 96/6 .*
- *Interrogatory 1697 CRO Incumbents Misc. P/7/7 Re. Saml. Daniel's pew 1697/8 CRO EDC 5/11 Sml.Daniel's will Ormerod Vol.1. p476.*
- *Cheshire Churches, RICHARDS, Raymond. Bishop Gastrell: Chetham Soc. Vol. V111 Notitia Cestriensis 1718 p345. Estimates for building Kn. Parish Church and Brief 1713 CRO QJF 141/4/76-80 Minutes re building Kn. Parish Church 1714-47 CRO P7/8/1-5*

There were three very different lively events in Knutsford which all arose from conflicting religious beliefs.

The Duke of Monmouth and the Whipping on Market Day 1685

When the Duke of Monmouth rode through Cheshire in September 1682, on his 'progress' in this part of the country, Knutsford and some Knutsford people were briefly part of events of national history. The Duke was the illegitimate Protestant son of Charles 11 and favoured locally above the King's Catholic brother James who was the next in line to the throne. The prospect of a Catholic King was not relished in Cheshire, even less in Knutsford where the many staunch dissenters abhorred anything to do with what they called 'popery'. Monmouth had made a similar progress in the West Country two years earlier to popular acclaim. In Cheshire he was accompanied at times by as many as 120 gentry on horseback and great crowds turned out in the streets to see him. After six days, on 14th September, he came to Dunham Massey home of Lord Delamere. Adam Martindale, Delamere's chaplain was there with other ministers and more crowds of people, some from Knutsford. One was Robert Thornley, then aged about 40, parish clerk and barber surgeon, who witnessed the Duke dining with about twenty or thirty gentlemen, their retinue dining in other rooms and 'a greate number of countrey people' the number of which he could not estimate, 'who were permitted to come into the roome where the duke dined to see him, to come in at one door and out at another, and so a presse continued passing and repassing most part of diner while'.

James Scott, Duke of Monmouth - National Portrait Gallery

He named five of the chief gentry there which he recognised, including Peter Legh of Booths Esq., John Mainwaring Esq., (Sir Thomas's son), and Col. Whitley's two sons. 'Most of these with some others that came the next morning accompanied the Duke to Mere, Mr. Booths, my Lord Delamere's eldest son'.

John Aldcroft, Knutsford innholder aged about 27 whose grandmother kept The George, continued the story. The Duke having stayed the night at Dunham dined the next day at Mere,

'and in the room where the Duke dined there dined about forty one of which ten were woemen, and in another room dined some twenty or thirty gentlemen of an inferior ranke, in other rooms were treated the retinnue belonging to them all, besides which were about two hundred neighbouring country people some of which were allowed to come in where the duke dined and walk round the table and view the duke: and several came into the room after diner to see him daunce. At his coming to the house for a good while the ordinary sort shouted a Monmouth a Monmouth and soe at his goeing away.'

He identified twelve 'of the chiefe persons' who were there and said that Mr. Booth's servants had (blue) ribbons at their cravats of the Duke's colours. They all set out then to Gawsworth through Knutsford where the streets were strewed with flowers and sand and there were two or three shouts of 'a Monmouth, a Monmouth'. A further account said,

As he pass't thro' Knutsford the streets were strewed with sand and flowers (to make his Grace's station more pleasant whilst he received a treat from one Harrison a felt-maker), and as he rode along the way, which was for the most part lined with great numbers of the people, some were sent before to instruct them how to know him, and the gentlemen that rode along with him frequently called upon them to shout, in which they were forward enough to gratify them.

News of this worried the Cheshire authorities who soon afterwards searched the houses of thirteen local gentry for arms, known sympathisers of Monmouth, including Peter Legh of Booths, Sir Thomas Mainwaring and the Rev. Mr. Swinton of Wallasey, of a Knutsford family. Few arms of any note were found here worth seizing.

Monmouth and the accompanying gentry wore blue favours in their hats. He was the nearest that most would ever see of royalty and was young and handsome. Charles 11 was displeased by the reports of this visit to the north west and Monmouth was arrested in Lichfield shortly afterwards. He went or was sent to Holland soon afterwards to keep out of trouble and harm's way.

Allegiance to Monmouth so publicly supported by so many at the time of his visit became increasingly dangerous particularly when three years later in May 1685, James 11 came to the throne. The Duke of Monmouth landed in Lyme Regis on June 11th in an attempt to fight for his Protestant claim to the throne. On June 20th King James issued a proclamation ordering the Lord

Lieutenant and his Deputies to 'seize all disaffected and suspicious persons' in Cheshire. Lord Delamere was arrested and taken to London.

Six days later the streets and heath in Knutsford were full of soldiers. A number of local gentry were escorted to Knutsford and held under house arrest. These included Peter Legh of Booths and Sir Thomas Mainwaring of Peover. Their families were allowed to visit them and on their first day, Captain Needham 'gave leave' for Peter Legh to dine at his own home at Booths with the other gentlemen, but they had to return to Knutsford again at night. They later made similar excursions to dine, at Peover, Joseph Harrison's, Dr. Smith's and on a further day at The Swan. Nonconformist ministers were also held within the county and Adam Martindale was gaoled in Chester Castle.

The rumour, gossip and speculation about Monmouth was on everyone's lips and the prime topic of conversation especially in inns, taverns and ale-houses. At this sensitive and uncertain time several Cheshire men uttered indiscretions which came out in arguments heated by drink, which words were to cost them dearly. One of these men was a Rostherne schoolmaster and his violent punishment was witnessed in Knutsford.

In Rostherne, Edward Cartwright schoolmaster, was drinking with Edward Massey gentleman, who was unsympathetic with any who supported Monmouth. An argument ensued and Cartwright became increasingly inflamed loudly declaring that 'I hope the Duke of Monmouth will be in the saddle when you die' and Massey replied frequently, he alleged, that he wondered that he who pretended to know this so well should speak such suspicious words of one who was a traitor. Cartwright exploded: 'The Duke of Monmouth is no traitor and if I hear any man call him a traitor, as I am constable I will put him in the stocks!'.

Massey had Cartwright arrested and brought before Thomas Needham of Venables JP, charged with speaking treasonable words. He was sent to gaol in Chester Castle to await trial of this serious charge at the next Assizes in Chester.

Talk about Monmouth was still on everyone's lips especially when they heard the news that he had been defeated, captured, taken to the Tower of London and beheaded on July 15th. The next day saw the 'restrained gentlemen' held in Knutsford bailed upon 'several single bonds and returned to (their) own houses' after twenty days.

In August at the Chester Assizes, Cartwright, Rostherne schoolmaster's case was called. It was Lord Chief Justice Jeffries (from Wrexham) who presided, hearing charges that day against seven Cheshire men of speaking treasonous and seditious words regarding the Duke of Monmouth against the lawful King James 11. The other men came from Altrincham, Congleton, Lawton, two from Northwich and one from Witton. The witnesses called to give evidence against Cartwright were Edward Massey, gent. of Rostherne, Edward Moss, fisherman of Rostherne, William Middleton, yeoman of Mere

and Thomas Drinkwater, milliner of Knutsford who had all overheard the
heated exchange.

After hearing the evidence, Judge Jeffries pronounced him guilty and
he was sentenced to be 'whipped at the cart's tail through the market town
of Knutsford at the high time of market on the next market day'.

Judge Jefferys - National Portrait Gallery

On Saturday 29th August 1685 when Knutsford's usual weekly market
was in full swing after mid-day, the town was very full, rather hushed and
very alert. Out of (probably), The George, Cartwright was led stripped to
the waist to the rear of a waiting cart in King Street to which his hands were
securely tied. The Deputy Sheriff of Cheshire, Rowland Waring, gent, came
behind with several of his bailiffs, one with a whip, others waiting their turn
to use it, carrying their staves of office. The horse was led forward and the
grim procession began. As the whip swished, nearby trading stopped and
people watched through their open shop windows, from behind their stalls
and from the roadside. The crowds, townspeople and visitors moved aside in
the narrow streets, children were held back with restraining hands to make
room for the steadily plodding horse, crunching wheels, rattling empty cart,
Cartwright with bowed head, his back taking the brunt of fearful cracking
whip and the upright dignitaries of the following Deputy Sheriff and bailiffs.
The crowd closed in behind them and before long some began to shout
insults at the Sheriff's party.

As they went round the town they came down by Thomas Leigh the dyer's
house. He was looking out of his window as they passed and incensed at
the sight he shouted out, 'Kill those bayliff rogues, killum, killum, knock
them in the head'. The following crowd took up the theme and renewed
and echoed the shouts.

As they completed a circuit of the town, the blood from the wheals flowed freely down Cartwright's back and by the time they got back to the inn and were loosening the cords to release him a great throng ran 'voyolently' and crowded up the street, blocking it and preventing the Sheriff, his officers and their prisoner from returning to their 'lodging'.

The crowd jostled, shuffled and pushed. The Sheriff commanded they gave way and made room but three men in particular stubbornly stood their ground and said defiantly that they had as much right and more so on the King's Highway. One said that he was near to his own house, had he not the right to be there? The bailiffs growing angry held up their staves about to strike, but some in the crowd called out, 'Have a care what you do, for if you strike we will strike again or words to that effect'.... The three foremost men gave 'very peremptory and saucy language' which caused the Sheriff to demand their names to be taken and eventually forced their way back into the inn. The crowd then gave a great shout and hurled insults after them, 'canting and spouting'.

Those whose names were taken were Robert Pollard, sharman, Robert Hall, baker and Samuel Steele, aleseller, all from Knutsford and with Thomas Leigh the dyer were brought before the Bench in October at the next Sessions for affront and contempt of the Sheriff and his officers. Their punishment was not recorded.

The punishments of the six other men who had appeared with Cartwright were likely to have been the same as his, to be carried out in their or their nearest market town but only in Knutsford did the townspeople dare to protest so vigorously against the sentence of the law of the land being carried out.

Lord Chief Justice Jeffries went from Chester to the Assizes in Dorchester in the west country in September where so many who had risen to support and fight for Monmouth, treasonously, were indicted. That came to be called 'The Bloody Assize', where hundreds were hung, drawn, quartered and tarred, hundreds more were transported for life to the West Indies and scores were ordered to be whipped not only through their market town but in every market town in the county. Lord Delamere was tried in London but was fortunate to be acquitted.

Knutsford may well have the distinction of being the only town in the country where its people objected vociferously against Jeffries' harsh punishment but that was before the Bloody Assize. James 11 as well as Judge Jeffries fled the country three years afterwards to make way for William and Mary in 'the Glorious Revolution'.

A witness to the market day whipping in Knutsford may well have been Hannah Bostock who lived just a few doors from The George in her father John's house, he was later one of the named Trustees of the Dissenter's Chapel. She may have been on hand to help to dress Cartwright's bleeding back but however it came about, she and Edward Cartwright were married by marriage licence in July, 1687.

References.
- Robert Thornley's examination re the Duke of Monmouth, CRO DLT 4996/15/9, and John Aldcroft's exam., DLT 4996/15/10
- Earwaker 1894 Trans. HSLC Vol. 46 1895 The Progress of the Duke of Monmouth in Cheshire Sep. 1682. Cartwright: 1685 CRO QJF 113/3/47 and 48 and PRO Cheshire Assizes 1685
- Seizure of arms: DLT 4996/15/58 Lists of arms taken: DLT 4996/15/53,54
- HODSON, J.Howard, Cheshire, 1660-1780, Vol.9 of A Hist. of Ches., Ches. Comm. Council 1978.

Riding Stang or Skimmity

With the turn of the century the old bitterness and rivalry still existed between dissenters and those of High Church persuasion of whom there were now more and Knutsford was home to men of many different beliefs. The Rev. and Mrs. James Peake had come to live here some time after William and Mary's accession to the throne. Rev. Peake MA, had been Vicar of Bowden and was a non-juror, believing it wrong to swear allegiance to the new monarchs while King James was still alive having earlier affirmed loyalty to him. The Peakes had friends in Knutsford of whom the bookseller, Peter Swinton was one, and presumably liked living here but their allegiance to King James still had the stigma of 'popery' about it and were regarded with some suspicion by many Knutsford people for this reason.

An incident occurred in Knutsford in December 1703 which stirred very un-Christian passion and fury.

'A Mawment or Figure done up into a rude shape of a child or baby was carried about the Town in a crude and ridiculous manner to expose, deride and reprove some Man in the Town who had abused or ill treated his wife by beating her'.

The object of this parade was Samuel Leadbeater, mercer of Knutsford, whose relative (brother?) was John Leadbeater gent, Attorney at Law, one of the Settlement Trustees of the Dissenters' Chapel who had been one of the Bondsmen at the wedding of Samuel and Hester Leadbeater in 1701, who had at the time of this incident just one son fourteen months old.

It is hard for us to see why a child or baby should be used to shame a man beating his wife unless it had caused her to have a miscarriage. This type of public entertainment, charivari, known as riding stang or skimmity often with beating pots and pans, had for centuries been used as a way of publicising a domestic matter and by the shame of it, putting an end to the offence, giving pranksters meanwhile an evening of fun. To Samuel Leadbeater this was no laughing matter and the message of the Mawment certainly struck its target.

He was convinced for some reason that Rev. and Mrs. Peake were the instigators. In shame and fury, 'offended at the Mawment', he stormed down to the new newly built White Lion for a drink to drown his humiliation and blurted out his accusations to two acquaintances who had gone there 'as neighbours together to drink a glass of ale'. They remonstrated with him and 'endeavoured to vindicate the reputation and defend the good name of' the clerical couple but Leadbeater 'with great vehemency and passion' uttered and repeated 'in a loud, violent and angry manner ... several scandalous words ... speaking of Mrs. Peake he called her a King James whore and a proud bitch, and speaking of Mr. Peake ... he said he was a Jacobite and a King James rogue and a knave'. At the raised voices and fearing trouble, the landlord sent for the constable who happened to be just next door at the Red Lion on business, and a neighbour who lived opposite who had been sitting by his fireside, on hearing the commotion went to his window overlooking the street to find out what was going on.

Samuel Leadbeater was not a dissenter like John Leadbeater. In 1698 he had bought a book of common prayer from Peter Swinton's shop after he had died. For his intemperance he was brought before the Consistory Court for libel the following June, 1704. The Deputy Registrar of Chester was (the Jacobite) Henry Prescott, brother-in-law of Rev. Peake (his first wife's brother), and he recounted in his diary in May 1704 that he rode to Knutsford on 'a sweet free morning' to take statements from the witnesses in this case and stayed with his 'Cousin Peake'. He made no comment on the Mawment incident but he enjoyed his 'cousin's' hospitality and meeting local clergy. Peake does not seem to have been an easy or very likeable man to some before this incident. Bishop Cartwright had a problem with him, mentioning 'another satirical letter' from Peake in 1686 and later when Mr. Peake preached an inappropriate sermon in Chester Cathedral it caused him some embarrassment. The Bishop reprimanded him and accused him of 'pride of spirit and petulancy'. Later the Bishop also tried to reconcile Peake with his in-laws but said that he found Peake had 'carried himself as ill to his father-in-law as ever he did to his Father in God', but all this had been more than 15 years before.

Leadbeater was ordered to make a declaration withdrawing and renouncing his 'scandalous words' and to be fully excommunicated from the Church until he did so. Leadbeater complied with these obligations and by 13th July it was recorded that the judgement had been performed. He was however not quite so ready to pay the demanded Court expenses, notoriously high, for he did not do that until 5th October.

Samuel and his wife were reconciled and the following September another son was born to them. They were to have nine children in all although not all of them lived. Hester Leadbeater became a registered midwife in 1718 having had another son the year before and yet another in 1720. She had plenty of practical experience of babies and their servants made good babysitters.

The 1710 Election Day Fracas

Religion remained an issue which continued to cause heated arguments and scenes during the early part of the 18th century and this was especially true at times of elections. The Tory candidates supported the Anglican Church and the Whigs supported dissenters and the Protestant Succession. A change had come over the scene in Cheshire since the reign of James 11 for many of the local gentry who had supported Monmouth, now supported the exiled King James. Knutsford people were keenly interested in politics with several ex Members of Parliament and candidates living locally.

In the elections at the end of October 1710 in the reign of Queen Anne, Knutsford's Parson Robinson was reported to Quarter Sessions as having said in conversation that he feared that if the new Tory candidates were elected, the Parliament might bring in Popery.

Election fever was high in Knutsford when the election results were posted up at 'The Cock'. Sir George Warburton of Arley and Charles Cholmondeley of Vale Royal, both Tories, were elected. The news was greeted with dismay by at least two Knutsford men, one who called Warburton a Popish Dog, and the other said Warburton had a Pope in his belly and uttered oaths about him. One of these, a linen webster Peter Leigh, was convicted at Quarter Sessions of cursing a profane curse for which offence he had to pay 2 shillings to the Overseer of the Poor for the use of the poor in the township.

A large bonfire had been built in the market place to celebrate the election but trouble ensued. People had come into Knutsford from surrounding rural areas including the servant of the Whig, Earl of Warrington (Lord Delamere) of Dunham Massey. Langham Booth his younger brother had been Whig MP from 1705 until this election. News of his defeat caused friction and sparks amongst the company and locals who were drinking their fill in the inns and taverns. Between 3 and 4 o'clock 'in the evening' (it was 30th October), quarrels were already breaking out in the market place where some people were saying they should not light the fire and were pulling down the wood laid in the unlit stack. Some were arrested then but the fire was lit after which the situation deteriorated into brawls with 'great quantities of stones, dust, water and other things' being thrown. A constable and another man were hit on the head with pieces of brick. Men took off their coats preparing for serious fighting and could only be restrained by two or three men apiece holding them back with difficulty. The witnesses who made statements called it a 'tumult' and a 'bristle or disturbance' which kept erupting and went on for some time despite the constables' appeals for peace and they themselves being attacked. The two constables, Thomas Green the glazier, the one who was injured, and John Birtles innkeeper of The Swan, could not have managed without help from other inhabitants. Eventually some sort of order was at last restored and fourteen men, ten of them from Knutsford were arrested. It is doubtful whether any of these men had a vote but that did not stop them having strong opinions and being prepared to fight for them.

References.
- *Riding Stang: Mawment: CRO EDC 5/ 1704/11*
- *Diary of Thomas Cartwright, Bishop of Chester, Camden Soc. 1843.*
- *Diary of Henry Prescott 22 and 23 May 1704 CRO T 225. Now Rec. Soc. of Lancs & Ches. Vol. 133 1997*
- *Consistory Court book EDC 1/101. With thanks to Dr. A. Thacker who helped to find and translate the outcome of the Mawment case.*
- *Election Day: CRO QJF 1710 138/4/44, 53-55 62-78 MP's for Ches.: Ormerod Vol.1 p.81 and 219.*

Two contemporary Knutsford men had links with the Church or Chapel but could not have been more different in character.

Peter Wood 1638-1706

Much of the information about Knutsford people of the 17th century comes from wills and inventories of the time. Inventories were made by neighbours, friends or those with special knowledge of a trade or profession shortly after a person had died appraising the contents of the house, the goods, cattle and chattels, the estate for granting probate. The information given varied, some being brief summaries but others full of detail, giving the rooms in the house and every item within down to, 'all the old lumber there'.

Between 1675 and 1706 a great many of these inventories and the wills, were written in the same hand and the writer was soon identifiable as Peter Wood. His handwriting and his name became instantly recognisable for of all the existing wills and inventories between these dates he wrote, and/or was an appraiser, a witness or an executor of about two thirds of them. He wrote and witnessed other legal documents too, leases of properties and land, apprenticeship documents and probably many others which have not survived.

He came from the family of Thomas Wood of Lower Peover, the fifth of six children, born in 1638. This family had been in Peover since before 1560 when Anne Wood was paying 6s. rent p.a. to the endowment of Sir John Deane's Grammar School in Witton, Northwich. · After his father's death when he was ten, his eldest brother Thomas became responsible for paying the rent but like many others during the Civil War he defaulted for nine years, although the rent had been paid continuously for nearly one hundred years but after being taken to Court by the Grammar School's trustees at the Restoration, he resumed payment once more in 1660.

Thomas later went to live in Church House next to Peover Church. He was Chapel clerk for Lower Peover from 1680 until his death in 1704.

It is not known where the brothers went to school, it may have been at Sir John Deane's in Witton as they had the rental connection there and it was a free school.

Peter Wood had a small house in Peover in 1664 and although he shortly afterwards moved to live in Knutsford he still kept the property there until his death. There is still standing in Little Peover a small black and white timbered house facing the green and near to the smithy which could possibly be the one in which he lived, the three fields immediately behind it were called, 'Near Wood', 'Middle Wood' and 'Top Wood' in a narrow strip. If these have nothing to do with his name then they could relate to one of the terms of a lease to him dated 1696 from Sir Francis Leycester for 'a demise lot and fearms in Little Peover'. The yearly rent was 6s.8d. payable on St. John the Baptist Day and St. Martins Day, plus two hens or 1s.0d, one day for mowing or 1s.0d., two days reaping or 1s.0d, and one day filling of muck or 1s.0d. Forty shillings were to be paid as a heriot and on the death of his wife. Some more of the conditions of the lease were that he was to fell no trees, was 'to lay and bestow one half of all muck, soil and compost' and was to raise within seven years ten young plants transplanted of acorns and raise in a nursery safely fenced during the next year, besides ashes and poplars, set or plant so many acorns or young oaks to plant into hedgerows. Could these have become the narrow Wood Fields? It is from Sir Francis Leycester and to landowners like him and their tenants, that we have the heritage of our tree studded hedgerows in much of the countryside.

This property was undoubtedly the same as 'the small messuage and tenement in Little Peover' which Peter Wood hoped would clear his debts at the end of his life and also where in his youth he had taken his bride Margery Crowther whom he married in May 1669, the daughter of Randle Crowther, a Knutsford shoemaker.

Unlike his brother, Peter Wood, his wife and mother-in-law were dissenters and early in his married life they were involved in a dispute about paying tithes to Rostherne on produce of hay from their land in Over Tabley. It was claimed that for seven years Peter and Margery Crowther his mother-in-law, did not pay these tithes and they were reported at last at a visitation and had to answer to the consistory court about this. The accuser was the troublesome Geoffrey Aldcroft, son of the Innkeeper of 'The George', so it may well have been a false accusation. The outcome of the case is not known.

The Woods moved to Knutsford some time around 1672 and he became a freeholder for it is from that time that Peter Wood became closely involved with the Manor Court and all the duties associated with it. A Jury man, six times a feoffee for Mr. Mann's money, often elected to inspect the town's bonds and at the turn of the century one of the newly set up committee to manage the town's affairs. Sometimes an Overseer of the Poor with whom he had a special affinity and interest, he wrote and witnessed documents for the Quarter Sessions in particular the long lists of poor people submitted to the Court at the time of Knutsford's epidemic. In 1692 he wrote out a petition for a poor, nearly blind man and his family in Tatton and in 1694 he was appointed by the Quarter Sessions with two other men to inspect the accounts of a late overseer of the poor of Pickmere. In 1698, the Scottish chapman Robert Blacklock from Dumfries left 20s. in his will written and witnessed by Peter Wood, 'to such poore persons in Nether Knutsford as Peter Wood, yeoman, shall think fit'.

He had sadness in his personal life. In 1676 in his own hand he wrote in joy of his son's baptism in Knutsford Parish Register on 25th January:

'Peter Wood, sonn of Peter Wood of Nether Knotsford'.

He had been married for seven years but his wife died in childbirth. Without its mother the child did not thrive and only lived for a month. In St. Helena's Churchyard there is a tombstone which reads:

'Here resteth the body of Margery, the wife of Peter Wood who died upon the birth of Peter her first child, January 21st 1676 which child died February 23rd next after, and is here laid by her'.

Peter Wood was an ironworker and a gunsmith. Writing legal documents was not a full time job and although it must have supplemented his income quite well the pay he received was probably not good compensation for the time he spent writing and working on them, some inventories must have taken at least half a day. His Manor Court posts and being Overseer of the Poor must also have taken many days, none of which were paid positions. When Sir Peter Leycester was building his Chapel at Nether Tabley between 1674 and '77, P. Wood supplied 'fans and all his ironwork', and later he was paid for new hinges and screws for the rails in the Chapel. In 1681 and 1682 he was calling himself a gunsmith. Elsewhere, throughout thirty years in Knutsford he is referred to as, and called himself yeoman.

He married again in 1681, Mary Swinton widow of Gorstich when he was called Peter Wood, gent., on the marriage licence. Her name appears with

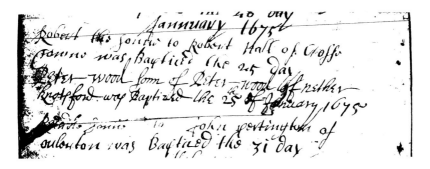

Part of the pages from Knutsford (St. John's) Parish Register, Baptisms.
Peter Wood's own writing entry of the baptism of his son 25th January 1675/6
CRO MF 32/1 25/1/1675/76

his as a witness to several documents for a short period, she was signing her own name. In 1684 they had a daughter Elizabeth but she only lived to be six years old. They had another son, Peter in 1685.

In 1698 when Mary his second wife died she is recorded as being buried in linen. This must have been a special gesture made by him, the 1678 decree being in force that everyone should be buried in woollen as a boost to the wool trade, a certificate being required to prove this. It would have cost him a fine of at least £2.10s. but some could not bear the thought of a loved one shrouded in rough wool. Peter Wood was a widower this second time aged 59, and their son Peter was not quite 13.

Peter Wood was one of Knutsford's chief dissenters, an articulate man called upon to speak at both the Interrogatories to do with the Church disputes. He was among those freeholders who brought a Court case against Peter Legh in 1686 to claim the right of presentation to the living of the Parochial Chapel and St. Mary's for themselves. When that claim was lost and the new dissenting Chapel was founded, having been one of the instigators of its building he was appointed one of its first Trustees in 1694. It is obvious from all sources that he was a highly respected and trustworthy man in Knutsford in his time, helping and working with rich and poor alike, a man to be turned to in time of trouble, honest and upright, public spirited and with deeply held religious views. He was left pews in the Chapel as a legacy in 1699. A house which he rented out in 1693 was registered at Quarter Sessions for divine worship for dissenters and in July 1694 a house in his name in the possession of John Bostock was similarly licensed. In 1697 at the second Church enquiry, Peter Wood gave evidence again even though he was then worshipping at Brook Street Chapel. He gave his age then as, 'about 50' when in fact he was nearly 60.

Five or six years later though, he stopped his activity at the Manor Court. In 1704 he wrote his own will and said then that he was, 'aged and weak'. He had made previous arrangements about his estate as the will concerned his 'temporal estate not heretofore settled', he had already dealt with his two lands in Whitebridge and the Damfield. He had become anxious about his debts which he mentioned no less than seven times and worried about his son not yet out of apprenticeship and about his servant who was looking after him so well. He was then living in a house which even then was the former Angel Inn (p124), two rooms of which were let off separately as dwellings of Daniel Gill and Randle Sutton which were included in the inventory. His total estate amounted to £63 16s.3d. of which debts were due to him of £29. He had £2 worth of books and his purse and apparel, £5.

His house consisted of five rooms plus the two of the other men. One room was 'the wash house', few of which occur in the Knutsford inventories of this period. There was 'a little tub and a smoothing iron and two heaters'. Among the items in his dwelling house was an armed chair with a drawer in and a little table with a drawer in and a new feather bed in the street chamber. In the still room, two stillages and the more valuable still in his street chamber, £1, with 8 quart bottles, could have been there from when it was the Angel Inn. This could well have been in the complex of buildings now known as 'Marble Arch', opposite the present Angel Inn.

When writing his will he made only the briefest reference to his Christian faith. This leading dissenter had written many declarations of faith in the preamble of many wills, but when it came to making his own on 13th September 1704, he wrote,

I, being aged and weake of bodie but of disposeing memory, praised be the Lord therefore, and being desirous to settle my worldly estate soe as to prevent strifes and contentions after my decease, doe make this my last will and testament in manner and forme following: my bodie I commit to the earth whence it was, to be decently buried by my executors as they in their discretion shall think fitt, and my spirritt to God who gave it.

He thought it would be necessary to sell or lease both his Knutsford and his Peover houses to pay his debts and appointed his dissenter friends Robert Kell of Marthall and Walter Antrobus, Nether Knutsford maltster, his executors, the power to do this if needed. He left all his books and the table that was his father's wherein he kept his deeds, and all his ladders to his son Peter and wished him to show kindness to his maid servant Hannah Stubbs according as his circumstances would allow. When he had finished writing he sent for his friends and neighbours to come to witness his signature, Samuel Leadbeater, Henry and John Long. After some conversation with them he was apparently reassured by the comfort of their company and his fears began to subside that perhaps his debts were not as bad as he thought and seeing things more rationally, came to realise also that his son would have no home base and no one to look after him, so he managed to squeeze in a codicil:

... that none of my household goods shall be sold during my son's Apprenticeship and that my servant Hannah Stubbs shall dwell where I now dwell as servant to my son during his Apprenticeship as occasion shall require and be paid by him or out of his estate she keeping herself chast and unmarried but this I leave to the discretion of my executors.

He died more than a year after this in February 1706 aged 68. His tombstone still, but barely readable, in St. Helena's Churchyard has inscribed upon it the epitaph: 'Death of the righteous end be like his'.

His son Peter later became a mercer in Sandbach and married well enough to have a marriage settlement part of which was the former Angel Inn and he sold off his father's lands, so the debts must have been paid.

Peter Wood's unassuming life but steadfast character was very much part of Knutsford life 300 years ago.

References:
- COX Marjorie: *A History of Sir John Deane's Grammar School, Witton.*
- *Parish registers, leases, Hearth Tax returns, CRO as before.*
- *Tabley accounts 1674 and 1677 CRO DLT/B/54 1648-1678.*
- *Dispute re tithes CRO EDC 5/9 (1675) Wills and Inv., CRO WS.*
- *Knutsford St. John Parish Registers.*

Joseph Harrison d. 1700

Joseph Harrison was one of five sons of Ann Harrison who when a widow lived at Tatton Old Hall which she held by lease with lands there. Her husband had been by status a gentleman. The Rev. William Harrison, possibly the eldest son, bought Cranage Hall near Holmes Chapel in 1676 for £1,800. In 1683 his brother Daniel and his large family lived there. Brother Samuel of Tatton and Cranage Hall, lived in Tatton Old Hall.

Joseph was probably the youngest son as he was 'in trade', a feltmaker and haberdasher, a hatter. He was in Nether Knutsford by 1664 in a house with two hearths and had one twice the size by 1674, having either enlarged or moved, and by 1677 had a servant and an apprentice. It is obvious that Harrison worked hard to cultivate his gentry connections and was proud to be hatter to the local gentlemen including Sir Peter Leycester who bought hats from him. Later he was very friendly with Sir Thomas Mainwaring and his family of Peover with whom he dined frequently.

Harrison made a good living in Knutsford and towards the end of his life he was calling himself, 'Gentleman'. His twelve roomed house was stylishly furnished but had no signs within it of the hatting trade although one of his rooms was 'over Leftwiche's shop' which was owned by him and may have been the hatters'. He may have handed over his business by then. His estate was worth £522, but of this, debts 'good and bad' were owing to him of more than £400, so not all his customers however, gentry or no, paid promptly. Harrison had ceased to work and had money and lands enough to live like a gentleman.

His house contents reflect this gentlemanly status, furnished in turkey work and leather upholstery and even the maid had a separate room. He had a pair of tables with men and dice for games with his friends while drinking coffee from the 'corfee can' kept in the buttery, the clock in the Hall enabling them to keep track of time. He kept a gun in his closet for outdoor pursuits with them. There were window curtains in the Hall and in the 'best room', his bedroom, there were two stands for wigs, a powder box and six patch boxes, with a looking glass. There was a sitting and a going wheel, and a churn in the drink house.

He often entertained the gentry to dinner and on possibly the first occasion in April 1680 he invited Sir Thomas Mainwaring, Mr. Ashton, Mr. Peter Legh of Booths, Mr. Bradshaw of Marple and Mr. Swinton of Knutsford when they had a barrel of oysters. At other times he invited Lord Delamere and even Squire Egerton (senior) of Tatton when he made a rare visit to the area.

Harrison owned or leased six shops and buildings in Knutsford, as well as land and building in Cranage and Tatton, a house in Allostock, a barn on Knutsford Heath, the Chapel Croft and land in Sudlow.

Harrison married but he and his wife Mary had no children. After he died his complicated will proved hard to administer.

At his death, his wife Mary was already entitled to her share of his lands in Cranage and property in Allostock under their marriage settlement, so his affairs in that respect were well organised. The rest was far from simple and most vitally, was there enough money to pay all his bequests?

Joseph's brother Samuel, then still living, had married twice and had a total of seven children, two of whom were lawyers. His brother Daniel had died before him and had left five children. Joseph remembered all these many nieces and nephews his sister and sister in law with varying degrees of generosity with money, annual rents from lands, and to one nephew his apparel. Above all he favoured his youngest nephew Benjamin not yet 21, son of the late Daniel. Even Harrison's widow's interest in the house in which they lived, in Nether Knutsford was to be subject to Benjamin's wish to reside there when he had finished his apprenticeship, and if he should wish, she should share the house with him. The larger part of his residuary estate was also earmarked for the favoured Benjamin. Harrison enjoyed the company of his brothers, their families and their mutual gentry friends. Being himself a younger son who had had to earn his living he empathised with his nephew Benjamin who was starting out in life as he had done.

As he made his will, Joseph may have wondered how the rest of the family would like it for he appointed trustees, none other than, 'my dear and honoured friends, Sir John Mainwairing (of Peover),and Peter Legh (of Booths)',

'to take care that nothing be done during the minority of my nephew and godson Benjamin which shall or may be injurious to him and that he receive all that part of my estate which is by me designed for him and hereby assigned and bequeathed to him and that upon occasion they would interpose on his behalf and act as Trustees chosen by me for him'.

He added a codicil a few days later on Christmas Day, stating that , 'If my now loving wife or any person whatsoever in her name or on her behalf do contradict or endeavour to destroy my Will, then my wife shall not have the legacies before expressed to the contrary notwithstanding'. But so much for the lengthy, carefully drawn will, trying to envisage every possibility, the Executors named by Joseph Harrison renounced their positions and his widow renounced her claim to take out Letters of Administration. Eventually his brother Samuel and Henry Long, chapman of Knutsford, were granted this duty with will annexed. Whether Benjamin got his inheritance without a fight we do no know but Benjamin did come to live and work in Knutsford some time after this and was known to be in Leftwiche's shop in 1714. However, the inventory of Harrison's house was not taken until nearly three years after his death.

Anxious to show his friendship and gratitude to the gentry he left bequests of a guinea to thirteen recipients, his friends Sir John Mainwairing, Peter Legh and Peter Shakerley of Holmes Chapel and several male members of their families also to the Rev. and Mrs Peake and to other people in Knutsford and 5 shillings apiece to sixteen local residents including his servant. He was on good terms with the Rev. James Robinson who witnessed his will and who was to have £5 for preaching the funeral sermon. There were to be 3 pence each to every poor person residing and dwelling in Nether and Over Knutsford, 'that shall come to my funeral'.

He made two generous charitable bequests: £50 to be invested for the minister in Knutsford provided he were

'Episcopally ordained and licensed and also nominated – by the majority ... of the inhabitants of the Chapelry of Knutsford according to ancient usage and custom'.

This provision is puzzling, for the whole point of the 1686 Court Case brought and lost by Peter Wood and his fellow dissenter freeholders was that they wanted the Minister to be chosen by Knutsford's people. After the case was lost, Peter Legh with others had the right to choose the minister. Harrison specified that any Minister not elected as above, 'irregular', in his eyes, should not receive this interest but the money was to go to Knutsford's poor instead. The Poor of Nether Knutsford were to benefit from the interest of £50 in a separate bequest and the Poor of Over Knutsford, of Tatton and of Allostock, £10 each. The Schoolmaster of Nether Knutsford was to have interest on £10 for the instruction and teaching of three poor boys to be chosen by the Minister of Knutsford. But the Charities list in the porch of the Parish Church only credits Harrison with just £10 for poor children, so it looks as if the executors had to make a compromise with the funds available. His generous wishes exceeded his estate. So at the end of his life he showed charitable concern for the less fortunate, whether he could afford it or not, but charity and kindness were not always evident in his life.

The six patchboxes may be clues to his character, a dandy, and there are also accounts in Quarter Sessions which show him as well as two of his brothers in not a very favourable light.

Brother Samuel aged 31 in 1676 was involved in a quarrel with Joseph Caldwell of Thelwall and had to appear before Magistrates because of it. In the spring of 1681, Joseph Harrison (of Knutsford, feltmaker and haberdasher), was with brother Daniel when they called upon one of their tenants, John Kelsall a silk frame knitter in Hale whose daughter Mary, pregnant, was sitting spinning in the house and her words tell what happened:

There came Joseph Harrison and Daniel his brother into the house where they executed a writ (upon Mary's father), they each of them having two sticks in their hands lifted up their sticks and bid him to obey them and he answered that he would. Yet notwithstanding the said Joseph Harrison struck him with one stick — whereupon Mary came and stept betwixt them. Then Joseph Harrison struck her with a very great stick. (She) being great with child was sore afraid lest she received great prejudice thereby. Joseph Harrison swore several times that he would lay her at the back of the fire and burn her if she would not hold her tongue, which he endeavoured to have affected.

This unpleasant arrogant behaviour was hopefully not typical, but perhaps Harrison's work as a freeholder and active member in Knutsford's Court Leet for many years helped him see some of the 'lower orders' more sympathetically. From 1672, he periodically served five, two year terms as a feofee for Mr.Mann's money and with Peter Wood, Henry Antrobus and Peter Swinton, was responsible for inspecting all the Town's bonds for charitable uses so we can understand that he would have liked there to be bonds perpetuating his own name. He would have had to work quite closely at times with people, particularly Peter Wood, with whom he may not have had a lot in common. From 1686 until his death in 1700 he was one of the grand jury at the bi-annual court leet meetings, although there is no evidence that he was an overseer of the poor or church warden or held any such local position. He may however, have had no choice but take on these responsibilities.

Another occasion when Mr. Harrison was mentioned in the Quarter Sessions was in 1699 when he was presented for laying a muck midden in the High Road in Nether Knutsford 'to the great damage thereof'.

There can be no doubt that Harrison cut a well turned dashing if not flamboyant, figure about Knutsford for nearly 40 years, so he would have enjoyed the memory of the highlight occasion when the Royal Duke of Monmouth riding through Knutsford in 1682, was greeted by Joseph Harrison representing the town, dressed in his best, who rushed forward with a flourish, resplendent in hat, patches and wig to offer the Royal Duke a drink, 'a treat'.

References.
- *Poll Tax as before.*
- *Tabley a/cs as before.*
- *Thomas Mainwaring's diary as before.*
- *Will and inv. of Joseph Harrison CRO WS 1703.*
- *Harrison's court charges: CRO QJF 1676 104/1/37 , 1681 109/1/51, 1699 127/2/105.*

Chapter Five
Families
Some of the Antrobus, Swinton and Birtles families

In the 17th century there were several families in Knutsford who had been in the vicinity for a hundred years or more, some having had many children had become almost dynastic. In this commercial centre, many of these families represent the rising middle class. These families were prosperous tradesmen and the family fortunes, property and business had come to command respect. There may well have been some rivalry between them but the families often inter married thus keeping the fortune and the business intact. As common for the 17th century it will be seen that agriculture was still economically important. Even though some of them were running successful trades and businesses which had no connection with the land, they or their servants farmed on their own fields or the common fields and kept livestock, fitting in the work required as they could.

The 1667 Poll Tax gives a close up view almost like a census, of Nether Knutsford families as they were at that time. It gives the names of 126 households, men, women and their children, 340 persons with their servants, journeymen and apprentices. The average size of a household that year consisted of 2.7 people which may be thought to be quite a low number, but there were 43 people living alone, 34% of all the households. 37 households had just two people, 14 had three people. 13 had four, and fewer with larger numbers, the largest household having 11 people under one roof. They all paid 1 shilling per head, poll tax whether adult or baby.

30 households had servants, 23.8% of them all. 21 had just one servant or apprentice but one had two apprentices and three servants. They paid tax on the wages they paid their servants each year at 1s. per £ or part of £, so their wages were stated. These range from 18 shillings to 30 shillings p.a. Three were paid more than this, up to £3, who could have been journeymen who had completed their apprenticeship and had not accumulated sufficient capital to start up their own business. There were eleven apprentices who received no wages as they were learning their trade. The total amount of poll tax collected in Nether Knutsford was £18 17s.

By contrast in Over Knutsford of the 32 named households with possibly four more there were about 100 people. A note says that the gentry family of Robert Venables Esq., his wife, children and servants were not included. This was the family of Peter Legh's mother who had remarried. There is a puzzling entry of a gentry family of John Brooks, gent. and his servants, of 16 or 20 in the household. In Over Knutsford eight families had servants and possibly four more whose servants were unpaid. Three had servants who were each paid £1. Apart from the gentlemen there were two households with 14 in each, four with 6 people, three with 3 people and five were living alone. The total tax collected in Over Knutsford was £6 2s.

Sir Peter Leycester's household in Nether Tabley consisted of Mistress Eleanor Leycester and their three sons, Masters Robert, Thomas and Ralphe also Mistress Birch and Mr. Bryon Leycester, for whom he paid 1s. each. He was one of the Commissioners who paid for his own poll and his title, £15 11s. Thomas Jackson his steward, paid 'for 4 wages, practise and poll, 15s'. There were 27 servants of whom seven received no wages but for whom their 1s. tax was paid. There were 35 in his household.

The Antrobus and Swinton families feature large in the life of Knutsford of this period. They will give an introduction to some of the shops and trades and illustrate seventeenth century family life, with marriage portions, children often dying young, paternal, brotherly and family love and loyalty and sometimes contentions, care of elderly mothers and widows receiving their lawful third of estate.

It was common for some of these in the same generation to be given the same Christian names which is confusing when trying to distinguish those who were contemporary

The Antrobus family. *See Family Trees 1 (p100) and 2 (p104)*

The story of the Antrobus family starts with the crucial figure of William Antrobus who was known to his Knutsford relatives as 'Uncle William'. He had come from a prolific Knutsford family, one of nine children who had left his native town to seek his fortune as a woollen draper in London where he died in 1665 aged 67. He may not have made a very large fortune by London standards but he had good income and capital from his flourishing business and shop in St. Paul's Churchyard. He was a Citizen and Merchant Tailor of London and had been appointed Alderman in 1659. He did not marry so his closest relations were his Knutsford family. In his lifetime he had taken his nephew George into partnership with him and had sent for his niece Hannah, George's unmarried sister, to be his housekeeper in return for a home and living.

The two branches of the family left in Knutsford that kept in closest contact with him seem to have been those of his brothers Thomas and Henry. This was possibly because both of them remained in the woollen drapery business and 'Uncle' William was a business as well as a family contact. Keeping this important connection with the capital was very advantageous in promoting their business. In this instance the connection proved beneficial both in 'Uncle' William's lifetime and in his death, for in his will he named 22 of his relations and left them all some legacy including his brother George and family in Ireland and another William Antrobus in New England.

To the Knutsford relatives he left his nephew Henry (2), an interest in money and lands in Barking, Essex who as we shall see used this and other money to benefit

the next generation. Nephews Isaac and Samuel, dissenting sons of brother Walter, were also left an interest in the Barking estate.

The residue from the sale of these Barking lands went to another nephew Henry (3) and his three children, Henry, Elizabeth wife to James Swinton, and Margaret Furness. His executors were his nephew John Eaton, son of his sister Parnell and Joseph Antrobus yet another nephew, brother to Isaac and Samuel of the dissenting family. Yet to the nephew most closely associated with him, his partner George, he seems to have been somewhat less than generous. For although he left him the house and shop in St. Paul's churchyard and half a share in the partnership, George was required to pay £1,000 for this to the executors and not unreasonably, to pay the rent of £100 a year for the lease of the shop property. George would probably have found it hard to raise so much ready cash in so short a time and this provision may have led to his later dispute with his brothers-in-law. William left niece Hannah his housekeeper, a debt of £300 owed to him by this her brother George. She could have had some difficulty in collecting this cash from her brother in the circumstances.

Nephew John, Walter's youngest son, was still an apprentice and 'Uncle' William, obviously a believer in the Protestant work ethic which had proved so successful in his own case, left him £100 when he set up in trade. The residue of his estate was to be divided between nephews Henry (2) (son of Henry), John Eaton and Walter's sons, Isaac, Samuel, John and Joseph.

A memorandum added to his will throws some light on how Uncle William lived. This records his verbal wishes which he had no opportunity to add to his will before he died two days later. He stated that he wished to leave money to Widow Webb and Widow Staple 'who have heretofore used to starch and mend my ruffs'. His best cloth suit, velvet coat and cloaks lined with velvet he left to nephew John Eaton, citizen and vintner of London. His seal ring, old velvet coat, his beaver lining and silk and woollen stockings and shoes went to nephew Joseph, citizen and haberdasher of London. William must have cut a fine figure in these splendid clothes, fitting for an Alderman of the City of London and a good form of self advertisement for his business, far grander than any tradesman in Knutsford at the time. While dictating the memorandum he relented towards Hannah 'his maid who kept his house', and left her £20 a year and the furniture 'of my chamber' wherein he lay sick. William Antrobus dictated this at the very end of January 1665, and the document states that 'he died of the sickness' very soon afterwards just before London's great plague which took hold in the April of that year.

'Uncle' William's will gives us an introduction to some of the Antrobuses of Knutsford and his influence on their lives and fortunes but they are all interesting in their own right.

Henry Antrobus(2). d. 1666. Nephew Henry was the son of William's brother Henry(1) 'of the Brook', Knutsford. He did not marry and had no children but he had five brothers and sisters. George was the only other boy who as we have seen had moved to London. There were two unmarried sisters, one of whom was Hannah, 'Uncle' William's housekeeper. Sister Sarah had married Charles Moreton and sister Elizabeth, John Norbury. It was these two brothers-in-law that Henry(2) chose as his executors, John having already been executor to his cousin, the other Henry Antrobus(3). They did not know what trouble was about to come.

One afternoon in September 1666, just after the great fire of London, this Henry Antrobus(2), yeoman of Nether Knutsford found himself weaker and 'did not know how the Lord would dispose of him' and had a mind to settle his estate. So he sent a message to the school for the young schoolmaster William Antrobus (no known relative) then aged 25, to come and write his will. When class was dismissed he came round and wrote out the will for the elderly Henry, going to an upper room for privacy. He started with a long, Calvinistic preamble, '... through the merits of Christ his death and passion, possess and inherit the Kingdom of heaven prepared for his elect and chosen ...' but it took 'until the time of lighting of candles' to finish and then the old man read it over and declared himself well pleased. Also present were his brothers-in-law John Norbury and Charles Moreton the appointed executors. They needed another witness to sign and they called up the labourer Robert Fentham who was threshing in the barn who came and put his mark.

He died about a month later and then his will became known. Henry's brother George in London had gone from a bad situation trying to raise the money for the share in his Uncle's business, to one that was much worse. He had survived the plague which followed immediately after his Uncle's death and then must have lost everything in the great fire, the shop being in St. Paul's Churchyard, so was in for a grave disappointment on hearing of his brother's death and the contents of the will. He had been lent £50 by his brother at some time but Henry in his will asked for it to be paid back and if recovered it was to be shared by the brothers-in-law, the executors. Not unnaturally, George disputed the will. The witnesses had to make statements to prove that there was no coercion by the brothers-in-law. In the event, George lost his case as the executors proved the will but we do not know whether they managed to get the £50.

Henry(2) had a picture of his famous Uncle William hanging in his parlour which he left to his cousin Henry(3) senior, who died later that year.

Thomas Antrobus, d.1654, William's brother was a woollen draper of Nether Knutsford. He leased various properties in the town from the Earl of Bridgewater in the late 1620's and early 1630's and some land lately enclosed out of the Heath.

His son was another Henry Antrobus(3) like his cousin and he also died in 1666. As described, one of his main assets was his share in 'Uncle' William's estate and when he made his will he left his wife Margaret an annuity and one cow. She had been Margaret Ankers from a family of 16th

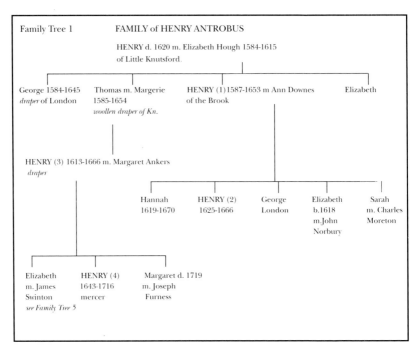

Family Tree 1   FAMILY of HENRY ANTROBUS

HENRY d. 1620 m. Elizabeth Hough 1584-1615
of Little Knutsford.

George 1584-1645   Thomas m. Margerie   HENRY (1)1587-1653 m Ann Downes   Elizabeth
draper of London 1585-1654   of the Brook
                    woollen draper of Kn.

HENRY (3) 1613-1666 m. Margaret Ankers
draper

Hannah   HENRY (2)   George   Elizabeth   Sarah
1619-1670   1625-1666   London   b.1618   m. Charles
                                   m.John   Moreton
                                   Norbury

Elizabeth   HENRY (4)   Margaret d. 1719
m. James   1643-1716   m. Joseph
Swinton   mercer   Furness
see Family Tree 5

century woollen drapers in Knutsford who, because they only seemed to have daughters give the deceptive impression of having died out. It is she who provided the connection with Market Drayton where her son Henry(4) was apprenticed. The bulk of the estate was left to his son Henry(4). To his daughter Elizabeth he left £10, as she had already received her marriage portion, married by then to James Swinton, chandler.

This son Henry Antrobus(4) d.1715, was a mercer but in addition to his continuation of the family business he was actively involved with his Swinton brothers-in-law in the property market in Knutsford as well as actually building. The house and shop that he built and 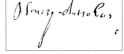 the one next to it are still standing opposite to the George Hotel, the handsomely decorated lead downspout now removed has his initials and the date 1697 upon it. His large dwelling house still stands at the Tatton end of King Street on the right hand side. He was also Knutsford's postmaster between the years 1689-97.

Henry Antrobus was in his youth at the time of his great Uncle William's death. After his apprenticeship he came back to Knutsford and expanded the flourishing drapery business but never married. He concentrated on his business and learnt to benefit like others from funerals, providing the necessary cloth for mourning deemed so important at the time, catering for all persons and all purses and clothes for other occasions. He provided the Leycester family with £37 9s. worth of mourning when Sir Peter died in 1684 and continued to supply the Leycester family for funerals and other occasions after that. He had sold garments made to the requirements of Sir Peter Leycester who bought 'a grate coat for Sam, £4, and a little black coat for little Frank, 2s.' Sam was Sir Peter's carrier and odd job man and little Frank, Francis, was Sir Peter's baby son.

Unfortunately his inventory has not survived so we cannot see what other range of goods he kept. He took over Peter Antrobus's failed business in 1683 and in 1687, appraised the inventory of Thomas Deane, mercer, who had 'cloth and stuffe' worth £122 being well placed to acquire some of that stock. By 1714, the year before he died, the collector of the double levy for the poor, after entering Henry Antrobus's legitimate 5s., added 'but nothing for stock worth £2,000'. Certainly his fortunes were considerable and he was lending money at interest to the Leycester family.

He died in 1715 and was particular about the attire of his household at his own funeral. To his servant Hannah Toft he left a legacy of £30 plus £10 to buy her a suit of mourning; to his servant, John Skellorn, (Skelhorn), William the joiner's son, he also left £10 for a suit of mourning of good broad cloth. £10 was more than the value of most people's entire wardrobe in Knutsford then so his two servants would have been a credit to their master in their good suits of mourning which would have lasted them for many years if not for life. John Skellorn was asked to assist the executors in the sale of the shop goods.

Dwelling House and the one beyond, out of sight, built by Henry Antrobus, near the north end of King Street

Going back to 'Uncle' William's will, he
had bequeathed all his lands in Knutsford to
his nephew Henry(3) for life and then to this
Henry(4); but if he should die without issue
then these lands were to pass to his cousin Isaac
Antrobus. Fifty years later all this seems to have
been forgotten. 'Uncle' William's fears for the
Antrobus line were well founded. Henry(4) had
no heirs and he left the residue of his estate and
all his lands and property to his only surviving
sister Margaret Furness. There seems to have
been no dispute about this and either Isaac's
heir forewent his inheritance or knew nothing
about it.

*Henry Antrobus's lead downspout
photographed in Knutsford's
old library September 1999*

As for his money, Henry(4) left £800 to and
for the use of the poor in Nether Knutsford. To
this day the accumulated interest of this money, under the name of 'The
Antrobus Trust', is still administered and distributed in Knutsford. His name
as benefactor lives on.

Elizabeth Swinton, *(Family Trees 1 and 5)* Henry(4)'s sister had married
James Swinton the chandler in 1665 and were together without children
when the poll tax was collected in 1667. Although Elizabeth had four
children, they all died as infants. At the end of her life when a widow, she
was living in the house of Richard Wrench, feltmaker of Nether Knutsford
to whom she left legacies and to his son. She seems to have been an old

Henry Antrobus's shop opposite the George Hotel the downspout was removed

lady frightened to be left to die alone for she left her household goods to Richard Wrench if she should die in his house. She died in 1710 leaving money to the Minister of the Church of England, the poor, for a schoolmaster and a small legacy to her brother Henry's servant, Hannah Toft who had obviously been kind to her. She left her property to her brother Henry and sister Margaret Furness.

Margaret Furness (sometimes written Furnace), Henry(4)'s sister, was married rather late in life to Joseph Furness who did not live long after the marriage. After her brother Henry died, his servant Hannah Toft with her £10 suit of mourning went to be servant to Margaret Furness having already helped sister Elizabeth Swinton when she was ill. As things turned out, Hannah Toft may well have blessed the day she went into the service of the Antrobus family for after Margaret Furness's death in 1718, she was left one of her houses to live in as well as her clothes to wear. She probably lived to a good age as she died in 1729. Her sister Mary, also a spinster, died aged 75 in 1719 and they both have tombstones in St. Helena's churchyard.

Margaret Furness, the last surviving member of this line of the Antrobus family, received all the family inheritance. She had six houses to dispose of as well as lands and a barn on Knutsford Heath. One of the houses that Henry(4) had built she left to cousin William Antrobus of Great Warford, old Isaac's grandson and the house next to it she left, to and for the use of a preaching minister of the Church of England and all successive ministers. Margaret was obviously Church of England. The house that Margaret lived in was leasehold together with its shop, and this was left to a cousin with instructions to let it out to John Skellorn, by now a mercer, so he must have stepped nicely into his master's shoes with a legacy of £50 to start him off. Another house in Toft, went to cousin Isaac Antrobus the schoolmaster.

The next branch of the family are the children and descendants of 'Uncle' William's brother Walter Antrobus. *See Family Tree 2.* This branch of the family were active dissenters.

Perhaps 'Uncle' William had a special sympathy with them for he himself was a staunch dissenter leaving 'to Mr. Fisher, late minister of God's word in Cheshire, £12 a year to be distributed to late ministers or preachers of God's word as had been ejected or deprived of their livings since Bartholomew tide 1662' and he specifically left a legacy to Mr. Hunter, the Minister ejected from Knutsford.

Walter had four sons, Isaac, Samuel, Joseph (in London) and John and a daughter Mary.

Isaac Antrobus d.1708, we have already met and know how he and his sons John and Walter came to found the Brook Street Chapel. He was a skinner by trade who in 1667 was living in Over Knutsford on his own for he just paid his 1s. poll tax at which time he was one of the assistant constables who helped to collect the tax. He must have married later that year aged 42 and with his wife Mary thirteen years younger, went to live in Brook Street where they were still living until his death aged 83. He was buried under the floor of the new chapel near to the pulpit. His will of 1698 was made 10 years before he died and his signature on it is very frail so he may have been ill during the last years of his life.

He had been a leading dissenter for many years and in 1667 the dissenting Minister Oliver Heywood had written that he had been 'sleeping at the house of Mr. Antrobus who used us exceedingly courteously'.

In 1697 and onwards, the Cheshire Classis minutes record many of their meetings being held in Mr. Antrobus' house. It had been licensed as a dissenting meeting place since 1693. Isaac and his wife lived there with son Walter, son-in-law Rev. Samuel Lowe and granddaughter Mary Lowe. His house included 8 beds, 9 feather beds, 15 boulsters and 4 pillows, 145 lbs. of pewter and 62 lbs. of brassware, 14 plates and 1 dozen trenchers.

Isaac had been an active man in Knutsford. He was involved with the Court Leet and took on the onerous jobs of Constable, Overseer of the Poor etc. but his strong dissenting views and faith dominated his life and involved him in active church and chapel life. He was not afraid to criticise and stay away from the established church in protest from time to time, incurring certain fines and risking imprisonment or even deportation when he faced

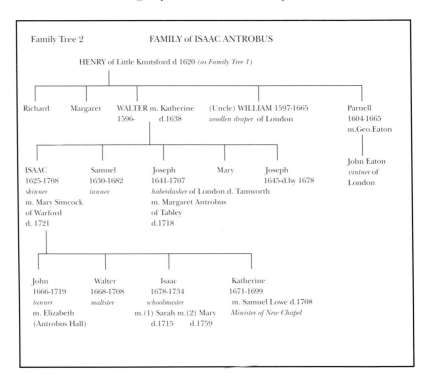

the daunting Judge Jeffries in Court in Chester. He supported the dissenters through all their times of persecution, gave the land and worked to plan, build and furnish the new chapel.

Old Isaac and his wife Mary had four children, three sons and a daughter. John Antrobus, Isaac's eldest son was also a tanner when he married and had already had his marriage portion when his father died. He and his wife Elizabeth built Antrobus Hall in Mobberley where he farmed.

Walter Antrobus d.1708, their second son was a maltster and never married. He had had an education and like his father was active in dissenting affairs and also like his father had witnessed wills and appraised inventories especially in the early years of the 18th century. He was one of the Trustees of the new chapel, executor of the wills of both Peter Wood and Alice Swinton, was a Juryman at the Manorial Court in 1701 and of the Quarter Sessions in 1702. He was still living with his parents and when his father died in July 1708, at which time he was farming with £40 worth of peas and barley growing. They kept three cows, two pigs, poultry and a mare, with £5 worth of hay. They had an apple mill, useful for making cider. Other foods were carefully preserved for winter use probably by his mother Mary, two flitches of bacon, 200 of cheese and a salting tub to keep vegetables and meat. He died only a few months after his father but unlike others of his family he was buried in St. Helena's churchyard. His tombstone turned up in 1916 used face downwards as a flagstone in somebody's garden. His mother Mary died aged 82 in1721.

Isaac Antrobus junior was Isaac's youngest son. He was still young when his father made his will. His father left him a house in Great Warford and provided a fund for the rest of his education and maintenance. He later became the schoolmaster who came back to Knutsford and kept the dissenters' school until his death in 1734.

Daughter Katherine had died young in 1699 aged 28, before her father. She had married Rev. Samuel Lowe who came as minister to the new chapel in 1696. They had one daughter Mary. Samuel Lowe had a room in old Isaac's house in which he kept a library of £23 worth of books equalling the value of his worldly goods much of which being linen must have been his wife's dowry. He died in 1709 not long after old Isaac and his son Walter. He had been minister at the chapel for 13 years. Matthew Henry the noted nonconformist minister, said in his diary that, 'There have been great breaches made upon that congregation this last year: this is the third funeral out of the same house in less than a year, old Mr. Antrobus, his second son and now Mr. Low his son-in-law'.

Very much against the odds, Isaac's granddaughter Mary Low survived, married and had children. She must have been looked after by her grandmother Mary since she was a baby.

Samuel Antrobus, Isaac's brother, was a tanner. Whereas Isaac had been to school and his literacy had given him many advantages in his life, Samuel was a tanner who could only sign his name with an unsteady 'S', so it is unlikely that he was literate although he was one of Over Knutsford's Overseers of the Poor in 1678. He left a legacy of £10 for the poor in his will. He was living on his own in 1667. Samuel had

a thriving tanning business in Over Knutsford with great quantities of wet and dry leather, £173 worth, and bark used in the tanning process. Some tan pits were found on the Welmar Estate off the Mobberley road although Samuel Antrobus was not the only tanner in Over Knutsford at this time. Tanning was a smelly business which must have been unpleasant to be near but he escaped the smell at times by working in his field; he had 'a land of barley yet standing' at the time of his inventory in August. He lived in a small house with two beds in it and two hearths but had made money during his life, with a mortgage of £103 owing to him on a house in Over Tabley when he died in1682.

This branch of the Antrobus family was clearly closely knit, staunchly dissenting and highly regarded in the community.

There was another branch of the Antrobus family living in Nether Tabley initially, but working in Knutsford.

Peter and Elizabeth Antrobus and a Treasure Hunt

See Family Tree 3 (p.108)

In the early part of the seventeenth century, two brothers from Nether Tabley Peter and Richard Antrobus were left as orphans and brought up by an uncle. When they grew up, Peter(1) married and had several children but Richard remained a bachelor. They were related to the previous Antrobus family.

During the Civil War, Richard who lived on his own in Davenham, began to be fearful because of marauding soldiers. He left his house taking with him his considerable fortune of £1,200 and 500 gold pieces, 400 angels and 300lbs in silver. He hid this in Peter's house in Nether Tabley for safety although Knutsford Heath nearby was a camping ground for thousands of Civil War troops. He hid the treasure very well and soldiers did not find it, nor even did his family for he died in 1645 without making a will and without telling anyone where the treasure was hidden. Although Peter took out Letters of Administration he himself died the next year without having discovered his brother's treasure.

Peter(1) had inherited his father George's woollen drapery business with shops in Knutsford and Warrington. He had married Ann Hough whose father had also been a prosperous draper in Knutsford. When Peter(1) died in 1646, leaving three sons and two daughters, Peter(2) the eldest was barely

18. He left his wife, 'the third of all goods and personal estate according as the same is due to her by law'.

He left legacies to all his children which were in fact their marriage portions but with the wording slightly different for each child. The legacy to his eldest son Peter(2) was prefaced with, 'in case he carry himself dutiful towards his mother and be a frugal and good husband', that to his second son George with, 'in case he be dutiful to his mother and will be ruled and directed by her and be not ill husband'. To his son Philip and his two daughters were added the proviso for them 'that they marry with their mother's and their friends' consent'. No mention was made of property.

Peter(2) inherited his father's and grandfather's business and on his marriage in 1648 moved from Tabley to Knutsford. He married very well, a woman of great character and competence, Elizabeth. She was daughter of Samuel Birch of Ordsall, who was a surgeon and a friend of Dr. Henry Newcome, the famous dissenting Minister of Cross Street Chapel, Manchester. Peter and Elizabeth had nine children, her firstborn being twins and all of them survived beyond infancy, no mean feat in those days. Elizabeth became a midwife from 1674, one of the few careers open to women at this time and one for which her medical background and practical experience must ideally have prepared her.

In 1667 their household was the largest in Knutsford which consisted of himself, his wife Elizabeth and seven children, (twins Peter and daughter Elizabeth were no longer at home), and two servants.

Peter Leycester of Tabley having been in this Peter's company on an occasion in 1653, said, 'Peter Antrobus of Nether Tabley who then lived at Nether Knutsford ... is a man of good Credit and repute among our Neighbourhood'. He patronised his shop.

Peter(2) did well with the business and had many properties. In 1656 and 1671 he owned eight houses and a cottage 'of his own freehold' in Lower Knutsford and the Cross Town. Then something unexplainable happened and his fortunes started to go downhill. He made his will in 1677 but did not die until 1684. Possibly he was in bad health. Whether of his own making or not, Peter turned out not to be 'a frugal and good husband' at the end, for when he died he was insolvent and had only three houses, one in Nether Knutsford, one in Crosstown and the one in Tabley, not enough money to pay his debts. The woollen drapery shop must have been sold to cousin Henry Antrobus. The family business died with him.

Peter(2)'s brother George must have shown great promise at Knutsford Grammar School before his father died for his legacy was greater than that of his brothers'. They went into business but George was destined for Brasenose College Oxford where he gained BA. He was then ordained and became headmaster of Tamworth Grammar School. He took his M.A. in Cambridge at Jesus College and also became Rector of Wollaton, Nottingham. He sent several students to St. John's College, Cambridge from the Tamworth school where he stayed until his death in 1708.

Brother Philip became a mercer in Knutsford and in 1671 issued a halfpenny trade token at a time when there were not enough coins of small value minted and in circulation. One of these coins with his name and 'Knutsford' stamped upon it and the Mercers' Arms, is now in the British Museum. He is believed to have retired to Tamworth near to his brother for that is where he died in 1683. Their sister Margaret also went there where she died in 1718.

When Peter(2) died in 1683, he had appointed his brother George an executor of his will but he renounced the executorship saying, 'Upon the account of my having the charge of a considerable grammar school upon me and several other weighty businesses, and living at so great distance from Knutsford, I do renounce the executorship that is in the said will imposed upon me'.

At his death, Peter's house in Nether Knutsford where he lived, had eight rooms, one of which was a schoolroom in which was a table, a form and some pictures. This could have been a 'petty school' where Elizabeth taught. Peter's goods were valued at about £50, many of the things in the house being described as 'old'. There was a board with a coat of arms on it, and in the barn and shippon outside were hay, beans and barley. He had a sword, but this, valued with his wearing apparel was only thought to

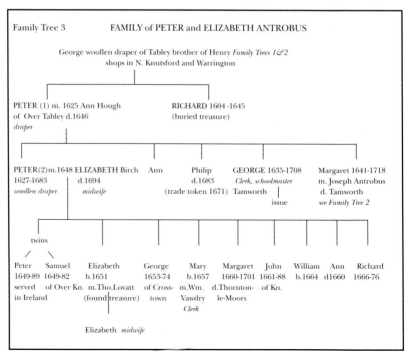

be worth £2. He signed his name on his will with a very good, clear, firm hand and his will covered every eventuality of his children dying and his wife remarrying but no mention of debts.

Peter's widow Elizabeth was an active dissenter and her house in Nether Knutsford was licensed as a Dissenting Meeting place in 1689 for the next few years.

She set to work with great energy and determination and with her daughter Margaret's help, paid off all her late husband's debts before she herself died in 1694.   As a midwife her name appears in several Quarter Sessions documents concerning attendance at births of bastard children and taking paternity statements for the Poor Law. She endorsed that she wrote and signed her will in her own hand, most unusual at that time, leaving everything in her will to her daughter Margaret in gratitude for her help. She had faced the death of all of her five sons in her lifetime, her eldest son Peter(3) having been a soldier involved in the fighting in Ireland had come home on furlough in 1689 but died a few days later.

Her three daughters survived her. Elizabeth married Thomas Lovatt who was later connected with the silkmill in Knutsford, Mary married the Rev. William Vawdrey, curate of Mobberley, and Margaret who was unmarried.

Meanwhile, what of the treasure? The house in Tabley that old Peter Antrobus(1) had lived in and where the treasure had been hidden, had had several tenants. It had a parlour, a lower chamber, the house, a buttery, a little chamber over the entry and a milk buttery beyond the entry. Outside there was a barn on the wall of which at the time of Peter(2)'s death in 1683 was an oak ladder of 24 stands. Peter(2)'s daughter Elizabeth and her husband Thomas Lovatt went to live there and in 1695, just a year after her mother Elizabeth's death, daughter Elizabeth found great uncle Richard's treasure and the Lovatts promptly claimed it for themselves. This galvanised Uncle George into action and despite his 'considerable grammar school in Tamworth', he applied for and obtained Letters of Administration to the estate of his uncle Richard, and called upon the Lovatts to account for what they had found. All this is known from the pleadings of the case in Chancery, but unfortunately the decision of the court has not survived, most likely because the family reached a settlement out of court. The money was probably shared amongst old Peter's descendants for it is just at this time that George embarked on a major scheme of extension at Tamworth Grammar School partly at his own expense.

The treasure was found too late to have helped Elizabeth, Peter(2)'s widow and it is hard to tell whether their daughter Margaret benefited from a share of it. She remained unmarried and died in Thornton-le-Moors, near the present Stanlow Oil Refinery. Why she had gone there is a mystery, but at least she harboured no resentment for she left her best pair of stays and an enamelled gold ring to her sister Elizabeth Lovatt and the residue of her estate to the children of her sister Mary Vawdrey. Her will was signed with her mark, although being 'weak and sick in body' at the time it does not look as if she could write, so her mother sadly, may never have found the time to teach her daughter although she may of course have been able to read.

The Swinton Family   *See Family Tree 4 (p.112)*

This family differed from the Antrobus's because one branch of them styled themselves 'gentlemen'. During the reign of Henry VIIIth an illegitimate daughter of John Leycester of Tabley had married into the Swinton family which with this gentry connection could have brought extra wealth and status to the Swintons from that time although most of them were in trade. Memories of this connection were probably handed down.

This was in 1538 when Thomas Swinton married Elizabeth one of three illegitimate daughters of John Leycester, and their son Thomas, mercer, left a widow Sibell (d.1570) who kept on her husband's high class shop in Knutsford stocked with more than £90 worth of cloth, worsted, velvet and damask, taffeta and sarcenet, silk fringes and lace, hats, gloves and leather etc., and playing cards. The stock sounds similar to that of Henry Burgess (d. 1612), although not in the large warehouse quantities which he kept. Sibell Swinton was a glover. She passed all her leather and wool skins and fells, dressed and undressed, all stock and tools, instruments and work looms belonging to the science and mystery of glover or whitauer on to her second son, Henry. Sibell Swinton's shop is evidence that there had been luxury goods for sale in Knutsford in Elizabethan times.

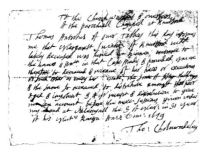

Thomas Cholmondley of Vale Royal informing the Churchwardens & Overseers of Knutsford that Margaret Swinton of Knutsford was buried in linen, contary to the law. 50 shillings was to be distributed amongst the poor, aged and impotent.

To the Churchwardens & overseers of the Parochiall Chapell at Knutsford

Thomas Antrobus of Over Tabley this day informes me that Margaret Swinton of Knutsford widd. lately deceased was buried in Linnen, contrarie to the laws & stats. in that Case made & provided, you are therefore to demand & receave of her heirs or executours or such other as enioy her estate, the sume of fifty shillings & the same so received, to distribute amoungst your poor Aged and impotent, & of your receipt & distribution to give me an account before the next Sessions, given under my hand at Valeroyall the 3 of Mar: in 31 year of his Maties Raign Ann Dom: 1679

Tho: Cholmondeley

John Swinton(1), a descendant of these, married Margaret Foxley in 1622. They had a family of six children and all were married except the youngest, Elizabeth, at the time of their mother's death in 1680. Both Margaret and her household were highly respected in Knutsford. She wrote her will in 1678 with specific legacies for all her family and carefully signed with her initials 'M.S.' called her mark, the best that she could do indicating that literacy was not always necessary for a mistress of a gentleman's household.

Her furniture and goods were worth £153 which included 3 cows and a swine and her clothes worth £10.

After her death, Thomas Antrobus of Over Tabley informed JP Thomas Cholmondley of Vale Royal that she had not been buried in wool as the law had required since  1666 and again in 1678. Cholmondley therefore wrote to the Chapelwardens and Overseers of Knutsford, via Quarter Sessions who demanded that her heirs and executors were to pay fifty shillings fine which was to be distributed amongst the poor.

The family thought it was worth paying the fine for her to be buried in linen.

John Swinton (2) d.1684, her son, gentleman but who was in trade in Knutsford as an ironmonger and grocer and could well have been a merchant, retail and possibly wholesale. In 1671 he was freeholder of Radbrook House. He had been in Knutsford for some years before 1667 at which time he was trading, having a substantial household which consisted of his wife Jane, two daughters and two apprentices, James Johnson and John Brook who later both went on to be grocers with their own businesses. The Swintons had three servants. When John Swinton married his first wife Jane Harpur from Wigan they were wealthy enough to warrant a marriage settlement from which he had benefited from several properties and lands among which was Radbrook House, but John Swinton leased this out like the others and at his death, goods at Radbrook and arrears of rent for Radbrook were listed in his inventory. Peter Leycester bought goods, grocery and 'shuger' regularly from him, Mr. John Swinton, and paid him for work done by his employees on his new Chapel which he was building in 1674.

John Swinton (2) and his first wife had three children surviving to adulthood, Jane, Elizabeth and John. Some time after 1667 his wife Jane died and John remarried Alice Shaw who had no children. John had been fined by the Church Court for keeping his shop open and exposing goods for sale on St. James's day in 1682 the year before he died, a conflict of business and tightening religious laws. Judging from his choice of second wife who was a strong dissenter, from the executors of his will and the guardians he appointed to look after his young son, he himself was a dissenter.

He and his sister Margaret Delves the apothecary's widow, died on consecutive days and had a double funeral.

In his inventory the shop was in 'the old house' with ironmongery valued at a considerable £215 (not itemised), this house having eight rooms. The newer house had six rooms. There was a clock in the kitchen. He was an educated, well dressed man who wore a signet ring, had a pocket watch and a grey Camlett coat like one Samuel Pepys had had made 20 years earlier. He kept a mare and had a special coat for riding. His apparel, watch, saddles and bridles were valued at £10. He left a long, complicated will which he made

while he was in good health a year before he died. He left his steel bow and
a rapier to his son John with his chest of drawers where he kept his writing
together with his books on Latin, law and divinity and a silver tankard to
James Harpur his first wife's brother. To Peter Wood who wrote out the will
(and the inventory), he left a set of broad plate buttons and 20 shillings for a
coat to set them upon. Out of his £32 of gold he left coins to several family
members and his son-in-law received the Camlett coat. He was concerned
about his daughter Elizabeth aged 23, that she might die unmarried and
made special provision for her. She may have been disfigured, deformed
or had some affliction. At his death he had £165 in ready money and silver,
quite a responsibility in those days before bank safes. He kept two cows, a
pig and poultry as well as his mare.

Having ten or eleven properties and lands, he was able to run his business
in a managerial capacity.

Alice Swinton, John's second wife died in 1699. A Swinton tombstone
of that date in St. Helena's may be hers. Alice came from a family where
there had also been a second marriage, not uncommon in those times and
she had half brothers and half sisters but she left considerable legacies
to her late husband's family and seems to have been on good terms with
her step children leaving them legacies when she died. Elizabeth her step
daughter who had pre deceased her the year before had left a legacy to her
step mother. Alice Swinton was a member of the new dissenting chapel

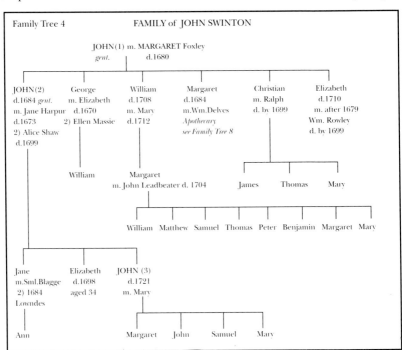

leaving legacies to her friends there, 'the Rev. Samuel Lowe, our minister',
to Hannah Kynaston the widow of the previous minister and to Peter Wood
to whom she also left her pews. For her executors she chose three of the
Chapel's first Trustees. William Skellorn who appraised her inventory was
a joiner who doubled as the local undertaker and lived next door to Peter
Wood in the former Angel Inn.

Since her husband's death she had moved to a smaller house where she
had four or five rooms most comfortably furnished. She had embroidered
(green) curtains, bedcovers, cushions, and couch chairs, and white window
hangings. There were chests of drawers, leather chairs and a bulrush chair.
She had pictures, looking glasses, a warming pan, bellows for her fire, a
toasting iron, snuffers for her candles, an hour glass, a maid(en) to dry
clothes, some books and two Bibles. There were a few agricultural items
and hay, £34 in ready money and her wearing apparel valued at £8 was all
left to others. Her inventory was valued at over £263. It was with Mistress
Swinton that Sir Thomas Mainwaring stayed while under house arrest in
1685 during the Monmouth Rebellion. She had not been widowed a year
at that time, so whether she was in this house or her husband's larger one
is not known.

Jane Blagge/ Lowndes was born in 1661, John's eldest daughter. In
her father's will of 1683 she is referred to as Jane Blagge. She had married
Samuel Blagge of Macclesfield that year and they had a daughter Ann. It was
Samuel Blagge who received the Camlett coat. By 1699 Jane had remarried
and was Jane Lowndes.

Elizabeth Swinton born 1665, was John's other surviving daughter who
died unmarried in 1698 aged 34 and is buried in St. Helena's churchyard.
One of the witnesses to her will was Parson James Robinson, so not all the
Swinton family were dissenters. Although
this was the daughter that her father was
worried about she disposed of her worldly
goods in a sensible and a complicated way.
She too left legacies to all her family even
including relatives by marriage. She had a
room in her step mother Alice's house and
made her will when she was only 29, being
at that time in 'in reasonable health'. There
must have been some reason why she did not
marry for she was an heiress of some worth
by Knutsford standards having specialties of
nearly £600. She wrote her name very legibly
and left a legacy of £10 for a schoolmaster
'until children can read well in the Bible'.
She kept a few sheep and a hive of bees. She
had an unusual collection of silver trinkets,

*Tombstone of Elizabeth Swinton
in St. Helena's churchyard*

all carefully listed but her father may have indulged Elizabeth to compensate for her disability whatever it was. After his death she was allowed to indulge herself for her wardrobe was extensive, probably of fine quality, its value at £22 10s. being more than double that of any other item for apparel in any inventory for Knutsford over a period of 60 years.

John Swinton (3) was John (2)'s only son. By 1698 when his sister Elizabeth died he was married with only three surviving children, John, Mary and Samuel. He, like his father and grandfather before him called himself gentleman. Although his inventory reveals a shop, unlike his father it seems to have been only the vestige of one with goods in it valued at only £2 and not specified. He may have been a merchant like his father, later on living on investment income from the specialties he had of £650. He had a comfortable house with set work upholstery in many rooms and he still had agricultural links like so many others still, with some poultry, a little corn, hay and fuel and eight measures of malt. He died aged 54, in 1721.

His wife Mary was co-executor with Isaac Antrobus the schoolmaster so he may have had dissenting views like his step mother. A witness of his will was his cousin Margaret Leadbeater, widow of one of the first Trustees of their new chapel. One of the items in his will was 'his silver tankard with his coat of arms engraved upon it' which had belonged to his father. He left this to his wife. Which coat of arms this was is not known.

Going back two generations, George Swinton was John (2)'s next brother who does not seem to have prospered as well as his elder brother John or his next younger brother William. Until 1708 he was remembered by his family in their wills but had probably died by 1710 when his sister Elizabeth Rowley died. He had been one of the chapel wardens who signed the petition in 1670 for permission to build a ringing loft for Knutsford Church when the ropes were making it unsafe for the people to pass below.

William Swinton the younger brother was the most prosperous business man of the family who left one of the few four figure estates in Knutsford, £1,279 6s. 4p. on his death in 1708. He was or had been a mercer carrying on a family tradition going back to the previous century, but according to his inventory the main asset of his estate was debts on bond. This was one of the ways that a wealthy man could both protect his money from theft and use it as an investment to earn interest. His large house had 18 rooms, a grand establishment, including the first mention of a dining room, with window curtains in every room. He had a very large number of chairs which could indicate that he did a lot of entertaining or used his house as a meeting place which could have been so, for whether he was a dissenter or not he specifically asked for a simple funeral, quite unusual in those days.

William and his wife Mary had one surviving daughter, Margaret who married John Leadbeater, Attorney at law, one of the first Trustees of the dissenters' chapel in 1694. They had a marriage settlement which formed part of the Title Deeds of the Golden Lion Inn which used to be in Knutsford's

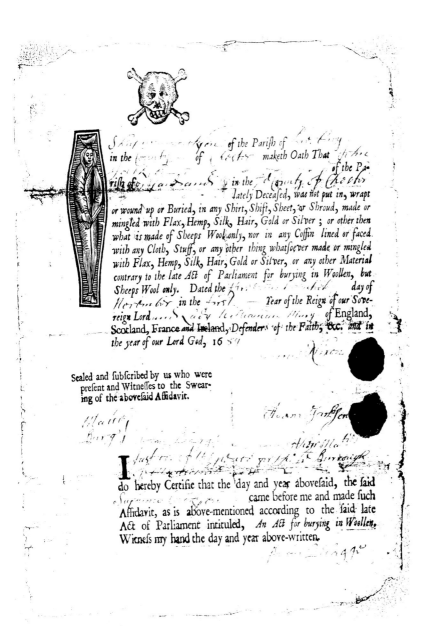

S...... ......y.... of the Parish of ....
in the .... of .... maketh Oath That ....
.... of the Pa-
rish of .... in the .... of ....
lately Deceafed, was not put in, wrapt
or wound up or Buried, in any Shirt, Shift, Sheet, or Shroud, made or
mingled with Flax, Hemp, Silk, Hair, Gold or Silver ; or other then
what is made of Sheeps Wool only, nor in any Coffin lined or faced
with any Cloth, Stuff, or any other thing whatfoever made or mingled
with Flax, Hemp, Silk, Hair, Gold or Silver, or any other Material
contrary to the late Act of Parliament for burying in Woollen, but
Sheeps Wool only. Dated the .... day of
Hovember in the first ...... Year of the Reign of our Sove-
reign Lord .... of England,
Scotland, France and Ireland, Defenders of the Faith, &c. and in
the year of our Lord God, 16 89

Sealed and fubfcribed by us who were
prefent and Witneffes to the Swear-
ing of the abovefaid Affidavit.

I ....
do hereby Certifie that the day and year abovefaid, the faid
.... came before me and made fuch
Affidavit, as is above-mentioned according to the faid late
Act of Parliament intituled, _An Act for burying in Woollen,_
Witnefs my hand the day and year above-written.

Certificate of Burial in woollen (Prestbury Parish) 23rd November 1689 old market place. John died in 1704 leaving his wife to bring up their eight children who were all mentioned in their grandfather's will of 1708. Their grandfather left money for all the children to be apprenticed. John Leadbeater's inventory depicts a house with ten rooms, comfortably furnished, six leather chairs and a form round the table in the hall, the children's presence indicated by a child's chair in the parlour, two little chairs in the kitchen, and a child's high chair in the buttery. In a closet was a box containing a bearing cloth, (these were sometimes red in colour), and child's linen, two christening hoods and four yards of lace.

His widow Margaret Leadbeater went to live next to Henry Long the chapman who mentioned this in his will of 1715. He may have lived in Drury Lane. By 1715 most of her children would have left home. In their usual way the rest of the family remembered her in her widowhood. She must have been a stalwart woman to have brought up all those children who grew to adulthood and founded the Leadbeater family, which name is still in Knutsford.

Margaret Swinton *(see Family Tree 8 p.160)* d.1684, the eldest sister of John(2),*(FamilyTree 4)* married William Delves who was a very successful apothecary. They had four sons and two daughters. Margaret survived her husband by nine years. After he died in 1675 she was lending money to Henry Antrobus, mercer. She could have lived comfortably with assets and bonds of £60 and plate, money, gold and gold rings worth £36.

In her widowhood she evidently occupied some time by baking biscuits among other things, to keep her independence. She supplied £3 worth in 1678 for Lady Leycester's funeral at Tabley and her 'biscake pans' are entered in her son Thomas's inventory when he died shortly after her. By the time of Margaret's death in 1684 her eldest son William had already died three years before. His widow Rebecca had two infant children, William and Margaret who may have been helped and befriended by William's bachelor brother Thomas who took out probate of his brother's will. The infant William grew to manhood and in 1701 was an assessor and afferator in the Egerton Manorial Court.

Christian was one of the younger sisters of William Swinton. By 1699 she had married Ralph Chesney and probably moved away from Knutsford, but she and her children were regularly remembered in all the family wills.

Elizabeth was the youngest sister of John(2) and William Swinton. After her mother's death in 1680 she married William Rowley but by 1699 when Alice Swinton her sister-in-law died she was already widowed. She left no children. She bequeathed legacies to her many nephews and nieces, many of them to be paid out of 'Hewitt's House' but the last item on her inventory is a debt of £50 secured on Hewitt's House, 'believed to be desperate' so it does not look as if many of them received anything. In 1710 when she died she was living with her servant maid in a 6 roomed house with books to read, a looking glass and pictures on her walls. She and her servant may have worked with linen as there was linen at the whiteners and linen cloth, a tear of flax (grown locally) and yarn valued at £8. Some of her clothes were bequeathed to friends, a large purse, a black and brown muff and her wedding ring, and to her servant, one mantle, and two petticoats 'an upper and an under not of the worser sort'.

At the same time there was another family of Swintons flourishing in Knutsford. *See Family Tree 5 p.119.* Possibly old Thomas and John(1) were brothers. By 1631 Thomas had married Lettice Burrows who by 1678 was a widow but she lived for twenty more years. They had three sons who each led very different lives, James, Peter and Thomas, but James and Peter both died before her. All were educated but Thomas went to university.

Thomas Swinton was in April 1669 a schoolmaster in Chester still keeping very much in touch with Knutsford. Possibly to give him capital to set up home there, he became a feofee approved by the Manor Court, of Henry Burgess's legacy, receiving £33 6s 8d from them instead of William Delves, Apothecary. He later became a clergyman and from 1674 until 1702 was the Vicar of St. Hilary's Church in Wallasey, Wirral. He kept up religious and political contacts in Knutsford sufficient for him to be suspected of planning to overthrow James II, for his house was searched for arms after the Cheshire visit of the Duke of Monmouth, at the same time as the gentry local to Knutsford.

He did not prosper as well as his brothers, possibly because he had a large family of seven children and could have been in a poorly paid living. As early as 1678 Thomas was in severe financial difficulty and had to sell off land and be rescued further by his brothers, for by a mortgage of that year the brothers agreed to pay off his debts in return for a mortgage on lands in Sudlow Townfields and a house in Nether Knutsford occupied by their mother Lettice and Dr. William Smith. In 1685 Thomas took a lease from Peter Legh of a house in Nether Knutsford. He paid a £10 premium for this lease, or rather he did not pay, for instead his is one of only two cases found where the tenant entered into a bond to pay the money owing.

His brother James Swinton was a tallow chandler in Nether Knutsford. In 1665 he married Elizabeth Antrobus. At some time he had a new parlour added to his house which he leased from his brother in law Henry Antrobus(4) *(Family Tree1),* but he must have made an unpleasant neighbour, for the smell of boiling animal fat for tallow was such that in the nineteenth century it is one of the noisome and offensive trades that is specifically forbidden.

He was Knutsford's main chandler. There was another James Swinton in Knutsford at this time, (see p.2 of the Poll Tax list at the end of this chapter), whose trade is unknown but one of these two James Swintons contributed to local trade by manufacturing octagonal halfpenny trade tokens. (Two other Knutsford tradesmen issued trade tokens which survive in the British museum, Philip Antrobus and James Johnson). James Swinton's candle house and brewhouse held a furnace to render the tallow and melt the wax, an engine, lead moulds, pans and ladles, vessels, wig yarn for wicks, weights and scales and some finished tallow candles for sale. He sent regular supplies to Tabley House yearly, candles worth £17.50s in 1680. Another account mentions candles in some quantity by the pound and by the dozen costing 4d. and 7d. a dozen. The more expensive candles were beeswax which burnt brighter and were less smoky than tallow. This needed purifying and then bleaching on linen strips in the sun for several weeks, a seasonal task.

Agriculturally he had some sheep and kept horses in the stable. There was hay, corn, malt, lime and muck in the barn. His house had seven rooms including the new parlour. They enjoyed the comfort of a warming pan and he had a few pictures and books.

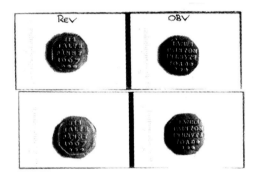

Trade Tokens of James Swinton in Knutsford
His 1667 halfpenny - Warrington Museum

Peter Swinton

Peter Swinton the third brother, was a bookseller and stationer in Knutsford, which was one of the few towns outside Chester in the late 17th century to have a bookseller.

His bookshop became a centre for all the educated men in the area, and he did a good trade amongst the many religious gentlemen and ministers who bought their Bibles, prayer books and works on divinity from him as well as taking their old well thumbed volumes to him to be rebound in local leather and calf skins and given marbled end papers. Sir Peter Leycester often bought books from him amongst which, an Antiquities Hibernica in 1673 and a Bible for his wife in 1675. Peter Swinton also catered for schoolmasters and their pupils, ABCs being disposed of from his shop after his death (see p.40). The only record of any publication that he made is that of Sir Robert Leycester's funeral sermon in 1684.

He sold stamped parchments and paper for legal documents and as a sideline to supplement trade, sold pictures and had 16 stands for periwigs for the full bottomed wigs of the time. (John Harpur was the local periwig maker in Knutsford at the time). He had several agricultural implements and garden tools. His cow house no longer housed cows but an apple mill and its accoutrements and also a stack of wooden boards. His barn held hay, barley and straw and £21 worth of corn on 11th October 1698. He was not married but with his brother as we have already seen, was involved with numerous business deals with property. He had a maid servant and was likely to have had apprentices.

His shop was part of a six roomed house with room for an apprentice and a servant. In his leisure he smoked, looked after his garden, made his own cider and played bowls, he had two pairs of bowls and a jack. Knutsford had a bowling green which existed until the last decades of the 20th century when an old persons' residential home was built upon the site opposite the Heath, behind Canute Square. He possessed a bridle, pillion and saddles for riding and his wearing apparel was valued with his tobacco box at £4 11 7d. possibly including a periwig. His 'dear and loving' brother James had left him part of his estate when he had died in 1690, and this he left as a charity to be distributed yearly for ever divided between a preaching minister, a schoolmaster and the poor of Knutsford. His dear and loving mother Lettice was remembered as well as his sister-in-law Elizabeth, also

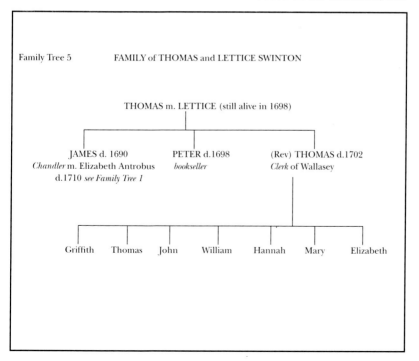

Family Tree 5   FAMILY of THOMAS and LETTICE SWINTON

THOMAS m. LETTICE (still alive in 1698)

JAMES d. 1690   PETER d.1698   (Rev) THOMAS d.1702
Chandler m. Elizabeth Antrobus   *bookseller*   *Clerk* of Wallasey
d.1710 *see Family Tree 1*

Griffith   Thomas   John   William   Hannah   Mary   Elizabeth referred to in affectionate terms. The rest of his estate he left to his 'dear and loving' brother Thomas the clergyman on the Wirral.

He appointed his loving friends Henry Antrobus, his brother James' brother in law, and John Leadbeater (Attorney) to be his executors and from the account which Henry Antrobus kept, the happenings at his death and funeral in September 1698 can be reconstructed. Peter Swinton was 54 years old when he became ill and sent for Dr. John Delves. He did not seem to be responding to treatment so thought it best to make his will. He was well looked after in his sickness by his servant who cooked him a breast of mutton and produced a bottle of cider to try to tempt him back to health. Despite this and Dr. Delves best ministrations and some medicine from Joseph Hough the apothecary, he died on September 29th. A message had to be sent to his brother the Rev. Thomas in Wallasey so a horse was hired and one John Moore went to break the news to him. The weather may have been bad at the time and Thomas must have had things to do because he stayed for two nights there before returning to Knutsford with the Rev. Thomas and his eldest son Griffith. Sixpence was allowed out of Peter's estate for a peck of oats for his horse.

Meanwhile in Knutsford the corpse was shaved and a coffin ordered from William Skellorn the joiner and undertaker. He was a tradesman who did quite well out of funerals, not only supplying coffins but also the ale at the wake afterwards. He often appraised inventories as he did in this instance with Dr. Delves and the Rev. Peake who were given 10d. between them for appraising the goods. The minister the Rev. Robinson was approached about the service and the funeral sermon, for which he was given £1, and the sexton at the Knutsford Church about digging the grave and helping to carry the bier.

The family and friends had to have suitable mourning clothes and the executor Henry Antrobus, mercer, was pleased to supply this from his shop. A burying suit was made, it does not say for whom, out of six yards of fine crepe at 15d. a yard and 2d for making, for which he only charged the estate 7s.10d. He supplied eleven and three quarter yards of Italian crepe at 2s. yard and three yards of Broad Allamode, an expensive smooth glossy silk at 6s.4d. a yard for the hatbands and 'love ribbon to the hatbands'.

Elizabeth his sister-in-law and her maid set about preparing the food, 10s. worth of beef and other provisions. They bought £4 worth of bread, asking Sarah Hough for some, and they went to John Brooks the grocer for butter, sugar and spice. Joseph Hough apothecary, supplied 27 pounds of biscuits and 6 and a half pounds of Naples biscuits so they were prepared for a great many people to come. And come they did, for Knutsford people and others from the area were sorry to lose their bookseller and Henry Antrobus made sure that his funeral would be fitting and memorable. No less than 20 gallons of ale were ordered and as this was quickly consumed, he sent out for 20 gallons more.

Henry Antrobus had a long task ahead of him as he settled the estate. He disposed of his property holding in Toft; he sold some of the items from his house to various people. Some of the stock of stamped paper was bought by Mr. Leadbeater,(Attorney) and Samuel Leadbeater bought a common prayer book and psalms at 4s.3d. Henry Antrobus also bought one for himself with two pictures for 12s. and some of the wooden boards. William Skellorn bought more of the wood. The corn was sold, Antrobus called it Rhombus corn and he was paid 14s. for two of Peter's old coats with the breeches and hat. There were many business letters from and possibly to London, debts to be paid and received from parsons and gentlemen, land tax and church and poor lays to be paid. He was still receiving money into the estate for several months.

The Birtles family   *See Family Tree 6 (p123)*

Although not as numerous as the Antrobuses and the Swintons, at the same time there were several families of Birtles. Some of these were tanners like Samuel Antrobus, and shoemakers who were part of the important leather trade in Knutsford. There were tan yards in the area of Drury Lane and 'the Brook' near Brook Street and on several sites in Over Knutsford.

John Birtles, tanner, died in 1666 at which time his tanning utensils, tanned leather and bark were valued at £55 6s. out of his total estate of £88 13s.8d. As far as is known he had just one son.

Son William d.1695, also a tanner, built up a far larger and more successful business. He was in 1667 living with his wife Mary, three children and two servants one of whom was possibly a journeyman. They were to have at least eleven children which Mary bore over a period of twenty years, their daughters unusually, dying young but seven sons grew to manhood. William's wife Mary died in 1686 in the same year that their eldest son William junior, died, he being twenty years older than their youngest, Hugh, who was only five at the time. It seems that all the boys had a schooling.

William had large stocks of leather, £193 worth in wet leather, £25 of dry leather and £24 in green leather. There was £100 worth of bark and in 'hair and tails and horns and all other necessaries belonging to the tan yard and the bark mill, £3 12s.6d'. He had supplied the Leycester household with six measures of hair for a bell rope in 1679 and 'a skin for the coach, 3s.6d' in 1692. He kept 4 milk cows, 2 twinters and a calf, 26 sheep, 1 mare, 1 nag, 1 swine and poultry. There was in August, £9 11s. worth of 'all sorts of corn growing and in the garner' and £7 worth of hay. His house was comfortably furnished to accommodate his family although Thomas and John had certainly left home at the time he died. He had pictures, a looking glass, a coat of arms, a gun, a £2 silver watch and books. Life was not always peaceful at home, his boys with a wide age difference between them were often bickering and fighting. William senior knew his sons and said in his will that, 'if any of my children do quarrel with or molest my executors ... they shall be cut off with 5s.'. He appointed sons, Thomas, Elias and Josiah to be his executors. He had already given Thomas, (born 1661), £95 and left him £20 more to be paid within 3 years. He was grateful to his maid servant Ann Pierson especially since his wife had died, and left her a calf.

William's eldest son, William junior who had died in 1686, had also been a tanner. He and his wife Margaret had a baby daughter Mary at the time of his death. Margaret took out a lease from Peter Legh five years later in 1691 and went to live in Minshull Lane with closes in Sudlow townfield. She may have taken the seven pictures and the map for her walls, and the looking glass and warming pan with her from their old house. William junior had been still building up his tan yard. He had 50 loads of bark, £33, twelve 'duker' leather and 5 hides of leather, £72, and nine green hides, £3 12s. His total inventory was valued at £156 16s. William was a dissenter who with his tanner friend John Rylands from Over Knutsford and shoemaker Thomas Harpur were responsible for breaking open the door of the Chapel in the town in 1684, but acquitted of offence at Quarter Sessions.

William's brother John, 1668-1720, married to Mary, became Innkeeper of the Swan in Knutsford who we will meet later. His father had left him £60 to be paid within 4 years.

Elias b.1673, and Josiah b.1678 were both tanners. In 1701 they were two of the three market lookers for green hides searchers and sealers of leather of the Egerton Nether Knutsford manorial court. Elias paid an unexplained sum of £35 and more to Henry Antrobus on the death of Peter Swinton but this may have been connected with brother Hugh, see below. In 1717, he was a yeoman living in Rostherne. Josiah married Mary Turner of Warrington in 1699. In 1701, Elias, Josiah and Hugh managed to agree between them to sell some of the land their father had left them in Whitebridge. Josiah went to London some time after this.

Hugh 1681-1703, the youngest, matured early and grew to be an independent and bright boy. Aged only 14 when his father died, was probably apprenticed to Peter Swinton, bookseller. When Peter Swinton was dying in 1698, Hugh was at hand to witness his will. He was hardly 17 but took over Peter Swinton's shop. If he had left school at the age of 11 or 12, he might have served five years of his apprenticeship but he must have been an able young man to contemplate taking on Swinton's shop and business. He must also have been considered competent to do it by his brothers and by Henry Antrobus. He had learnt the trade and knew the business contacts. He had already received his portion from his father. Hugh went with one of his brothers, probably Elias, to see Henry Antrobus, Peter's executor about the shop. Henry bought them a drink while they discussed business and this was included in his expenses out of Swinton's estate. Hugh was married by licence when he was only 18 to Elizabeth Pierson of Bowden, one of his bondsmen being John Leech another bookseller older than Hugh who had bought marbled paper, ABCs, pasteboard and leather from Swinton's estate. He was probably also a previous apprentice of Swinton's and was Knutsford's main bookseller for many years in the 18th century. Hugh Birtles now stationer, and Elizabeth's high hopes of married life were cut short when he died unexpectedly barely four years later. He was very young to have taken on this business and aged only 22 when he died.

His shop contained £82 worth of books to be sold in the shop, counters worth 10s. and two dozen pictures with frames which, as Peter Swinton had done, supplemented the trade in which he seems to have made a promising start. He had debts owing to him good and bad, £60. In his house were two 'childs chairs' in hopes of a family and six knives in a case and six forks in a case. He had wearing apparel and a pocket watch, £5. His brother Thomas appraised the inventory with Walter Antrobus.

Another Birtles family were also tanners, they may have been cousins. *See Family Tree 7 p.126.* Hugh Birtles, had married Ann. They must have been elderly when they died for they had grown up grandchildren, at least one of whom was married. Hugh and Ann had had four children but one may have died in their lifetime. Daughter Elizabeth married Jo Barber and it was their daughter Hannah who was married when her grandfather died. He had handed his tan yard on to his son William and the house he then lived

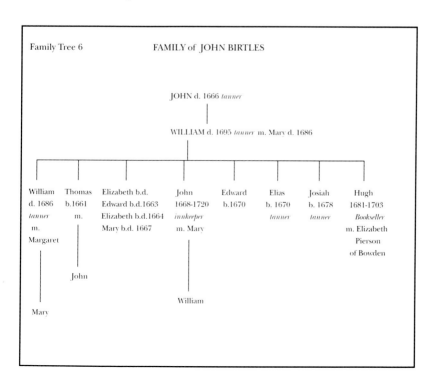

Family Tree 6   FAMILY of JOHN BIRTLES

JOHN d. 1666 *tanner*

WILLIAM d. 1695 *tanner* m. Mary d. 1686

William	Thomas	Elizabeth b.d.	John	Edward	Elias	Josiah	Hugh
d. 1686	b.1661	Edward b.d.1663	1668-1720	b.1670	b. 1670	b. 1678	1681-1703
tanner	m.	Elizabeth b.d.1664	*innkeeper*		*tanner*	*tanner*	*Bookseller*
m.		Mary b.d. 1667	m. Mary				m. Elizabeth
Margaret							Pierson
							of Bowden

John

William

Mary

in with the 'torf house and swine couts'. Whether or not Hugh was leading a life of leisure, when he wrote his will he called himself, gentleman. He was living in a comfortable house with 8 rooms and 7 beds. He had £45 of gold and silver by him and kept a cow, a calf, a horse and poultry with hay and corn etc. worth nearly £15. In 1664 he may have been the 'Captin Birtles' listed as having 4 hearths in 1664 and listed as Hugh Birtles in 1673/4. He had bonds and debts due to him of £175. Hugh died in 1680 and Ann the following year.

Their son Thomas died in 1682, only two years after his father. He was a shoemaker who married twice, his first wife Eleanor, was sister of Margery Crowther who was Peter Woods' first wife. Peter Wood was uncle to Thomas and Eleanor's three children. In 1667 Thomas's family were established with a servant.

Thomas's father-in-law, Randle Crowther had been a shoemaker and when he died in 1666 he had leather, lasts and wood heels in his shop worth £16 2s.6d. but debts by specialty due to him of £364, a great sum then, for not many shoemakers became so prosperous.

Peter Wood's house, the old Angel known as Marble Arch

Thomas married his second wife Margery and had three more children. When Thomas Birtles died they were living in a 5 roomed house with 7 beds and 2 cradles. He was busy on his fields when not in his shoemaker's shop with £33 worth of wheat, barley, peas and hay and kept a nag, 3 milk cows, 13 sheep and 8 geese. He had two hundred of cheese and a cheese tub. In his shop were leather shoes and goods valued at only £2 10s. and he had debts owing to him of £67. He named Peter Wood as his trustee to his wife his executor.

His son Hugh (1661-1687) by his first wife, became a mercer. After his father had died, Hugh, unmarried, the eldest son was master of the house while still in his twenties. He lived with his 'mother in law' Margery, his step mother, his brother and sister and his half- sisters and brother. Death threatened him while still young and when writing his will, left £40 to his sister Alice and his house, a land in Whitebridge, a field in Over Tabley and a land in Damfields, eight occupied cottages in Nether Knutsford with named tenants, all the rents of these for eight years to go to the education of his three (half-)brother and sisters, aged 11, 9 and 5, with permission for his brother Edward, 'if he please' and Alice, 'for as long as she shall keep herself unmarried', to remain and dwell with their (step)mother. After eight years these rents were to go to his brother Edward giving him leave to 'settle a jointure of all or part of the lands and premises upon a wife or wives he shall happen to marry, suitable to her portion'. He named his sole executor his Uncle Peter Wood.

There are gravestones in St. Helena's churchyard of Thomas Birtles, shoemaker died October 1682, and of Hugh Birtles his son, died May 1687 aged 26.

Hugh's brother Edward, 1666-1727, also a shoemaker, married Catherine Ashton in1691. It was their son John, 1696-1717, who was the scholar from Sir John Deane's School, Northwich who was a student at Trinity College Cambridge. His tombstone still records this in the old Knutsford church yard.

There were also other Birtles in Knutsford at this time.

References:
* *N.Kn.Poll Tax, CRO. 1667 DLT F/71.*
* *Much information from ANTROBUS SIR R.L.. Antrobus Pedigrees 1929, family trees and quoting Chancery proceedings P.R.O.*
* *Knutsford Parish Registers CRO. Wills Supra, and Inventories, W/S CRO. Leases.*
* *Peter Swinton's funeral accounts: A/cs of Henry Antrobus, DET 303/4 CRO. Peter Swinton's publication of Sir Robt. Leycester's funeral sermon 1684: Dictionary of Printers and Booksellers PLOMER Henry R. OUP 1968*
* *Sir Peter Leycester's Accounts and lists of charterers, Tabley Papers, C.R.O. DLT B/52, 54, 55, 56.*
* *Diary of Sir Thomas Mainwaring CRO. DDX 384/2.*
* *MITCHELL IAN, The book Trades in Cheshire 1680-1830, Trans. of Lancs. and Ches. Antiq. Soc. Vol. 95 for 1999, p. 23-38.*
* *SWANN, JUNE, Shoemaking, Shire Album 155, 1986.*
* *J. Swinton's trade tokens, Warrington Museum and the British Museum.*
* *Cheshire Sheaf, 3rd series 3555, p.9, quoting Randle Holmes, Harlean Mss..*
* *CRO ZCR/60/26/32. Register of Dissenting Meeting Places CRO QDR/7 MF 96/6*

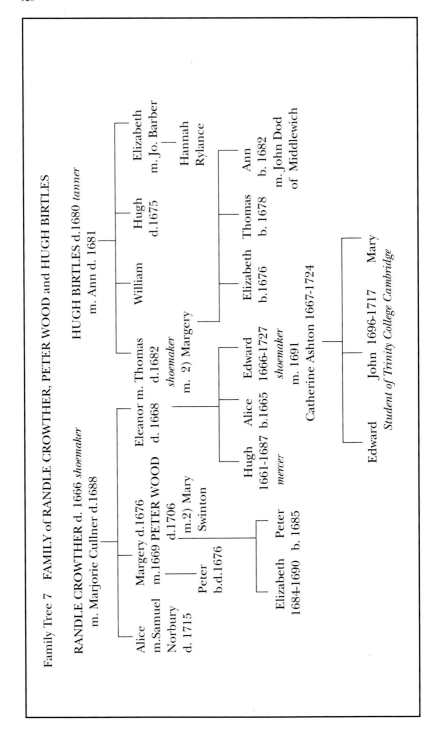

Family Tree 7   FAMILY of RANDLE CROWTHER, PETER WOOD and HUGH BIRTLES

Nether Knutsford Households with Servants and /or Apprentices in 1667

Information from other sources	Name and family	Servants, Apprentices and wages	
	Jeffrey Mottershead, wife Ellin, daughter Anne	Sibbell Berry, servant	21s
CURRIER Crosstown 2 hearths '73,'74	**William Daniel,** wife Jane, son William	John Bostock, apprentice Alice Hibbert, servant	20s
1 hearth '73,'74	**John Norbury,** wife Elizabeth	Elizabeth Lowndes, servant	20s
BLACKSMITH Crosstown	**Adam Mottershead,** wife Margaret	James Parsivall, apprentice	
TANNER 1 hearth'64,'73,'74	**William Byrtles,** wife Mary, 3 children, William, Thomas, Elizabeth	James Houseman, s'vant £2 16 8 Mary Newall, servant 22s	
	Thomas Crosby, wife Ellin, daughters Martha, Dorothy.	Robert Barlow, apprentice	
FELTMAKER 1 hearth '73, '74	**Henry Orrell,** wife Isabell, daughter Mary	Elizabeth Acton, servant	18s
2 hearths '64,'73, '74	**John Cowpe,** wife Elizabeth	Elizabeth Wyatt, servant	30s
MERCER, DRAPER POSTMASTER 2 hearths '64 4 hearths '73,'74	**Jeffrey Aldcroft,** wife Elizabeth, 5 ch. John, Theodorus, William, Dinah, Mary 'Agent to the Post Office'	Esther Nusse, servant	20s
DYER 2 heaths '64, '73,'71	**Thomas Gandy,** wife Cisley, sons William, Thomas	Hugh Robinson, apprentice Peter Deane, servant 40s Alice Taylor, servant 20s	
	Anne Huett	Elizabeth Hughes, servant	18s
WIDOW,freeholder '71 2 hearths '64	**Margaret Brownfield,** ch. John, Mary	Mary Toft, servant	18s
PHYSICIAN 2 hearths '73,'74	**William Smith,** wife Isabell, 3 ch. Alice, Samuel, Henry	Emma Heppard, servant	18s
GLOVER 2 hearths '73,'74	**John Toft,** wife Hanna	Peter Anderton apprentice	
4 hearths '64, ('73 &'74 in Sarah's name)	**William Bostock,** wife Sarah, 3 ch. Ralph, Mary, Hannah	Elizabeth Meire, servant	18s
INNKEEPER 8 hearths '73 ,'74	**Thomas Pollard,** wife Margaret, 3 ch. Thomas, Robert, Sarah	John Bramhall, servant 22s Anne Burgess, servant 20s	
BLACKSMITH'S WIDOW 2 hearths '64	**Elizabeth Stubbs**	John Turner, apprentice	
MALTSTER? 2 hearths '64 ('73, '74 in Margery's name)	**William Antrobus,** wife Margery	Elizabeth Woomer, servant 20s Israell Lowe, servant 20s	
SILKWEAVER 1 hearth '64,'73,'74	**Ralph Mourton,** wife Ellen, 3 ch. Ralph, Ellen, Mary	William Longworth, apprentice Francis Gatliffe, servant 26s	
SHARMAN 2 hearths '64 3hearths '73,'74	**Thomas Mourton,** wife Sarah, 3 ch. Thomas, Mary, Elizabeth	Samuel Deane, servant 26s Anne Smith, servant 26s	

WOOLLEN DRAPER 2 hearths '64 3 hearths '73, '74	**Peter Antrobus**, wife Elizabeth, 7 ch. Samuel, John, George, William, Richard, Mary, Margaret	Hannah Browne, servant Jane Strongitharme, s'vant	22s 22s
VINTNER'S WIDOW 'THE GEORGE' 8 hearths '73,'74	**Mary Aldcroft**, daughter Jane	Mary Cookson, servant Mary Curbishley, servant Edward Piers, s'vant 'no wages'	30s 20s
APOTHECARY 3 hearths '64, 5 hearths in '73,'74	**William Delves**, wife Margaret, 6 ch. William, John, Thomas, Robert, Margaret, Elizabeth	Anne Horton, servant	26s
IRONMONGER GROCER son of John Swinton of Radbrook Hall 4 hearths '64,'73 '74	**John Swinton**, wife Jane, daughters Jane, Elizabeth	James Johnson, apprentice John Brook, apprentice Jeffery Stockley, servant Alice Barlow, servant Jennett Hargeave, servant	£3 40s 22s
(Mother and sister of above John) 2 hearths '73,'74	**Margaret Swinton**, daughter Elizabeth	Richard Byrchall, servant Marg't Ogleshaw, servant	53s 4d 26s
INNKEEPER 'RED LION' 4 hearths '64,'73,'74	**Robert Royle**, wife Alice, 5 ch. George, Samuell, Robert, John, Alice	Margery Swan, servant	19s
INNKEEPER 2 hearths '64 4 hearths '73 '74	**Henery Warburton**, wife Ellin, ch. Henery, Dorothy	Mary Ashton, servant	18s
SHOEMAKER 2 hearths'64, '73,'74	**Thomas Byrtles**, wife Elianor, ch. Hughe, Alice	Abigail Bentley, servant	18s
SKINNER? 3 hearths '64, 2 hearths '73, '74	**James Swinton** (not the chandler)	William Leftwiche, apprentice Elleanor Guildbody, servant	30s
FELTMAKER HABERDASHER HATTER 2 hearths '64 4 hearths '73,'74	**Joseph Harrison**	Benjamin Hobson, apprentice Katherine Barton, servant	26s

Nether Knutsford Poll Tax, 1667: Total of 126 households, 340 persons

30 households with servants, 23.8%
    11 apprentices
    37 servants of whom probably 3 journeymen: William Byrtles servant Houseman   £2 16   8
                                                                    John Swinton's servant Stockley   £3
                                                                    Margaret Swinton's servant Byrchall   53s 4d

Number of people in households

	1	2	3	4	5	6	7	8	9	10	11	
How many of that size	43	37	14	13	5	4	5	2	2	-	1	= 126 households 2.7 average h'hold size

'John Leigh trayned souldier and wife Ellin'
'Ralph Bower trayned souldier and wife Mary'

'Jeffery Alldcroft Agent to the post office in Knutsford, his sallary is £4 per annum soe he is to pay
for £2 13 4 for which he payes to the monthly Tax and for his poll that whole is 3s.0d'.

All paid 1s. each, poll, and 1s.per £1 or part of £1 for annual wages. £18 17s. collected.

N. Kn. Poll Tax, CRO DLT/F/71.

Chapter 6
The Poor

As already seen, Knutsford people, particularly the tradesmen and the middle classes, left bequests in their wills for the minister and the schoolmaster but by far the most left money for the poor. The Parish Church boards in the porch today list many of these.

Some of the benefactors had substantial means but others had comparatively few worldly goods themselves. John Aldcroft, Over Knutsford bachelor shoemaker, left £5 to the town stock for the poor of Over Knutsford out of his total estate of about £25 after his 'debts good and bad' had been resolved. Mary Colley, spinster, in 1719 preferred the direct approach of giving out money to the poor. Although in very reduced circumstances, after leaving five bequests amounting to 51s. she requested '50s. to the poor of the Township of Nether Knutsford to be paid into the hands of Mr. Robinson, the minister for Knutsford, and Mr. Ralph Seddon ... by them to be distributed amongst the said poor people as they shall think fit'.

However, gentlemen were mostly better placed to be more generous. Sometimes the poor could benefit by attending a gentleman's funeral. Some gentlemen chose the traditional form of benevolence, among them John Venables of Knutsford of the Kinderton family, who having requested his own genteel funeral at Rostherne, left '6d a peece to all poor that shall come for a dole'. Having watched the giving of doles though, Sir Peter Leycester did not approve. He wrote his own will in 1672 (he died in 1678) and made it very clear:

... because at Sundry Burials of Gentlemen it hath beene Accustomed to give money to the Poore, sometimes 4^{den} sometimes 6d a peece; which as it is very little benefit or advantage to the poore, so it attracts a numerous Confluence of Beggars at such times, many Cominge a dozen or sixteene miles waytinge such Dole, and oft=tymes these who have little or no neede, havinge an estate to live uppon; as hath beene often observed: and for as much as those kind of Persons are never satisfied at such doles, but make greate Confusion & Clamour, sometimes bitter Cursinge as I my selfe have heard.

Therefore my will is that there be no Portions of money distributed among such beggars how small soever, who shall come out of their owne Places of abode: if any shall come but my mind & will is that all such be admonished to returne to their owne homes, without expecting my Dole: and tellinge them, that it was my Expresse Will to relieve the Poore of my owne Towne onely , & no other: ...

which he went on to do.

There was another more obscure form of charity. In most of the inventories of tradesmen and medical men there appears an often substantial item, 'debts good and bad', 'debts believed to be desperate' or some similar phrase listed as an asset. Customers were allowed to buy goods or receive services without payment at the time, the formalities completed by the debt being duly entered into the 'shop book', both parties aware in many cases that there was little possibility that the money would ever be paid. This must have been consciously acknowledged and carefully regulated by the retailer because he could have refused to serve anyone who could not pay and too many customers in this category would soon cause a business to fail. It was nevertheless a recognised if unspoken way of helping the poor. Some gentlemen though, expected to be given credit even by those they knew could ill afford it.

The 1601 Poor Law laid down the basic framework for relieving the poor which lasted until 1834, making each parish responsible for its own poor. Churchwardens and 'substantial householders' were to be nominated each year as Overseers of the Poor to be answerable to JPs. The duty of the Overseers was to provide for the poor by collecting a rate, a ley, approved by the magistrates, on all occupiers of property which money was to be for the aged and infirm, widows and orphans and to bind pauper children apprentice at the age of 12. These were relieving and preventive measures but its working at parish level was difficult and onerous.

Before 1662, Knutsford was in the 'vast' parish of Rostherne which at that time comprised ten townships, the poor law of the entire parish being organised from Rostherne. After that date and a petition to the Court, Knutsford and Over Peover church wardens and overseers were given permission to make provision for the poor within their own respective townships.

Knutsford would seem to have been as good a place as any in which to have lived in Cheshire. In the late 17th century, Gregory King estimated that one fifth of the population were in receipt of poor relief at one time or another. Knutsford's Hearth Tax returns for 1664 give a picture of Knutsford's society, see Fig 2 p.13 and Fig 8 p.175. In Nether Knutsford 112 households were charged on their hearths, and 85 households were not chargeable, Over Knutsford more rural, was poorer. Those non chargeable were the people who had a house was worth less than 20 shillings a year, or who occupied land worth less than 20 shillings a year, or who had property worth less than £10. These Nether Knutsford numbers show that 57% were chargeable and 43% non chargeable. Macclesfield had 55% non chargeable, Stockport and Nantwich, 50%, and Congleton 45%, showing that Knutsford was nearly as 'prosperous' as Chester with 40% exempt. Hoskins suggested that those with only one or two hearths were homes of the poor whether chargeable or not, which alters the figures. Nantwich and Congleton had 93% in this category, Stockport and Nether Knutsford had 85%, and Chester 67%. The average number of hearths per household was 2.6 in Chester and 2.1 in Knutsford, where 15 houses here had between three and five hearths and 4 houses had between six and nine hearths, these, mostly inns.

However, many living in Knutsford who lived in one hearth cottages could not be classed as poor. Some were running a business or service and raised families to adulthood. Robert Thornley barber surgeon and chapel clerk, lived in such a cottage for at least twenty years and brought up three children there before moving to a larger house. Dr. Smith lived in a similar cottage when he was first married in Knutsford. Ralphe Mourton silk weaver, was living in such a cottage between 1664 and 1674 with his wife, three children, a servant and an apprentice. He was not one of the needy poor although silk weavers often were poor, their loom and necessary equipment costing little initial outlay with which to start work. Ralph Nixon was a silk weaver who left goods worth £8 8s.10d. but he had managed to support a wife and raise three children in his two roomed house with just an upper and lower chamber. His widow survived him eleven years. William Hurst another silk weaver, was only slightly more comfortable with an estate worth £18 12s. of which £11 was the valuation of his stock.

Not all those exempt from charge in the hearth tax were in receipt of relief but were the ones living at subsistence level with a meagre standard of living, vulnerable to illness, accident or the slightest change in circumstances or fortune. Inventories survive of some of these cottagers, which indicate how some of them lived, having estates worth only about £10 or even less. Apart from the bed with typically '2 old blankitts and a coverlet', these cottagers had little other furniture beyond chairs and stools and few possessions. Some did have a small item, a bible, possibly an 'old' one, and others a book or two, or a clock (worth little), which may have given self esteem in an impoverished, bleak existence. Some of them had a few sheep. Some men, working at or from home, labourers, had their tools of trade included in their small estates.

Edward Owen tailor, had a smoothing iron, 2 pressing irons, 1 pair of tailor's shears, 2 cloth yards and one 'ell board'. His clothes were valued at £1 and all his total goods were worth £3 16s.3d.

Samuel Ryle, cutler died also in 1677, his smithy contents listed hammers, bellows, anvil etc., rapier blades and swords worth £3 11s 3d, debts were owed to him of £5 17s. He was boarding with someone and apart from his linens and clothes, £2 10s., his bible worth 1s 6d was his only personal possession.

Peter Alexander hosier, d.1666, had shop contents:

18 pr. mens worsted stockings @ 3s.2d. pr		£2 17s 0d
2 prs. linen drawers	4s 0d	
13 pr. childerin's hose	4s 4d	
35prs. of womens hose	£2 18s 0d	
11 pr. cloath stockings white and watchett		
@ 4d. and a pr. of gray knit ones @ 14d.		14s 0d
2 shop chests at	6s 8d	

His total estate was valued at £13 5s.2d. which included these shop goods.

He had a clock and bell, an old bible and another book.

Widows and elderly spinsters lived sparsely. The goods of Mary Long, spinster, were valued at £4 16s.10d. Her entire possessions were, her bed and bedding, 3 old coffers, 2 boxes and a cradle, 2 chairs, 2 stools, a grate, tongs, a flesh fork, a spoon, some pewter and wooden ware, a brass pan, a candlestick, 1 bible and a little bodkin, her clothes worth 13s.4d. and her two sheep.

Shusannah Partington d.1661, had a similar list but no table, chair or stool but 'one historie booke and wax candle 6d'. Her apparel, linen and woollen was valued at £2 13s.4d and her appraisers who included Isaac Antrobus wrote as the last item, 'Some few clothes taken off the deceased person which the woman that stript her hath as her due, 3s.4d'.

In 1664 there were 85 if not more, cottagers like these in Knutsford. In 1719 the Overseer of the Poor, Robert Shaw of Over Knutsford gave account of the goods of Ann Taylor, a pauper, late deceased, which he sold to the value of 13s. and a farthing. She was among the poorest.

They made money as best they could. On the Tabley estate, Jane Ryley in the 1690's was spreading molehills, sometimes called 'moldiwarp hillocks', and was filling sacks of moss 'for the slaters' at 3d. a sack.

Some left their homes in order to find a job when there was no prospect of employment locally and at least two of these had travelled to Knutsford which offered the opportunity for them to settle successfully. Hugh Pritchard the bread baker from Welshpool, in 'the Kingdom of Wales', and Robert Blacklock, chapman, came from Dumfries in 'the Kingdom of Scotland'.

The elderly, often widows, were sometimes taken in to live with a married daughter and family. Peter Wood's mother-in-law had a room in his house and stayed even after her daughter died, still being there after he remarried. Others were dependent on the kindness of neighbours to provide food, 'table', and sometimes shelter, paid for by the Overseers.

At the end of their lives, the prime concern expressed in the wills, was that their debts and funeral expenses should be paid. Widows and spinsters with few household goods and possessions had savings in the form of a bond, had lent money so that it was a debt to them, or had saved money towards covering these expenses. Of the wills and inventories that exist, only three of Knutsford's fifteen or so poorest women had no such provision.

The prevalent attitude to the poor in these centuries was shown by the building of Houses of Correction. After 1610, Constables were to 'search out rogues and apprehend vagrants and shall send them before the Justices who shall commit them to the House of Correction'. 'Lewd women that have bastards may be sent; if they have another they shall be sent'. Houses of Correction were built in the 17th century in Chester and Middlewich and for about thirty years there was also one at Nantwich which closed in 1718. These were terrible places and by their very nature open to abusive practices.

In December 1681, Sir Robert Leycester wrote to the Master of Correction at Middlewich: 'Herewithall the body of Richard Rylands late of Morley being a person distracted in his senses, wandering about and disorderly behaving himself to great terror of his Majesty's subjects ... very abusive language and actions at Meyre Hall ... committ him to the House of Correction and punish him by putting fetters or gyves upon him and moderate correction'. A note beneath this letter shows that he relented: 'Discharged. Ordered to be sent to Wilmslow to be taken care he do no injury'.

In 1662 the Act of Settlement made official a practice which had been in force for some years. The poor law had become a matter of money, who should pay for whom, who should be responsible. The Act decreed that each parish must be responsible for only those born within its bounds and that any stranger must be able to afford to rent a tenement of £10 a year or have a certificate from their parish of birth agreeing to take them back should they become impoverished and chargeable to the overseers. Every traveller required one. A stay of 40 days in a parish constituted a settlement. Robert Blacklock, the Scottish chapman, had an estate in Dumfries in Lockmabengate which would have been sufficient security for him to have settled in Knutsford.

Accident, misfortune, illness or death of a breadwinner could befall any, and to some whilst away from home. In 1654 the York North Riding Sessions reported a woman taken wandering in the Constabulary of Pickering who said she was born at Sandbridge (Sandlebridge), in Chester (Cheshire) not four miles from Knutsford, and

was the daughter of a carpenter there, being committed to the House of Correction as a rogue and a vagrant, doth appear to be a person under distraction and distempered in her senses, and nothing appearing to require further detention, to be conveyed from constable to constable to the town of Sandbridge aforesaid, there to be provided for: to the constables of Pickering, Malton, Hutton upon Darwent, Whitwell, Flaxton and all other constables in the way leading to Sandbridge.

Sir Robert Leycester wrote in June 1680, to Middlewich House of Correction:

The constables of Nether Tabley hath brought before me a wandering idle person calling himself Thomas Saunderson being a crate carrier or petty chapman and denies that he ever had any settlement nor knows in what parish he was born. I therefore send you herewithall the body of the said Thomas Saunderson and in His Majesty's name, strictly charge you and command you to receive him into your custody and him safely keep to hard labour until the next general quarter sessions with moderate whipping giving him so much allowance as he may deserve by his own labour and any work according to the statute in that case provided.

The Act of Settlement did not stop the rogues, vagabonds and beggars from wandering the country and the JPs were given powers to send them not only to the houses of Correction but to the plantations. They caused fear wherever they went and one of the bellman's duties was to keep watch for them. In 1674, James Swinton, constable that year, confessed that he had been misled by false passes shown to him by '17 sturdy rogues and vagrant beggars ... people commonly called Gypsies, besides small children more which were carried on women's backs'. He had delivered them on to one of the constables of Over Knutsford forthwith. They had been passed from constable to constable from Appleton near Warrington through ten townships including the two Knutsfords and then on to Chelford, possibly 15 miles. In 1694 and again in 1696, the magistrates in Cheshire were still alarmed about them and issued orders to the constables to be more vigilant.

Different sorts of people came to be in need of help. The unemployed were sometimes taken on as casual agricultural labour but another means of gainful employment was later, to be enlisted in the Army. In 1708, with Churchill leading the Wars of the Spanish Succession on the continent, men were enlisted,

not having any Lawful calling or Imployment ... or making use of any Lawful means for their support or maintenance nor having a vote in the Election of any Member of Parliament, ... were delivered before us by the Constables of several Townshipps ... and Delivered over to Capt. Lawrence Saintlow in the Hon. Col. Phineas Bowles Regiment of ffoot to serve as Soldiers ... and Twenty shillings paid to every man and likewise Twenty shillings to the Constables.

They would feel rich. Articles of War against Mutiny and Defection were then read to them. James Hobson and George Cockeran of Knutsford were among those delivered into this Regiment on 22nd April, 1708. By 1745, the amount given to soldiers recruited for the army was only one shilling.

Forty years earlier than the events above, in 1667, a Nether Knutsford widow Francis Leycester, whose daughter's husband had been

a soldier under the command of Col. Daniel in his Majesties' service (that now is), and was with the Regiment transported to Portugal where he dyed, leaving a wife and three small children and nothing to maintain them ... since, the petitioner's daughter had died and the poore children very destitute and only the petitioner to care for them. (She) is now old and not able to labour and take pains as formerly, her small estate exhausted and spent in maintaining the said children, that she and they are likely to endure great hardship and misery if not perish and starve for want of necessities if not relieved.

They were granted a weekly allowance from the overseers.

Misfortune could soon cause great distress to a family with limited means. John Woolmer, a labourer in Over Knutsford, had his cow taken from a field which brought him, his wife and two small children, 'into great exigence for want of milk to relieve and supply the great necessity of his poore family'.

The Act of Settlement, in attempting to solve some problems, caused more, of endless wrangling and litigation between parishes, trapping the unemployed within the parish and involving constant moving about of people who could not prove their place of birth. There are examples of Knutsford people caught up in these problems and of the overseers and constables dealing with them. The Overseers for Over Knutsford show how their time was involved with their duties, travels and account keeping, punctuated by visits to the inns for drinks, to discuss business.

In 1710 they were concerned with the place of settlement of Elizabeth Barrow singlewoman:

Spent going to New Barn upon having a summons about Elizabeth Barrow	2s.0d.
Paid to Joseph Acton when he went to Chester with old Elizabeth Barrow	10s.0d.
Paid to Joseph Acton more what he had laid out in his journey to Chester about old Elizabeth Barrow.	$6^1/_2$d
To Richard Rylance for going about old Elizabeth Barrow	11d
For getting a copy of an order	2s 0d
Paid for horse hire to Chester	2s 6d
Spent at a town meeting about her	1s $2^1/_2$d
Paid for writing a copy of the advice from the sessions at Chester their order being reversed	4d
Spent in bringing her to Ashley	8d

Her travels were not finished. In 1711 there was a court order stating that the last legal settlement of Elizabeth Barrow was in Over Knutsford, 'being a hired servant and continuing there in the said service for one year and upwards'. She was to be conveyed to Over Knutsford accordingly as she had lately come to dwell in Nether Alderley.

Old servants obviously formed a part of these problem poor people who having spent their lives in other people's homes had nowhere of their own when they were aged and unable to find a position, unless fortunate enough to be kept on as an old retainer such as Hugh Yarwood had been in John Swinton's household, or those who were kept on and paid no wages, mostly in houses of the gentry.

In 1712, Mary Taylor was the Over Knutsford's Overseers' concern. The parish thought that Lymm was responsible:

Spent in bringing Mary Taylor to Lymm	3d
(but) Pd. Wm. Gibbon for his cart going to Lymm to fetch old Mary Taylor's goods back	4s 0d
Spent that day we both going and old Mary Taylor along with us in meat and drink	1s 6d
Pd. for a bed board for old Mary Taylor's bed	1s 0d

Thereafter, back in Knutsford, Mary Taylor received 6d from each Overseer per week, with occasional entries to buy her two penny worth of turves or coals. She died in 1715.

There is another example in 1713:

Pd. Wm. Gibbon for hire of a horse to Goostry about Sophia Holford	1s. 0d
(4 weeks later): Spent in going to Goostry with John Rylance about Sophia Holford to prove her settlement.	8d
Pd. John Rylance for horse hire there	6d
Spent at John Birtles on same account	4d
Spent at Thos. Writes on same account	4d
Pd. Wm. Gibbon for his horse for 2 persons to the Three Greyhounds upon the same	1s 0d
7 weeks later:	
pd. for 5 week for Sophia Holford Table before she lay in	5s 0d
for 2 of the first weeks she lay down and attendance	6s 0d
for 2 of the last weeks she lay down at 2s 6d the week	5s 0d

The other overseer said that they spent 3s at the Three Greyhounds about her with Mr. Birch and witnesses in meat and drink and 4d in going by order to John Birtles' to enquire about the matter, and 2s 6d to Mr. Lovatt for laying her in childbed.

Illegitimate children were a great problem for the Overseers. Without a father to support a child, he/she was liable to become the responsibility of the parish where it was born which would have to pay maintenance until old enough to be put apprentice. Hence the anxiety that no such child should be born within the bounds of the parish and the duty of every midwife to obtain the name of the child's father who should provide maintenance, exacted at the moment of birth when the mother was in the extremity of her pain.

In 1704, Ann Johnson of Over Knutsford named 'John Holford of Plumley, husbandman' who did beget her with child'. He was ordered via the constables 'to appear at quarter sessions and if he refuses, to safely convey him to the Gaol and safely keep until he shall find sufficient security'. Some woman were also required to give surety. Elizabeth Taylor of Knutsford in 1682,

poor petitioner, being got with child by one John Morton who promised marriage but at the last over run her and ... delivered of a male child in the township of Over Peover and because (she) could not give security as that township did require, (she) was sent to Gaol to the Castle at Chester where (she) remains to her utter undoing. ... she humbly prayers to take her sad condition into your gracious and tender consideration to order the Overseers of the Poor of the Parish of Rostherne or Churchwardens to take (consideration) of her plight ... at the next month's meeting ... that she may have her liberty to get her living and maintain her child as far as she is able ....

In 1676, James Ridgway of Toft was the reputed father of a bastard child upon the body of Susannah Hill of Toft, spinster, 'for as much as the said child may become burdensome to the parish of Rostherne', he was ordered to pay 30s. p.a. by quarterly payments for 12 years, then £3 6s.8d. for the cost of binding the said child apprentice. The father and mother of the child were required to give security 'to save the parish harmless from all charges and prejudice that could happen by reason of the said child'.

This was the standard Court order, the money payable to a mother varying from 30s. to 40s. a year at this time, probably according to the likelihood of the father being able to pay. Sometimes the child died. In 1655, the Justices made a different decision. Thomas Cadman of Ollerton, husbandman, had gone to the court at Middlewich with his two brothers who were standing surety. He had fathered a 'bastard woman child begotten on the body of Alice Oakes of Lower Withington, spinster ... likely to become chargeable'. It was ordered that 'Thomas Cadman shall forthwith take the child into his own care and sufficiently keep the same' ... and further ordered him to pay the Churchwardens the sum of £5 for binding of the child an apprentice.

Another case occurred in 1673 when two constables of Toft had 'in their custody and charge John Stubbs by virtue of a warrant ... and suffered him to escape, the said John Stubbs being the putative father of a bastard child begotten upon the body of Elizabeth Norrel, spinster' .... The Court ordered that the two constables should pay for the maintenance of the child with John Stubbs until further order.

At the time the child was born, the midwife and her assistant(s) who were present at the birth were required to make a statement of affiliation to the local JP. On 5 Dec. 1682:

Isabell Smith wife of William Smith of Nether Knutsford, Physitian, ... a professed midwife - on Friday last was a three weeks, sent for to the labour of Mary Grantham of Over Knutsford, spinster, to act the part of midwife and that she charged the said Mary Grantham in the extremity of her pains in travail to declare who was the father of her bastard child ... (she) did affirm that Richard Massie of Denfield is the father.

The woman or women who assisted at this birth also affirmed as above. It was felt to be the duty of the unmarried mother to affiliate her child. Midwife Elizabeth Antrobus in1682, admonished one patient in dire extremity that 'she could not expect God to ease her' unless she 'fathered her child right', having stubbornly until then, named a man falsely.

Illegitimate births were comparatively rare however, only about twenty in sixty years from the Knutsford locality.

The regulations about the House of Correction for a second bastard child were applied to Ann Johnson (above) of Over Knutsford, single woman. The Sessions at Nantwich gave an order that she was 'convicted of bastardy (affiliated upon John Holford), having had a (second) bastard child, refusing to give security therefore this order is to receive her into safe custody and safely keep with due correction and hard labour during the space of one month'. Her first child had been born in 1701 and the second in1704, but both died. Some of these women were inadequate, simple, most were under nourished, but others were brazen and defiant.

In 1678, Sir Peter Leycester in the year in which he died, was taking a statement from Sarah Adamson of Mobberley about the fathering of a child. She accused him of abusing her and said he was not fit to be a JP.! Outraged and indignant he angrily denied it. He wrote the whole episode in his own hand.

Bastard children had a low chance of survival, for the fathers could not be made to pay as in the case of William Tomlinson, apothecary, (p.167).

The old and infirm who were no longer capable of sustaining themselves were candidates for regular relief from the overseers but required an order from the JP's to give the authority. Carefully composed petitions were sent to Quarter Sessions:

1676. "Humble petition of Joane Owen of Nether Knutsford ... hath inhabited the said town the space of 52 years and upwards and is above an hundred years old and through extreme pains in her head hath almost lost her sight, so that she is not able to aske relief and through age and decrepidness altogether helplesse and not having anything of her own to support her - humbly begs your worships will be pleased to take her poor and wanting condition into their wise and judicious considerations and appoint her such relief as you shall judge meet amongst other pentioners of the said town and she will ever pray for the worships' health and remains faithfully to command whilst I am: Joan Owens.

In 1661, two Knutsford brothers, John and Henry Grange were receiving weekly payment from the Overseers but claimed that it was not enough to live on. ' - poor petitioners, ... the small goods that they had is all consumed and spent and their allowance formerly ordered for their maintenance being but 9d. a week is farr short for their relief to subsist on, so that they are likely to perish and starve for want of necessities'. The Court awarded them more.

In 1692, the dissenters Isaac Antrobus, Peter Wood, John Bostock and John Leadbeater sent this petition to the Court:

Humble petition of Phillip Armstrong of Tatton: - hath been a painful and laborious man ... and hath maintained himself and four children by his own fare ... now having lost the sight of one of his eyes and the other being grown too dim that he cannot follow his trade ... or possibly maintain himself and his said children (whereof two are but little ones), - humbly desire and bequest ... and grant some assistance to him in this strait ...

This was followed by a note from the Rev. James Robinson:

We whose names are subscribed do believe that this petitioner is an object of charity having not been able to follow his trade of some time for the reason above mentioned and therefore do recommend him to your worships' charity.

It is reassuring to know that the leading dissenters and the parson were co-operating in this charitable plea. It is also evidence that the dissenters were not in a position to maintain their own poor as they did in some larger places. It also shows that they still had concern and authority for those beyond their own township boundaries but still in the parish of Rostherne. The usual order when granted by the JPs was in the following form:

To the Overseers of the Poor of the Township of Nether Knutsford. Whereas complaint hath been made ... that Mary Coppack of the Township is an aged and impotent person and hath not wherewith to subsist or keep herself - we charge you to pay the sum of 1s. by the week towards the maintenance of her after this date, 11th May 1688.

Not many of these orders exist in Quarter Sessions. As it appears that such an order was necessary for a person to receive regular relief, it is most likely that the monthly Bucklow Hundred Court dealt with many cases.

Knutsford's famine/epidemic, 1685-6.

In the spring of 1686, Knutsford was in the grip of a severe infectious epidemic which caused the deaths of many people. The usual average number of burials a year was 28, but in 1686 this rose to 96. The average number of

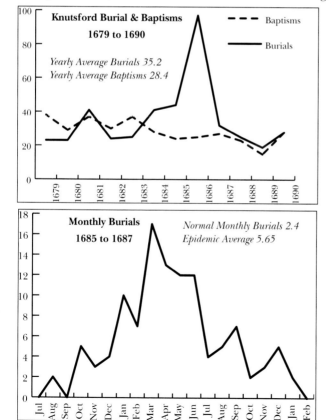

Fig. 6

burials a month in Knutsford was about two, but in March that year there were 17, the numbers having been rising since the previous autumn. There was probably a famine following a poor harvest the year before and stocks of food were at their lowest in the spring so that many were in a poor state of health and susceptible to infection, but both rich, or comparatively so, and poor were dying so famine was not the sole cause. Husbands died leaving widows with small children, wives died leaving husbands with children to rear, children died, others were orphaned. Some breadwinners who survived the sickness were left weak and unable to work, putting the whole family at risk. This epidemic was not the Plague which had so badly smitten London in 1665 and reached other places like Eyam, Derbyshire. After it died out in 1666 with the Fire, no more cases are thought to have occurred anywhere in this country.

The effect of this infection on Knutsford was a huge increase in the numbers who needed help from the parish. In Nether Knutsford, 61 families were in distress, involving 209 people. In Over Knutsford their numbers were also high, 27 families, 91 persons. 300 people altogether were in need in both townships, one third of the population. The resources from the usual poor rates were inadequate, and a plea was made to Quarter Sessions, not only from Nether and Over Knutsford but also from Altrincham who were similarly stricken, for extra help. Peter Wood submitted lists of the names of the poor in immediate need to the Court, two pages long. The Court charged the petty constables within the townships of Bucklow Hundred (there were 82 townships in the Hundred) to collect a levy. Extra mizes were to be collected from Knutsford itself.

The following year, 1687, the situation in Nether Knutsford had improved slightly but was still serious. After a harvest, one third of the grain was needed to be kept for seed the following year but when the crop was poor, this was

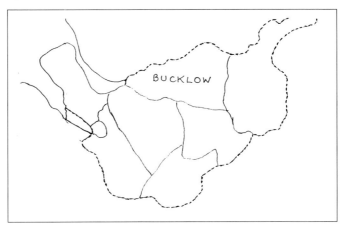

Fig 7. Area of Bucklow Hundred in Cheshire
(sketch from CRO Guide 1994 p12)

not always possible, resulting in an even smaller harvest. This situation could take many years to overcome, a bumper year being their saving. There were still 52 families, 141 people receiving relief, of whom there was a core of about fifteen who were old, weak, lame or blind, one had his house rent paid and two were paid for attendance. Four orphans, three from one family, were boarded with families who received payment for their food and clothes. There were 32 people in Nether Knutsford receiving a weekly or monthly pension to sustain them. In that year, of the 61 families who had received relief in 1686, 30 families were still on relief but there were 22 new ones on the list. The Overseers were still paying out more than they received. Once again they required help from other townships in the Hundred. The Court again ordered the Hundred to assist but exempted six townships as they themselves had 'an infinite number of their own poor'. John Bostock recorded:

Received out of the Hundred	£30 0s 0d
Received from the Towne in monyes	
Amounting to 43 mizes Eleven shillings and Eleven pence	£29 5s 0d
The total,	£59 5s 3d

But the Overseers disbursed £62 01s 03d, all carefully itemised with how much was paid to each person or family, including what was spent on coffins and Church dues. They were awarded £10 more from the Hundred in October to make up this deficit and Altrincham also received £10 extra that year.

Years of crisis arose fairly frequently. There had been one in 1674 when Nether Knutsford petitioned the Court for extra mizes, their 'poor so numerous'. Also in the years, 1694, 1708, (which year also included Altrincham), 1710, 1711, 1714 and 1715.

The town was often at these times ordered to raise extra money by itself. On 7th September 1708 at the Knutsford Sessions, Langham Booth and Edward Thorneycroft, magistrates, ordered that 'half a mize should be paid to Joseph Strethill of Mobberley, yeoman, upon 2nd October next at the Cock in Knutsford' and similarly in 1711, quoting part of the original 1601 law that 'the inhabitants, Parson, Vicars and occupiers of lands, houses, tythes ... should similarly pay by one of the clock at the house of Judith Shaw's (the Cock), in Nether Knutsford'. In 1714 another double levy was paid in Knutsford. They paid according to their rateable value at a rate which fluctuated.

Badges

In 1697, an Act was passed in parliament following reports and complaints that some of the poor were found begging even though they were receiving relief from the parish. Some even complained that the poor were receiving more money for doing nothing than they could earn by their honest hard

work. In order to stop begging, this Act required provision that in future
every pauper, his wife and children, 'shall wear upon the shoulder of the
right sleeve of the uppermost garment ... in an open and visible manner, ...
a large Roman 'P' together with the first letter of the name of the parish ...
in red or blue cloth'. Any refusing to wear the badge was to lose relief or
be sent to the House of Correction to be whipped and do three weeks hard
labour. In Over Knutsford these items appear in the accounts:

1710: Pd. Peter Lowndes for drawing a list of poore and for finding cloth and cutting letters for the poor to wear	6d
1712: Pd. for making badges for the poor	3d
1729: Pd. for badges and setting on	1s 0d
1733: To four badges for Gatley's children	8d

And when Mary Taylor (above), had arrived back from Lymm, a badge
was made for her to wear.

The overseers paid for a variety of things and in Over Knutsford, each of
the two overseers paid their part of the costs. In the early 18th century each
was paying about £1 15s. for rents for their poor half yearly. They were each
paying about 9d. a week for about three women and several children, some
orphaned and 'fostered' with families. For those not able to get their own
meals, money was paid to someone for their food. They paid for clothes and
fuel and the getting of it, other miscellaneous items and coffins. A child's
coffin cost 1s 6d. The business expenses were recorded, horse hire to spend
a day at Court, meat and drink while there and sometimes for witnesses,
meetings in inns with the Head Constable and others and the extra drink
after the monthly meeting, 'being the day we went out of office' and even,
'for writing the accounts in this book, 4d.'

One sorry family can be followed through the accounts, the children
becoming old enough to be put out in apprenticeship, probably as servants,
but first of all being given new clothes from head to toe. On this occasion
they were fortunate enough all to be sent to the same house (possibly not
in Knutsford) but no-one knows how they were treated. There were no
checks that we know of.

The Birch family

In 1709, Margaret Birch of Over Knutsford, was widowed. She and her four
children, Martha, Esther, Hannah and John were receiving relief. Money
was paid for 5yds cloth for shifts for the children, and Robert Fogg the
prospective employer was paid £3 10s 'for the children'.

The next year, the Overseers bought new clothes, two shifts, stockings and
shoes for the eldest child, Martha, and hose and cloggs for Esther. Later in
the year, Peter Lowndes was paid for stamped paper for writing indentures
of apprenticeship for Esther Birch and a Justice of the Peace was paid for
signing them. Then Esther was bought new clothes, a pair of 'Bodeys', a

mantua and petticoat, shifts, shoes and stockings, a straw hat, apron and caps, totalling 18s 6d.

10 months later it was Hannah's turn. She, too, was apprenticed and clothed and Robert Fogg was bought drinks on several occasions in the process.

In 1711, Margaret Birch and child John were paid 9d per week by each overseer. In 1712, 'old' Martha Birch, the mother, died. The Overseers had each paid for a quarter's 'table' for her. Robert Fogg was again approached and was prevailed upon to take in 'Birch's young child'.

How 'old' Martha Taylor was is not known. Her youngest child was not old enough to be officially apprenticed.

The office of Overseer of the Poor, was in Over Knutsford taken on in rotation by the freeholders of the houses there. Sometimes it was a woman who took on the position. Mary Hewitt, widow of Over Knutsford was Overseer in 1717, not altogether unusual. Women overseers were appointed in nearby Hale. Those who could not or did not wish to take on the job, hired someone to do it for them. 'The accounts of Benjamin Birch Overseer of the Poor with Saml. Hoole and serving for Ashton's House and beginning office 5th May 1710'.

The accounts of the Overseers were submitted to the Justices for acceptance. Sometimes these were not passed and in 1694, Peter Wood and John Swinton were asked by the Court to inspect the accounts of one of the overseers in Pickmere. This they duly did and reported with a written statement presented at the next Sessions.

Housing

Some of the early records of the Manor Court show its concern about the letting of cottages. The anxiety was that no one should come to live in the manor who was going to become a pauper and dependant on the town financially. Although paupers were the financial responsibility of the Overseers of the Poor, the Manor Court jury as freeholders, all paid the Church rates, leys, for the relief of the poor so it was in their interests to keep potential paupers out of the town. Responsible people undertook to give security for incoming tenants upon condition that they did not become burdensome to the town. In other words, prospective tenants were 'vetted'.

1643:- 'Whosoever shall let any stranger, forrener his house or any part of his housing without consent and allowance of both constables with four sufficient men whom they shall choose to approve the same, on penalty of 10s. to the Lord of the Manor so long as they shall continue there'.

1654:- 'John Gandie of Agden and Richard Edge of Nether Knutsford bound themselves for £10 to save harmless from Owen Brundrett, his wife and children inhabiting the manor of Knutsford. Witnessed by Thomas Dale and Robert Royle and signed by John Gandie and Richard Edge'.

If a family's fortunes took a downward turn, those who vouchsafed them were required to make a further bond.

1656:- This bill binds Wm. Ridgeway and John Pickering, yeomen of Tabley, for £10, to the constables of Knutsford on condition that if Thos. Hudson of Knutsford do not remove himself, his wife and family out of the manor of Knutsford at or before 1st May next' ....

Assurances and bonds of this nature appear before 1666, after which they disappear but they may have been kept elsewhere after that. They certainly did not lose interest in who was coming to live in the town.

Small one roomed cottages, cruck framed, wattle and daub walls with thatched roof and earth floors were the normal living accommodation of many labourers and cottagers. Some built up a loft space reached by a simple wooden ladder either for storage or extra sleeping room. Many cottages were built by those who were going to live in them with help from neighbours. They did not take long to build having once obtained permission from the Lord of the Manor. Requests, petitions for these dwellings, came before Quarter Sessions.

Peter Legh gave permission on at least two such occasions for people to build within Over Knutsford. In October 1681, he gave 'leave and liberty to Robert Williamson of Over Knutsford, labourer, being devoid of habitation also considering his former case and difference together with his wive's lameness and poverty, to erect and build a cottage or house to dwell in on that part of the wast ground in Over Knutsford as I have appointed'. In this instance, permission alone was not quite enough for him and he put in a further plea for help with 'Margrett his wife ... poverty so great they need assistance to erect the said cottage', which petition was also granted.

In deepest winter, 8th January 1693/4, another house was being built. 'I Peter Legh Esq. ... do give my full and free consent that the cottage erected or now in erecting in Over Knutsford on the Town Heath bee erected and finished for the only habitation and use of Peter Norbury and his family, poor inhabitants in the said town'.

These dwellings could last a long time, home and shelter for several generations if necessary but storms, weather and rot took their toll. Perhaps this is what some Lords of the Manor counted on.

In 1682 a petition to the Sessions for relief describes the state of the house.

George Hale of Knutsford and Ann his wife ... of a very great age, the younger being 84 years old and upwards. By reason whereof as also decrepidness of body and sight are not able in the least to work or get anything towards their livelihood, also the house they now live in is (if not timely) repaired, in danger to fall to the great damage if not affliction of the petitioners ... beg ... speedy relief according as you shall think fit.

Their petition was granted, 'to be provided for accordinge'.

In the October Sessions in 1690, Jane Chorley of Mobberley put in a pitiful plea that she was removed last Christmas from Chorley to Mobberley and was almost starved 'at that extreme cold snowy season for want of convenient housing for her and her three small infants'. One of them died, her husband had left her and her house 'falleth and raineth through'.

The townships needed a cottage in which to house the suddenly homeless or those brought back to their place of birth or settlement. In 1688 it was

Ordered by this Court that the cottage for the Township of Ollerton ... which is to be erected upon the waste of Ollerton ... is referred to the two next Justices of the Peace for the County to direct and appoint where and what part of the waste ground the said cottage shall be erected.

In Nether Knutsford, orders like this do not occur (or survive), but the Court Leet had considerable powers. In 1687, just after the epidemic and the great pressure on the town's resources, the Manor Court made this resolution,

Being sensible of the great prejudice that comes to the town by erecting of cottages it is therefore ordered that no cottage shall for the time to come be erected within the liberties of Nether Knutsford, and that if any person do erect any, they shall be proceeded against according to law

A further injunction was made against anyone who made an addition to his cottage. The resources of the town were considered to be fixed; they only had so much land on which to grow crops and if more people came to live and share this land it would mean less for those already here.

Some Lords of the Manor were more ready to allow houses to be built than others. Sir Peter Leycester in 1666, said of Altrincham, 'There are so many cottages erected here by permission of the Lords of Dunham Massey that it has become a nest of beggars'. However, not all obtained consent and Sir Peter listed eight cottages which had been erected in Lower Peover between 1640 and 1677 without consent of any Lord.

Further into the 18th century in order to solve the problem of finding places for the poor to live, Parliament decreed that a local Poor House should be maintained. In 1739 Over Knutsford accounts begin to record items relating to it.

1739: April 16th.	1 load of coals for the poor house	1s 2d
	pd Tho. Jackson for work at the poor house	1s 2d
1740: Jan.1st.	pd. for a load of coales to the poor house	1s 2d

Later entries are for daub and daubing, thatching and glazing, and for land tax for it.

These are for Over Knutsford's Poor House. The Nether Knutsford Poor Law accounts have not been found but evidence of its Poor House exists as two fields and a small one on the Nether Knutsford Tithe map of 1847 called the Poor House Fields. They were within the circuit of the racecourse on the left hand side of the road, opposite the Heath on the road going towards Tabley. The problems of helping and relieving the poor, continued.

Referencess:
- *Over Knutsford Poor Law accounts, Cheethams Library.*
- *Quarter Sessions files, CRO QJF and Indictments and Presentments QJB*
- *Nether Knutsford Court Leet.   Hearth Tax returns.*

Benjamin Hobson

Benjamin Hobson was given a good start in life as he was apprenticed to Joseph Harrison the feltmaker and haberdasher, hatter, to receive his training. Hobson had already joined this household some time before 1667, at which time Harrison was not yet married but was established in a house with two hearths and his shop and a servant. Hobson may have been a relative of Francis Hobson, gent., of Prestbury who was to became Harrison's brother-in-law.

Hobson completed his apprenticeship, often a time of hard work and long hours not only learning his trade but also out in the fields. After receiving wages as a journeyman for a few years he became able to find and lease a property in Knutsford and set up in business on his own. Perhaps his father had given him his portion. There were two hatters already in the town, Joseph Harrison his previous master, and Henry Orrell, with his wife, family and servant, so Hobson was not without competition.

By October,1675, he was in a position to take on an apprentice of his own to help with the work and give him a chance to increase his stock. At this stage in his life he must have felt some satisfaction that he was doing well and he relished and enjoyed the freedom of being his own master at last. Beyond his working life he began to court young Ann Swinton in the town.

Ann Swinton was not, unfortunately, the best practical choice for him business-wise for she had no prospects of a portion or dowry, but when he was with her he was not listening to cold economic reasoning. Ann became pregnant. This was a disaster for both of them. Ann would soon lose whatever position she held, and for Hobson, so early in his career, just building up his business he knew he could not yet afford to support an apprentice and a wife and child. The shame and disgrace of a bastard child would be hard enough to bear, and bad for business, affecting his good name and he knew too that he would have to pay maintenance even if he did not marry.

Ann Swinton had her confinement in Nether Peover where Elizabeth Antrobus was with her as midwife when the child was born in June 1677. 'In the extremity of her travail', Ann affirmed several times that Benjamin Hobson was the father of the child 'and no one else'.

When Hobson heard of the birth of his daughter, the reality of it we can only surmise put him into a state of panic and in desperation seeking to escape the situation, leaving everything he ran from the town.

Declarations of Elizabeth
Antrobus and Mary Deane
who attended the birth of
Anne Swinton's child, the
father named as Benjamin
Hobson. 7thAug 1677

Cond Cester.   Examinacons taken before Sr Peter Leycester Bart & Edward
Legh Esq. two of his Maties Justices of the pease & quorum for the sayd
County at Meyre Aug 7 1677

Elizabeth Antrobus wife of Peter Antrobus of Nether Knotsford
in the sayd County of gen. upon her oath sayth that about six weekes
since shee this examinant was p(re)sent att the labour of Anne Swinton late of
Nether Knotsford in the sayd County spinster who was then in labour of
a bastard child and in this exam t p(er)formed the office of a midwife to
her, and this exam(inant) in the extreamity of her travaile did
demand of her who was the father of her sayd child and shee
answeared and affirmed severall tymes that Benjamin Hobson late of Nether
Knotsford aforesayd feltmaker was the father of the sayd
Child and noe one els, and therupon shee was afterwards delivered
of a Bastard female att Peover aforesayd in the Parochiall Chappellry
of Nether Peover

                                             Elizabeth Antrobus
Mary Deane wife of Thomas Deane of Nether Peover aforesayd
gen. upon her oath sayth that shee was likewise pr(es)ent about the tyme
aforesayd att the labour of the sayd Anne Swinton & heard her
affirme & say in the extreamity of her travaile that the sayd
Benjamin Hobson was the father of the sayd child & shee was
afterwards delivered of a Bastard female Child att Nether Peover
aforesayd.   Mary Deane

Taken before us   her marke
P. Leicester
Edw. Legh

Richard Shaw the innkeeper's son, Hobson's apprentice was left alone in the shop. He was not yet two years into his training and having been abandoned, his terms of apprenticeship were broken. He petitioned the Quarter Sessions for official discharge from his master, telling the Court that his master had, 'fled the country having fathered a bastard child'. His apprenticeship discharge was granted.

At the next Quarter Sessions in October 1677, the Court heard of the bastard birth and duly ordered Hobson absent or not, to pay Ann Swinton 30 shillings a year, at 7 shillings and 6 pence a quarter from the time of the birth for 12 years, 'if it shall so long live', and then £3 to put the child apprentice.

Hobson in due course returned to Knutsford to face the town and his neighbours, and the consequences of events. There would be obligations connected with his property lease and his business for he would not want to loose his home and place of livelihood as well as his apprentice. He would soon be aware of both of the Quarter Sessions' judgements and he probably had to repay the original down payment of Richard Shaw's apprenticeship fee. But before long there was even more shame to face.

In December 1677, the Church in the role of maintainer of public morals, summoned Ann Swinton and Benjamin Hobson before the Archdeacon at his Visitation in Knutsford, and the Correction Books record that they were fined for fornication. Although this would have hit them hard in their current financial straits, with court fees to pay as well, they might possibly have been somewhat relieved knowing that only a few years earlier a public confession and penance, wrapped in a white sheet with a wand in the hand, would certainly have been required of them.

Into the new year, Hobson shouldered his shame, worked hard in his shop and pulled himself together. In June, the banns having been read he and Ann were married.

Life would not be easy for them after such unplanned events. Hobson would never be able to develop the good shop with earning capacity and the prestige he had hoped for, as his best business hopes had been shattered.

The family grew as they had five more children although two died in infancy. When famine and sickness came to Knutsford in 1685/6, the Hobsons were badly affected as there were no customers with money for his hats and no crops. In April 1686, Benjamin Hobson, his wife and four children were listed among the many Poor of Knutsford who were named in need of assistance.

These hard times took their toll and in November 1689 Ann Hobson died, their youngest son not yet three years old.

Hobson married again quite quickly to Mary, to ease the household burden and to look after the children, but she too died after a very short time in February 1691. The children would have been a little older then and better able to fend for themselves and to help their father. Their first child would have been twelve, old enough to be put apprentice if her father could spare her from household tasks.

Benjamin Hobson himself died five years later in 1696.

References.:
- *Francis H., J.Harrison.'s brother-in law; J.H.'s will, 1700. Hearth Tax Returns, P.R.O. 1664.*
- *Apprentices: Poll Tax 1667, DLT/F/71*
- *A Swinton, child and birth, R. Shaw, and Poor List, CRO Ches. Quarter Sessions, QJF. Visitation and Correction Book, CRO EDV 5 Dec.1677.*
- *Elizabeth Antrobus' statement, CRO 1677 QJF 105/3/103*

Elizabeth Cowpe and John Poole

There was an inkling of trouble brewing in October 1689 in Robert Pollard's Inn where some Knutsford townsmen and gentry were drinking and discussing something other than Knutsford's forthcoming fair.

Around a table was a group of men, Mr.William Leicester of Toft, Robert Thornley surgeon barber and clerk, a constable that year, John Highfield of Bexton and young tailor John Poole on the defensive but defiant, with his father Richard Poole from Toft trying to sort things out between his son and an aggrieved Nathan Cowpe, barber. Local collarmaker William Ridiard came upon this group and stood by to find out what was going on.

Mr.Leicester had just served a warrant on 23 year old John Poole and read it aloud to him. John Highfield got pen, ink and paper in order to draw up a bond for Richard Poole to promise to take his son John to Bullock Smithy(Hazel Grove), on the following Tuesday to 'undertake to save the township harmless from supporting a bastard not yet born on the body of the daughter of Nathan Cowpe'.

For some reason the bond was not sealed that day but Richard Poole did agree to bring his son to Knutsford on Monday morning 'by 10 of the clock' to seal the bond then, to Nathan Cowpe and the constable, but young John Poole was a slippery customer. He was nowhere to be found on either Monday or Tuesday.

Nathan Cowpe the barber had plenty to worry about. His daughter Elizabeth had confessed a few months previously to her parents that in April, six months before this warrant was served, that she had entertained her swain John Poole in her parents' house upon at least two occasions. She was then aged 17, a virgin living at home with her parents. She had known John Poole from childhood for both were born in Knutsford. Her words were that, 'Upon the promise of marriage to her (he) had carnal knowledge of her body, and also about a moneth after'. It soon became clear that she was pregnant, but John Poole aged about 23 years would not marry her. Apart from inclination quite possibly he was in no position to do so being either a servant or an apprentice he had in any case not yet received his portion from his father, and had no money to marry and set up home.

The Cowpe family had to come to terms with this and at length after much discussion, Nathan wrote letters to his brother in London. By August arrangements had been made for Elizabeth. Like many before and many since, she travelled to London where she hoped to hide in anonymity. She stayed initially with her 'Uncle Cowpe' in Little Britain near St.Paul's.

There was at that time in Little Britain, an acclaimed spacious school/ factory built by a philanthropist Thomas Firmin, draper, for the employment of the poor in linen manufacture. Children were taken from the age of three. They were taught to read as well as spin and could earn 2d a day, adults, 6d. 'Uncle Cowpe' would certainly have known of this and this may possibly have offered hope for some future independence for Elizabeth, but not yet. She soon found a lodging in the Parish of St.Andrew's Holborn, Co. Middlesex where her child was born in January 1690, a girl she christened Alice.

Even in 1690 it was not possible to live entirely unnoticed in London. The midwife from St.Martin in the Fields who attended the confinement was obliged to submit her information on the birth of the bastard child and it's named father to the Middlesex JP.s, in whose presence Elizabeth Cowpe with four month old Alice were summoned in May. The paternity of the child had been freely given and the midwife also gave her testimony of the same, 'declared in the time of her sharp pains'. John Poole was ordered to pay maintenance, the actual order was for £5 to cover costs since the birth and then 2 shillings per week for 8 years, then £5 to put the child apprentice. The papers were sent to Cheshire. (It was more expensive even then to live in London comparing Benjamin Hobson's order 13 years earlier who was to pay 30 shillings a year, with this order of 104 shillings a year. Also the age of apprenticeship in London was 8 and in Knutsford it was 12, and the cost of apprenticeship £5 in London, £3 in Cheshire.)

But John Poole paid not one penny.

In October 1690 Nathan Cowpe as a freeholder, was one of the Jurymen, as he had been on several occasions before, at the Quarter Sessions when the Court sat in Knutsford. It was here that he heard the statements of his daughter Elizabeth and of the midwife, and of the order which was issued for the arrest of John Poole for failing to pay anything for his child.

Martha Cowpe, Nathan's wife, had signed her name as a witness in 1672 when she was 24. Had daughter Elizabeth learned to write and was she able or could she have afforded ever to write home to her parents?

The Bread Bills for their Majesties' prisoners in the Castle of Chester tell the next part of the story. 'John Poole charged with a female bastard', was billed quarterly there for bread at 7d. a week, from 6th October 1690 until 11th July 1691.

No more is known of Elizabeth and Alice Cowpe. Elizabeth and/or the child may have died, or were they sucked into London's underworld? Death or disappearance would have allowed Poole to be released from prison, freeing him from obligation. Poole did not return to Knutsford, wisely perhaps.

We have not heard the last of John Poole who in 1706 was in High Leigh, then a labourer, where he gave sufficient bond of £40 with security to 'save harmless the township of High Leigh from a bastard child, male, born on the body of Sarah Johnson, single woman of High Leigh'.

John Poole's father Richard died in 1718. His will bequeathed unto his eldest son John,'£2 in full satisfaction of all his claims either to my real or personal estate–and the reason why–I give no more is because I have heretofore in my lifetime preferred him according to my ability'. He had been a long time grief and worry to his father.

References:
• *Thomas Firmin's establishment in Little Britain: WEBB Sidney and Beatrice, English Poor Law History, 1927 Longmans Green & Co. Part 1, p 106.*

Thomas Poole and John Highfield.

Thomas Poole, ironmonger and nailer of Knutsford was Richard Poole's brother, and he too had family problems.

His daughter Mary married John Highfield junior of Bexton in 1688. The Highfield family, yeomen, had lived in Bexton for several generations. William Highfield, John's grandfather and most likely his father John farmed 20 acres there, leased from the Leycesters of Toft. On the west side of the

steeple, (tower), of the Knutsford parochial Church, under the window where the bells hung, was written on the stone, 'William Hefeld and Margery his wife'. They were probably two of the benefactors to the building of the tower in stone in the reign of Henry the eighth.

John junior and his brothers probably went to Knutsford Grammar School as had their father and grandfather. John junior was 28 at the time of his marriage and he and Mary set up home possibly in Plumley at first but later they too went to Bexton. They had six children, four of whom survived infancy. Both Highfields, senior and junior were on good terms with the Poole family as was evident in 1689 when one of them stood bail for Richard and John Poole in the case with Elizabeth Cowpe. John junior became quite a man of property for within 10 years he held no less than three properties with lands in Bexton, Plumley and Nether Knutsford, this last being left to him by an uncle. He was letting them out on lease. It looked like a promising and financially secure household.

But all was not as it seemed and something was very much amiss. By 1703 he was heavily in debt. At the end of that year he became very ill and by the 15th December with the possibility of dying, 'being weake of body', he made his will. The will indicates the seriousness of his debts because he asked his executors, his 'dear wife Mary', his father-in- law Thomas Poole and his brother Ralph Poole of Macclesfield, to sell all these properties, the goods and cattles 'for the best price that can be gotten' in order to pay off his dues. He hoped that there would be enough money over towards the support and livelihood of his wife and children and their education. He was too optimistic.

John Highfield did not die for another nine years until September 1712, in what state of health in those years we cannot tell. John Highfield senior died in 1704 but apparently did not leave enough to his son and family to make a substantial difference. He had given his son his portion when he married.

By 1710 the family were in dire straits. The children had become chargeable to the township of Bexton being supported by the Overseers of the Poor 'by reason of their poverty and infancy'. A yeoman's family had become paupers. A Court order was sought and the J.P.s decided that 'Thomas Poole, (Mary's father), grandfather of Samuel, William, Hannah and Ellen Highfield, was of sufficient ability to contribute towards the maintenance of the said children'. It was therefore ordered by the Court that Thomas Poole should pay £3 yearly to the Overseers by equal quarterly payments till further order to the contrary. (Nearly 4d. a day for four children is comparable with the cousin John Poole's 1d a day for bread in Chester Castle twenty years before.)

Thomas Poole had two other married daughters and two sons. He pre deceased his son-in-law by a couple of months. In his will he left only one shilling to his daughter Mary Highfield, 'and no more because I have given her all ready a sufficient portion and paid for her and her husband John more than my ability'. To his granddaughter Ellen Poole he left 5 shillings, 'the reason why I leave her no more is because I have given her father and paid for him a deal more than his share of all my effects both real and personal'.

Ref: The Highfield's estate of 20 acres, Ormerod.

Chapter Seven
The Medical Scene

Wonderful little when all is said
Wonderful little our fathers knew
Half of their remedies killed you dead
Most of their teaching was quite untrue
                              Rudyard Kipling

The surgeon has his round of thirty miles and sleeps at Cranford. Cranford ch.1. Mrs.Gaskell

Knutsford had long been a local centre for medical treatment as there were doctors in Knutsford in the 14th century. It was certainly such a centre in the 17th century. Medical knowledge was scanty compared with standards today although knowledge of anatomy and physiology was growing. Harvey had demonstrated to Charles 1st his discovery of the system of circulation of the blood. Advances and successes were trade secrets to individual doctors, part of the mystery of their profession and their livelihood. Knowledge in the provinces may not have been as advanced as in London but it is possible that discussions with other doctors of their experiences may have led to changes in the practice and theory of medicine.

They believed as in centuries before in the four humours, the imbalance of any one of which, they thought, caused disease and for which there were four main remedies, bleeding, blistering, vomiting or purging. Often the cure was as unpleasant as the complaint if it did not cause the death.

There were plenty of medicines, herbs, potions, pills and ointments, infusions, many of them cures which had come down from medieval times from the monks if not before, concoctions and distillations made from flowers, herbs and chemicals, many ingredients being imported from far overseas. A few cures were known and some doctors found that certain things were effective, they were skilful and knowledgeable for their time. Families had their own recipes and remedies and educated people, gentry and aristocratic families collected these with others recommended by friends. They very often tried these first, before calling and paying a doctor or seeking advice. Herbs and flowers were grown in many gardens, specialised herb gardens having been in existence for many years. Wise women in towns and villages gained reputations for being able to help some conditions.

Some doctors consulted astrology and some wore all black to sustain an air of mystery. Not everyone went to a doctor or apothecary immediately or at all and even sensible, educated men undertook strange remedies and were willing to try anything for a cure. The Rev. Adam Martindale sought unorthodox help for his young daughter who would seem to have contracted polio and was paralysed. She was placed in the carcass of a newly killed calf while it was still warm.

There was no idea of germs or how disease was transmitted, hygiene standards were low or non existent. There was little hand washing for eating or food preparation or washing at all in some cases. There were a few washing turnells in the Knutsford inventories and just one widow had a basin and ure, another had a clothes maid(en) 'to dry clothes'. Pepys only washed all over, once in the six years of his diary. Poorer people had no opportunity or inclination to wash, many even believing it to be harmful. Houses were often ideal breeding places for pests of all sorts which were accepted as a nuisance of life, fleas, lice, rats and mice abounded, also intestinal worms. Even the gentry had their problems, Sir Peter Leycester paid a man 'for stopping the holes against rats in Mr. Pocklington's study'.

Drainage and sewage disposal was non existent or rudimentary. In Knutsford, several households had chamber pots and close stools, but where were these emptied? The middens of household refuse in the streets attracted the inevitable flies.

They tried to keep wells free from contamination but most realised that water was not safe to drink, drinking only ale or beer which had fermented. Milk was drunk mostly by children but that was not always safe from the cow with tuberculosis or brucellocis. In Knutsford everything drained downhill to the brook by the Moor, waste products from the leather industry, skinning and tanning, dyeing, tallow chandlery, slaughtering and butchery, poured into it. Waterborne diseases had every chance to flourish. Knutsford's wells could not have been kept completely clean despite efforts and decrees by the Manor Court. Smoking related illnesses may have been prevalent although no connection with these and tobacco was then known. No wonder people became ill and plagues and epidemics flared up. Under nourished poorer people were affected first, always more susceptible to disease and illness and malnutrition caused other problems, so it is a wonder that any survived to old age.

Knutsford's epidemic of 1686 could have had several causes but we will never know what it was for certain. The parish registers give no cause of deaths during that time. It could have been many diseases such as influenza, smallpox, scarlet fever, diphtheria or even measles. The Pilgrim Fathers in America had a measles epidemic in 1670 reported by Thomas Sydenham which had a monthly pattern similar to that of Knutsford's, rising to a peak in March and finishing in July. Smallpox was a most dreaded infectious disease in the 17th and 18th centuries.

Mortality was high especially among infants and children, childbirth was hazardous and there were many miscarriages. Midwifery was one of the few jobs which was open to women, maturity and experience being the main qualifications but inevitably problems were met which resulted in the death of the mother and /or the baby. It is to be hoped that they did not often have such a brutal, gruesome task as that reported in the parish register for Rostherne in 1697 under 'burials': ' a child pulled piecemeal from Elizabeth

Boone of Bucklow Hill'. Elizabeth Boone herself was possibly glad enough to die the next day. Most would have seen death from a young age which coloured their attitude to life and may account to some extent for the strong religious faith of many.

There were several types of doctor, apothecaries, surgeons and physicians and various combinations of these. Apothecaries started historically as grocers, pepperers and spicers. This was until James 1st granted them a charter for a seven year apprenticeship to be followed by an examination in pharmacy and medicine which enabled them to be licensed by the Society of Apothecaries in London. Grocers left this society in 1617 but the links still lingered, many imported herbs and spices used in cooking were also used in medical prescriptions.

Apothecaries could treat patients but not charge for attendance. They were to display the tile of admittance to the Society in their window or their premises, a diamond shaped glazed tile upon which they made pills, replacing a pestle and mortar which had been the previous medieval symbol. Medicine was symbolised by carboys of red and green, lit from behind by candles, and large gilt jars were also used by one Knutsford apothecary in the shop window, these making attractive High Street shops which drew in customers and where most people went with their ailments as they were cheaper than physicians. Apprenticeship was the usual training in the provinces although this differed throughout the country.

Surgeons on the other hand were more practical and were allied with barbers in a City Company in 1640. The barber's pole outside their shops was the symbol of an arm bound by a tourniquet holding a bowl for lather for

Barber's Bowl c. 1700 - Picture from the Thackray Museum

shaving or blood, for blood letting in the arm or hand was one of their chief tasks. Some learnt at home with their fathers, for others apprenticeships were with other barber surgeons, sometimes in hospitals or in the army or navy during times of war, the wounded providing them with practice. Fractures were set without anaesthetics apart from alcohol. During this and the previous century amputations and wounds were sometimes cauterised but they were learning to tie off blood vessels, advances were being made. Tooth drawing was another of their skills. Surgeons broke away from the barbers about a century later and gradually obtained more recognition.

Physicians since 1522 needed a university degree. Like the clergy they went either to Oxford or Cambridge or if a dissenter, to a Scottish university where they were not required to belong to the Church of England. Afterwards they went as apprentices either with a doctor or into a hospital of which there were several in London. A diary was kept by Dr. Kay of Baldingstone near Bury, 1716-1751, of his experiences of medical training. He found the London hospitals were unpleasant places, neither clean nor restful, with drunkenness among patients being just one of the problems. He went as a pupil to an apothecary in Guy's hospital in London and attended patients in other hospitals in the city where he found the whole experience harrowing, little in hospital but affliction and death.

Some physicians had their own pharmacy in competition with the apothecaries. They all had shops which were in effect their surgeries and many physicians also took in patients at home like a cottage hospital, for care, rest, medication, diet and isolation if necessary which gave patients as good a chance as any of recovery, even if it took a long time.

A contemporary account of this practice was recorded by William Blundell, local squire of Crosby, north of Liverpool, 4th July, 1691 :

My daughter Brigid, being reduced to a very dangerous state by sundry distempers, removed to the doctor's in Wigan about 8 or 9 weeks ago, since when she hath been better and worse by turns. She is now (blessed be God), in a very more hopeful way and we expect to see her at Crosby before it be long.

In London there was rivalry between these professional bodies but in Knutsford and in other provincial towns, doctors practised in more than one branch of the profession calling themselves apothecary surgeons, or physician surgeons, probably to maximise their earning capacity, filling local needs and niches. It was not as important to maintain professional barriers beyond London, especially as there was a kind of fraternity amongst them in nearby towns, many of them as we will see, intermarried within medical families in the neighbourhood.

The Bishop initially authorised doctors, surgeons and midwives, like the clergy and schoolmasters, their licence to practice thereafter renewed by the Archdeacon at the visitation. After 1662 they were also expected to take the oath of allegiance and affirm to the 39 Articles and the Book of Common Prayer. Many of Knutsford's doctors and medical men at this time were dissenters which may account for the fact that these records are incomplete and only a few years refer to Knutsford's men in the medical profession.

Dr. William Smith, Physician and Surgeon, 1637 - 1701

Dr. Smith was a physician, his education and background unknown but licensed in 1665. By 1667, he and his wife Isabel in Knutsford had three children and a servant although in1664 his house had only one hearth. By 1673 they had two hearths and by 1678 were in Minshull Street sharing a house with and/or looking after the elderly widow Lettice Swinton. Shortly after this, he and his wife moved to a freehold house on King Street which had six hearths and about 15 rooms. These included chambers over the house, pantry, kitchen, shop, and entry. His house had a yard, gardens, orchard and buildings standing on the backside of the house. Moving to this larger home would have given them room to take in boarding patients. Possibly to celebrate this move, they invited guests to dinner in May 1680, who were Sir Thomas Mainwaring, the Rev. Kettleby Turner, Mr. Gatley, a minister, and Joseph Harrison.

Dr. Smith was a frequent visitor to Peover Hall to attend Sir Thomas Mainwaring, his children and grand children. Sir Thomas was let blood, given pills, purging pills, 'physick' and a vomit at different times. When Sir Thomas's married daughter was taken ill on one occasion, both Dr. Smith and his wife, a midwife, were sent for, staying at Peover for two nights until 'they supposed that (his daughter) did miscarry'. Isobel Smith was a licensed midwife from 1674 but unlike her contemporary midwife Elizabeth Antrobus, she could not write her name, using only a capital 'I' crossed in the middle.

William and Isabel Smith had eleven children, three of whom died as babies, but when William Smith himself died in 1701, he had only two married daughters and one unmarried daughter still at home.

Dr. Smith built another freehold house in 1697 in Whitebridge with a barn next to it. This house was registered in his name as a Dissenting Meeting House in the possession of Samuel Lowe, clerk, the minister then of their new Chapel. William Smith was named as one of the dissenters in the church and chapel disputes in 1686, was a witness of the will of the ejected minister, Rev. Peter Legh in 1694 and nominated three foremost dissenters, Peter Wood, John Bostock and Walter Antrobus to be his executors with his wife when he came to make his own will.

He had a large agricultural stock, £30 worth, with corn threshed and unthreshed (in May), £3 14s., a winnow sheet, hay, 2 mares, 4 cows, 1 young swine and poultry. The Leycester family bought four loads of lime from him in 1682 and he even supplied sugar loaf to them. He needed horses for travelling to see patients, travelling sometimes as far as Lymm about 10 miles away where once he was up all night when Captain Daniels died.

He attended patients of all ranks of society. In 1693 he had been to Bostock where he expended £3 4s. 'In Chirugicall Medicines - in the cure of Martha Lamb, a poor inhabitant of Bostock which she is in no wise able to pay', the overseers there were to include this sum in their assessment of the poor and pay Dr. Smith as soon as it was collected.

A close stool, a chamber pot within a cupboard or box. Dr William Smith had three in his house

His household goods indicate his boarding patients with eight beds numbered with all their corresponding bedding, bolsters, pillows, blankets and coverlets. There were six other beds for the family, the apprentice and servants and 19 pairs of sheets, pillow beares, 9 towels, 15 diaper and 9 huckaback napkins and tablecloths. A wash house with a furnace pan and coopery ware (barrels), indicates some washing facilities. It was one of the conditions of his apprentice that washing should be done for him. Three close stools would be for sick patients' use. One of his rooms was the Garden House which had a grate in it, somewhere for him to escape, perhaps from work and patients or somewhere for isolating an infectious patient. The house had 10 leather chairs and others, stools, backstools and cushions and 9 tables one of which was three and a half yards long. There was a warming pan, a clock and case, pictures, 130 lbs of pewter and £5 worth of books. His instruments of surgery, £5, shop goods, £40 and debts good and bad owing to him, £44. His wearing apparel, ring, saddles and bridles were valued at £16, he was well dressed, the total, £242 19s.

In 1698 William Smith took on an apprentice, although probably not his first. The indenture written out by Peter Wood, is an insight into the expected behaviour of 17th century medical students and their hopes of training:

The Indenture of Apprenticeship for a term of five years was drawn up between William Brookes of Adswood (near Stockport), yeoman, and Legh Brookes his son, and William Smith of Nether Knutsford, Physician, on 15th July 1698. William Brookes, put his son Legh to be an Apprentice or Covenant Servant to William Smith in the 'Science, Art or Trade he now useth' to be taught and to dwell with him and serve after the manner of an apprentice for a term of five years, during which time, Legh Brooks was to:

1. Well and truly serve William Smith's secrets
2. Keep his commandments close
3. Gladly doe and perform, lawful and honest everywhere
4. Not doe nor suffer to be done, hurt to his Master, to the value of 12 pence or more by the year, but shall hinder the same if he can or else immediately admonish his Master thereof
5. Not inordinately waste the goods of his Master, nor lend them to anybody
6. Not play at dice or any other unlawful game whereby his Master may incur hurt
7. Not contract Matrimony
8. Not frequent taverns or Alehouses
9. Not absent or prolong himself from the service of his Master day or night without first obtaining license and consent of his Master
10. Bear himself to his Master and Mistress and all his, as a good and faithful apprentice in all things during the said term.

The father promised to pay £20 during the first year and £6 a quarter for the following four years and to provide his son with clothes. William Smith promised to teach and to find his apprentice food and drink, shelter and washing.

William Smith died before the end of the five years, in April 1701, but the legal terms of the document would have enabled them to come to some agreement as to Legh Brooks' future.

William Smith was 64 when he died and was buried in Knutsford, his epitaph reading, 'one time useful, faithful and successful in the practice of Physic and Chirurgery'.

Keeping medicine in the family, William and Isabel's middle daughter Mary married Richard Green, surgeon and apothecary of Neston, Wirral, 1693. Some time after their marriage they moved to Altrincham and Mary came home to her parents' house either to have a baby or to bring a sick child with her. Unfortunately the medical Smith family could not help for the little son died and was buried in Knutsford, his father then being named as Richard Green, Apothecary of Altrincham. They moved to Knutsford soon after William Smith's death, Green being registered as surgeon for Knutsford in 1701,1712 and 1716. He became an active member of Knutsford's literate community witnessing wills and appraising inventories. Richard and Mary

had three more children but none of them lived. By 1714, Richard Green
was owning property and wealthy enough to be a voter of the shire.

The Delves family.   *See Family Tree 8*

William Delves(1), apothecary of Nether Knutsford was one of Knutsford's
most wealthy men. He had an estate of £1,470 of which £987 was in bonds
or securities.

   William Delves had a well stocked shop containing £60 of 'druggs', £35
in compositions, £20 in 'oyles, strongwaters and domestick preparations'
and other items including stills. He had £100 of debts in shop books good
and bad. Among his domestic goods were £5 worth of books, his mare, a
cow, and some corn growing in 'Downes Croft', (in August) and £106 2s
10d in silver and gold.

   He lived in a house with five hearths in 1664 until his death and in 1667,
his household consisted of himself, his wife Margaret, (nee Swinton), six
children and a servant.

   He was one of the Knutsford Chapel (Church) Wardens at the time of
the Restoration and was mentioned several times by Adam Martindale who
called him 'my civil and courteous friend notwithstanding our different
judgements'. When discussing Martindale's successor, Benjamin Cross's,
addiction to drink, Martindale alleged that Benjamin Cross bought gills of
brandy from his ingenious friend Dr. Delves. When he refused to sell him

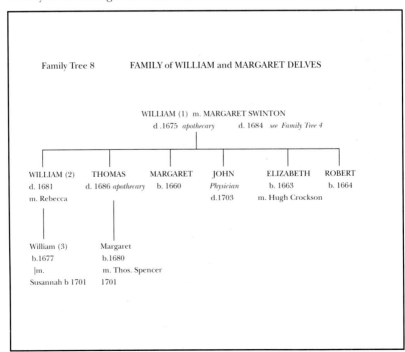

Family Tree 8   FAMILY of WILLIAM and MARGARET DELVES

WILLIAM (1) m. MARGARET SWINTON
d .1675 *apothecary*   d. 1684 *see Family Tree 4*

WILLIAM (2)	THOMAS	MARGARET	JOHN	ELIZABETH	ROBERT
d. 1681	d. 1686 *apothecary*	b. 1660	*Physician*	b. 1663	b. 1664
m. Rebecca			d.1703	m. Hugh Crockson	

William (3)
b.1677
|m.
Susannah b 1701

Margaret
b.1680
m. Thos. Spencer
1701

any more he got some from elsewhere but Benjamin Cross died still owing William Delves £10. William Delves supplied 'Physick' for Mistress Ann Legh of Norbury Booths in 1662. Apothecaries sold brandy, strictly for medical purposes of course, including veterinary uses. At one time five bottles of brandy were bought for a horse at Tabley which had 'the pole evil'.

William and Mary Delves had eight children; two having died as infants but the others received a good education and inherited substantial legacies from their father. The eldest son, William(2) inherited the shop but what his trade was is not clear. He died in 1681 calling himself gentleman and Sir Thomas Mainwaring attended his funeral.

The shop contents and the shop debts went to his brother Thomas who was already a practising apothecary in his own premises in Knutsford when his father died. Thomas died unmarried 11 years later in Knutsford's epidemic year, 1686, at which time his shop goods were worth £150, with books, £8. He had a screen in his shop possibly for examining patients in privacy. His house was very well furnished with green bed and hangings in one room and 'sett' purple curtains and a purple rug in another. Among his possessions was a goffering iron and a smoothing iron. His apparel was worth £10. Thomas kept six horses and mares which he may have been hiring out, his saddles, bridles and swords were valued separately from his clothes. His estate was worth nearly £600. It is no surprise that his 'very loving friend' was Joseph Harrison the hatter. They would both enjoy riding or racing their horses dressed in fine clothes..

There were also 10 biscuit pans amongst the kitchen utensils. His widowed mother provided the fashionable Naples spiced biscuits for funerals in some quantities at several times to the Leycester household where Thomas also supplied various 'apothecary stuff' over the years.

He was a religious man who started his will with an especially long religious preamble, leaving legacies in very loving terms to his brothers and sisters. He must have been in his forties, in February being then 'sick and weak of body'.

There was still one other brother of the Delves family, the youngest, John. He also was in the medical profession, a doctor with a degree, BA and a Licentiate Physician. His exact dates in Knutsford are unclear as the records do not exist to tell us, but he was practising in 1698. He attended the bookseller, Peter Swinton in his final illness for which he was paid a fee of £4 6s by the executor. He too died young and unmarried in 1703.

Robert Thornley, Barber Surgeon 1634 - 1695

Robert Thornley was contemporary in Knutsford with Dr. William Smith, of a similar age. He was barber surgeon from a medical family, his brothers and nephew were surgeon barbers, (the significance of the order of description is not known), in Macclesfield and his wife's uncle had been a surgeon in Rostherne. He was in Knutsford in 1656, aged 21 or 22 when he married Alice Hunt of Rostherne during Adam Martindale's time but their banns were declared in Knutsford's market place during the Commonwealth. In 1667 they were living in a small house, cottage, with one hearth, his family consisting of his wife Alice and three children with no servants at that time. He may have had a separate 'shop' in which to work, then. They stayed in that cottage for about 20 years until after 1674 after which they moved to a much larger property with five grates and 10 rooms including the garret and cellar.

Thornley was a barber employed by Sir Peter Leycester from 1663 until Sir Peter's death in 1678, being paid quarterly. On his regular rides back to Knutsford Sir Peter entrusted him with payments for Peter Swinton for books and James Swinton for candles. After Sir Peter's death he was at Tabley Hall again for he was given money to pay James Harvey for ale after Sir Peter's funeral.

Robert Thornley was engaged with all the Manor Court duties at different times and was given charge to keep the Town chest in his house. He was paid by the Court to keep the town clock in good repair and Sir Peter Leycester also paid him to mend his clocks, the Leycester family still calling on him for this service in 1694. Thornley obviously liked clocks, he had a watch and a clock and case of his own, worth 50 shillings which his son still had at his death.

Robert Thornley had another great interest in life, the Church. In 1669 he was licensed as surgeon and as Parish Clerk for Knutsford, which position he held until his death. He represented the laity's role in worship during difficult and sensitive times. A Clerk's duties varied from place to place but he held the keys of the two chapels and took an active part during the services. In April 1671 a license was given to him as Parish Clerk, to Church women and to bury the dead in Knutsford when the minister the Rev. Kettleby Turner was ill. Clerks' duties elsewhere involved reading the lessons and leading the responses during the service, assisting the Minister by arranging Christenings and Confirmations and they had duties at burials. Literacy was a requirement, a Clerk appointed for Over Peover was once described as 'a literate person', as another duty was often to write the parish register or to keep a copy of it.

Robert Thornley was contemporary with the dissenters and despite their split with the established Church, remained on very friendly terms with many of them. Thornley asked Peter Wood to write his will and after he had died Isaac Antrobus and Peter Wood came to appraise Thornley's inventory. He and the dissenters had been together and held many discussions for more than 30 years through the difficult times and their presence in his house at that time is proof of their friendship. Thornley was one of two 'loving friends' of Isaac Antrobus.

Robert Thornley kept a valuable gelding worth £10 as well as a cow, a pig and 9 sheep and grew a quantity of corn and had hay and malt. His house was comfortably furnished and he had two guns. He had £120 worth of bonds, £38 in gold and silver and his wearing apparel, watch, saddle, bridle and canes were worth £6.

One of the rooms in his larger house was 'the Parson's Chamber'. The Thornleys had taken in young Parson Robinson when he had first come to Knutsford four years earlier. He left 20 shillings for Mr. James Robinson 'our Minister', to preach his funeral sermon. When Thornley died aged 59 in August 1695, his books were valued at 6s.8d, reflecting the less academic nature of surgeons. The £2 worth of 'Instruments belonging to his Imploy' were not identified, neither were the goods in his shop, £40. Thornley bequeathed his house in Knutsford to his son William, apothecary, and another house leased from the Egertons to his daughter and her husband Joseph Hough apothecary. Thornley's estate was valued at £282.

The Thornleys had had five children but only their son William and daughter Mary (Hough), were still living when their father died. surgery ran in the family as his wife's uncle had been a surgeon in Rostherne probably where he did his apprenticeship. Robert had brothers in Macclesfield, Thomas and William (Aldermen), both surgeon barbers as was one of their sons, Nicholas. He played a significant and important role in Knutsford life during difficult years in the church, with problems with the appointed Ministers, Squire Peter Legh and the serious dissent among the congregation but steered them all through it and remained Parish Clerk. His relationship with the gentry, Sir Peter Leycester and others, must have been discreet during the politically sensitive times, reporting on his visit to Dunham on the Duke of Monmouth's visit.

William Thornley, Apothecary Surgeon 1663 - 1710

Robert's son William inherited his father's house and was soon expanding, building on a new room to the house. This may have been built after his marriage in 1698 aged 35, to a young widow, Mary Gandy of Great Budworth. They were to have a family of five, but in 1710 when he was 47, he became ill and wrote his will, 'being at present surprised by sickness', from which he died shortly after, his widow giving birth to their sixth child a few days later.

William had turned one of his father's parlours into a smart 18th century dining room with a round table and a large oval table with 12 rush bottom chairs, pictures on the walls and a new item of furniture for Knutsford, a 'press to hang clothes in'. William had a substantial brewing pan fixed about with lead in the kitchen and in the cellar were 14 gallons of wine, a dozen bottles and five little barrels. They were able to entertain guests in style. He had a fowling piece and a musket which may have been his father's 2 guns.

The goods in William Thornley's shop were valued at £65, nests of drawers, pots, bottles and other utensils, and the instruments for surgery and his books, £6. He also had agricultural crops, livestock and agricultural implements worth over £31. His estate was valued at £544 but over £300 of this were regarded as partly desperate debts.

Joseph Hough, Apothecary Surgeon, d 1699

Robert's daughter and William's sister Mary, was also married into the profession, to Joseph Hough apothecary surgeon, whose half sister Sarah was married to John Booth apothecary in Warrington. Joseph and Mary were married in 1687. It was Joseph's second wife, but they were to have no children.

They were not quite as prosperous as William Thornley but lived in a 7 roomed house, the lease left to them by Robert Thornley. Mary's widowed mother Alice had come to live with them. Joseph and Mary, or possibly Mary and her mother, had taken over Margaret Delves' (d. 1684) biscuit making for funerals. They had supplied 27 lbs. of them and six and a half lbs. of Naples biscuits for Peter Swinton's funeral in 1698. Joseph Hough also supplied physic for the bookseller in his last illness, prescribed by Dr. John Delves.

Joseph Hough was among the minority but significant number in Knutsford who had no agricultural items whatsoever and when he needed to hire a horse he had a hackney saddle and a side saddle and a lanthorn to find his way at night. He had interests of a different sort, a gun, a pair of pistols and fishing rods. He liked to hear his wife play on their pair of virginals of which there was only one other pair in the existing Knutsford inventories.

His well stocked shop goods were valued at £74 16s 8d.:

Druggs in boxes	£30	Chemical preparations	£5
Compound medicines in the potts and bottles			£25
81 shop potts	£3	Bottles	£4
6 nests of drawers	£4	2 counters	£4
4 mortars	£4	1 pair of scales and weights	6s 8d
1 pewter still	£1	1 copper still	£1 10

These goods in his shop were appraised by William Thornley and John Booth his apothecary brothers-in-law, who valued his estate at £109 8s. including his debts, some of which were desperate, £81 10s.

John England, Apothecary Surgeon d.circa 1711

John England was an apothecary and surgeon in Knutsford for just a few years before 1711. He came to Knutsford from Northwich where things had not gone well with either his business or possibly his marriage.

Apothecaries jar, dated 1684. The jar is for Oleum vulpinum (Oil of foxes),
which was used for chest complaints. From Thackray Museum

John England was not a good business man. Medical men usually made a
very good living but John England had a soft heart and found that he could
not deny his help to the needy, money or no. Word soon spread and some
poor people travelled from distances around in order to seek help from him.
Soon his business was in desperate straits and he was allowing drugs, services
or credit in return for goods and food which he himself needed.

His wife Elizabeth may have been disgusted with her husband's inability
to make a decent living, a grave disappointment to her high hopes and
expectations when she had married a medical man, and they moved to
Knutsford hoping to make a new start. In May 1710 a daughter was born
to them, baptised in Knutsford but Elizabeth may have taken the child to
Northwich soon afterwards as their Knutsford home was quite unsuitable
for a child. She and the baby were certainly was not living there when her
husband died.

John England's burial registration has not been found although his horse
was at his house when his inventory was taken. He was living in a state worse
than many paupers, in the meanest condition. When his wife heard that he
had died she seized the opportunity to make a quick visit to Knutsford to take
mercury from his shop to sell. She renounced her right of administration
of his estate and appointed two of her husband's principal creditors from
Northwich in her stead.

This they did with admirable thoroughness and took infinite pains.
The inventory they made of John England's estate is most detailed and the
probate clerk called it 'full and perfect'. His personal goods and chattels
were meagre:

One mare, an old saddle and bridle appraised at	£2 1s 6d.
Two old chairs,	6d.
His wearing apparel and boots,	13s 4d.
One feather bed,	6s 8d.
Ready money,	3s 1$\frac{1}{2}$d.
One iron brewing pan,	13s 6d.
One iron pot	3s.
Total,	£4 1s 7$\frac{1}{2}$d.

No bedstead, pillow or blankets are mentioned. He may have lodged in Hollingworth's inn. Then follows the exact contents of his apothecary shop, 201 listed drugs and chemicals with valuations. 63 have been identified: laxatives, purgatives, emetics, something for worms, embrocations, inhalations, pain killers. Senna, rhubarb, castor oil, aloes, camphor, laudanum, absinthe. Many herbs not in the modern pharmacopoeia were listed with, oils, palm oil, lead salts, liquorice, aniseed, fennel, coriander, cardomon, orange rind, colouring, cochineal, rosemary ointment, (Unguent Nervin), and many chemicals which are still today used in medicines. A remarkable list, all the items valued at only £23 but some were in a decayed state.

Apart from these, his shop tile and chirurgeon sign, large and small gilt bottles, pots for oil, syrup and ointment, bottles, a brass mortar and a stone mortar, an iron furnace, 3 nest drawers, 2 counters, a copper still and worm, 3 tin bodies and surgeons instruments were all valued at £7 10s and his books were worth 10s.

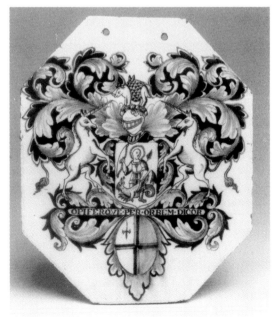

Apothecary's Tile c. 1700 - 1720. From Thackray Museum

Then there was appended a list of 153 debtors whose names had been entered in his shop book. The administrators did their best to track them all down but 25 denied the debt, 14 were not known and 26 were described as poor. A look down the list tells its own story. These are some of them:

Mr. Robert Hewit of Knutsford who says there's as great a sum due to him from Mr. England,	13s.
Sam Peacock who says nothing's due,	£1 8s.
Jos. Booth of Waverham,	1s.
John Crownes sister of Chester,	3s. 9d.
Mr. Arrowsmith who denies the debt,	7s 1d.
Esther Lewis of Stretton and we can't find any such woman,	7s.
Henry Henshaw's friend but know not who is meant,	2s 6d.
Ellin Redson, very poor,	1s 6d.
Mr. Burton, watchmaker of Sale who was long before Mr. England removed from Northwich and is very poor,	£1.
Sar. Sadlers servant but do not know who it is,	6d.
John Gorst, waller, very poor, (A salt boiler)	10s. 6d.
Sarah Miller kept on the town,	1s.

There was a debt from Sir Samuel Daniel for £3 5s, John Hollingworth, Knutsford innkeeper, 'who has a greater sum due to him and agreed to be stopped in his lifetime, 3s 10d.' and Mr. Leech, Knutsford bookseller, 'who says the same, 5s.1d.' He was supplying his goods to a wide spectrum of society.

The last item on the list was 'Quick sylver sold by Mrs. England since her husband's death before an inventory was taken, which she has accounted for to the Administrators, 8s. 9d.' Quick silver, mercury, was a well known treatment and cure for 'the pox', or venereal disease.

Ol: Syr. And oyntmnt. potts pill potts & large
pots and shop Tyle large guilt bottles and
Small ones brass mortar and stone mortar   £7.10.0
an Iron furnace, 3 nest Drawers two Counters
Coppr. Still & Worm 3tin bodys ye Chirurgeon
signe and Surgeon's Instruments

Books   £0.10.0

Part of the inventory of John England, apothecary of Knutsford

Not all apothecaries were wealthy and successful.

William Tomlinson

William Tomlinson was an apothecary whose background is unknown but came to set up his own practise in Knutsford c.1677 until c.1690.

We have seen that marriages in the medical profession were often within their own circle, but whether Mr.Tudman gentleman of Toft had had any connection with medicine is not known. In 1667 Mistress Tudman his widow was living in Toft with her son Thomas, daughters Elizabeth and Martha and their servant. It was daughter Martha who became Tomlinson's bride.

Martha brought with her a very good dowry or marriage portion which in itself would have made it possible for Tomlinson to set up his own practice. Martha and her family had every right to have had high hopes that this would be a good marriage with expectations and prospects of a better than average lifestyle with a servant or two before long as soon as her husband became established in his career. In this case this was not to be.

After their marriage, William and Martha lived in Toft where their first son was baptised in 1677. Toft was then as now, a rural area with scattered houses and farms about a mile south of Knutsford. William had his 'shop' in Knutsford.

During the next six years as a professional man, Tomlinson's standing in the community seemed to increase and in March 1683 he was called out to give assistance and medical advice to an elderly man who had been seriously assaulted. The case was brought to court and his statement as a medical witness told of the condition in which he found this man and went on to give the prognosis that pleurisy was likely and his recovery was doubtful.

Their family had grown during this time and their fourth son Charles was born later that year in September 1683. When this baptism was recorded the child's father was named as Mr. William Tomlinson. He had been accorded the status of a gentleman but sadly, his behaviour was very far from gentlemanly.

Tomlinson had a very violent temper causing Martha to be what was, or became, what today we would call a battered wife. Whether there was a drink or drugs problem, (he certainly would have had access to both of these as all apothecaries had a still, which would have given him the means of making potent spirits), how long it had been going on can only be conjectured, but his behaviour seems to have deteriorated dramatically in quite a short space of time.

In October 1683 barely a month after Charles was baptised there was a noisy and unpleasant scene overheard by Martha's mother who tried to come to her daughter's rescue but was herself turned upon. Mistress Elizabeth Tudman said that she tried to intervene but was 'affrayed of her life or the hurting of her body'. The incident had been so serious it had been taken to

court, who ordered Tomlinson to find sufficient sureties to keep the peace
and to appear again at the next Sessions.

Within two months things went from bad to worse, the situation
deteriorated appallingly and Martha and her children were turned out of
the house. In the last days of the year she made a petition to the court for
'surety of the peace' against her husband, and also for maintenance. These
were her desperate words:

Your petitioner's husband enjoys by her two parts of three of a tenement in Toft,
and he has by her four small children, (they were ages 6, 4, 2 and 3 months at
this time), and that he hath very often beaten and abused her whereby she hath
been necessitate for fear of her life to pray he might give security for the peace
and that upon hopes that he would live peaceably with her she permitted him to
be discharged at the last Sessions. Since then he hath so beaten and abused her
that she is now afrayed he will kill her. He hath taken away from her all the said
two parts of the tenement now worth £16 p.a. and hath sold and taken from her
all the cattle and household goods and not left a bed for her or her children to
lye on. When she brought her children to him for some relief he would afford
them none, but in the late great frost and cold caused the fire where the children
were to be slacked out whereby they were necessitated through extreme cold to
seek relief elsewhere. Your petitioner hath nothing to relieve them withall but
what out of pity and charity is afforded by others' ....

It is no surprise that their neighbours, Martha's mother and her brother
had also become involved for he, Thomas Tudman of Toft, gent., petitioned
for surety of peace against him, also afraid for his life.

The Overseers of the Poor also put in a plea:

'It is found that the children of William Tomlinson of Nether Knutsford,
Apothecary, are likely to become burdensome to the parish of Knutsford ... the
said William Tomlinson neglecting to make provision for them notwithstanding
his ability to do so, he being possessed of an estate of the clear yearly revenue
of £10 or upwards'-.

Tomlinson was ordered to pay his wife a yearly sum of £5 quarterly and
this he may have done for about 18 months. Martha and the boys must
have found refuge somewhere and all was quiet as far as we know until two
years later when once again he attacked her and he was bound over for £40
to be of good behaviour. This was during the time of Knutsford's epidemic
and famine and there must have been difficulty in finding food for them all
during this period as for the whole neighbourhood. Her living conditions
may also have been poor, and in July 1688 Martha died. She could not have
been very old. Her death precipitated another crisis as all the boys then
needed looking after. The three older boys, aged 6, 8 and 10 were possibly
considered employable or at least useful, but Charles the youngest aged 4
was not. Their father was instructed to maintain all the children, and to
take care of and provide for Charles.

In October 1690 yet another Court order revealed that Tomlinson had failed to comply. The boys were probably boarded out and made to work for their food which was paid for, minimally, by the Overseers of the Poor. Tomlinson could not be made to pay and owing money for their upkeep, he was ordered to be arrested and committed to the Castle at Chester.

At the same time, one John Barlow of Castleton was appointed 'to maintain his children, (Tomlinson's) and to seize out of Tomlinson's estate either real or personal ... what was requisite for their maintenance.' Who was this ? Was he a relative or a complete stranger hoping to do well out of this arrangement? Not long after this however, there was an order for the removal of John Barlow, his wife and 3 children, (three of the Tomlinson boys?), 'lately come to reside in the Township of Ollerton with a rent of £10, to be removed to the parish of Great Budworth'. It does not sound to have been a very secure home for the boys.

Tomlinson did not languish very long in Chester gaol. By the middle of June 1692 only 18 months after his committal, he had already been at large for quite some time and was being sought throughout the County for trouble of a different kind. He was apprehended and questioned about it at Peover, by Sir John Mainwaring.

Tomlinson after losing his home in Toft, seized to pay for the maintenance of the children, was lodging then with John and Alice Leicester in Nether Knutsford in their ale house. Tomlinson said that he was then about 42 years old, and 'confessed' to the following events: On Thursday afternoon of the previous week, Margaret Hughes of Broken Cross, Macclesfield widow, came to the house where he was lodging, carrying with her a young female bastard child about a week old and said it was born of her daughter, Ann Hughes at a house on the side of Stockport Moor. Tomlinson was charged with being the father of the child but he denied it. He then asked Alice Leicester, (with whom he was lodging), to take the child and go with him. They 'carried it the next day to Handford Bridge and lay there all night, then took it on Saturday to Chester and returned back with it that night to Tarporley and there left it in a basket by the side of an outbuilding about 11 of the clock in the night.' (It was June).

Alice Leicester said the child was brought into her husband's ale house by Margaret Hughes at Mr. Tomlinson's request and that she, Alice, had gone with him to Chester and to Tarporley and was with him when he left the child but when he went out from Knutsford he had said that he would go with her into Lancashire to set the child out to be nursed, 'for he must take care of it being it was laid on him, though he was not the father of it'. She said that 3 weeks or a month before Ann Hughes was delivered of the child, Hughes had come to the Leicester's house and enquired for Mr. Tomlinson and declared that he was the father of the child.

At the next Quarter Sessions in Nantwich, the above statements were read following the finding of 'a young female bastard child of about a fortnight old

– exposed and left in the road and common street in the town of Tarporley' the Court having instructed 'all constables, headboroughs, Bailiffs and their Majesties' officers in the County of Chester to seek out William Tomlinson Apothecary of Knutsford, reputed father of this child to go before a J.P. and be examined ...'.

The Leicesters may have begun to regret taking in Mr.Tomlinson as a lodger. John Leicester was charged with laying Tomlinson's bastard child in Tarporley.

The Chester Sessions do not record the outcome of this sorry saga. Tomlinson did manage to keep out of the courts after this but did not die in Knutsford so there is much that will never be known.. It is certain though, that Knutsford gossips would have had plenty to talk about, not to mention the scandal of having to pay more poor rate in order to support a gentleman's family.

References:
- *14th century Dr.: JRL. Mainwaring Manuscripts, Hand List, No. 23. Knutsford lease by Wm. De Huchtrinton, physician in 1342.*
- *Books of recipes etc., and William Blundell's daughter at the doctor's: 'Cavalier', Letters of William Blundell to his friends 1620-1698, ed. Margaret BLUNDELL. Longmans Green & Co. 1933. Ps 56-59 and 268.*
- *'A Study of the English Apothecary from 1660-1760'. Medical History No.3 1983, Juanita G.L.BURNBY. London, Wellcome Inst. For the History of Medicine.*
- *The Diary of Richard Kay 1716-51 of Baldingstone near Bury. Remains of Hist .and Lit. of Lancaster and Chester Vol.XVI 3rd series printed for Chetham Soc. 1968 Man. Univ. Press.*
- *Diary of Sir Thomas Mainwaring, CRO as before.*
- *Inv. of William Smith, CRO WS 1701. Apprentice indenture, CRO DDX 52/1.*
- *Parish registers, Poll Tax as before.*
- *William Smith grave inscription, Manc'r Local History Library, Owen Mss. Vols. 13-17. No. 7*
- *Diary of Adam Martindale, as before.*
- *Peter Swinton's funeral a/cs. CRO and Sir Peter Leycester's a/cs. CRO.as before.*
- *Nether Knutsford Court Leet a/cs. and Hearth Tax returns as before.*
- *Inventories of William and Thomas Delves, Robert Thornley, William Thornley, Joseph Hough, and John England all CRO WS*
- *William Tomlinson, from Quarter Sessions, CRO QJF and QJB/3.*
- *Clergy Call Books, (Visitation), CRO EDV/2/7-12.*

Knutsford's Medical Men c.1660 - 1720

		(Clergy Call Book dates)
Physician/Surgeon	William Smith d.1701	1674, 1677,1686
	John Delves d.1703	
	John Skelhorne	1709, 1712
	Thomas Kingston	1712, 1716
	Andreas Lowe	1712
	Robert Penny	1716
Apothecary	William Delves d.1675	
	William Tomlinson, practising 1680's.	
Apothecary/Surgeon	Thomas Delves d.1686	
	Joseph Hough d.1699	
	William Thornley d.1710	
	John England d.1711	
	Richard Green	1701, 1712. 1716
Surgeon/Barber	Robert Thornley d.1695	1669, 1671, 1674, 1677
	Nathan Cowpe d.1698	

Some Knutsford Midwives

Sibell Brookes 1665 (in Quarter Sessions)	
Elizabeth Antrobus d.1694(1677,'82,'83 in QS,)	1674, 1677
Francis Aldcroft (1678 in QS)	1676
Isobel Smith d. 1711 (1682, '96 &'97 in QS)	1674, 1677, 1686
Margery Hewitt (1690 in QS)	
Elizabeth Lovatt (1708 & '9 in QS)	1712, 1716
Elizabeth Lever (1709 in QS)	
Margaret Leadbeater (1719 in QS)	
Elizabeth Hatton	1712, 1716

Chapter Eight
Inns and Innkeepers

Traditionally Knutsford was a commercial, market, fair and court centre where accommodation, food and drink were required for a variety of people in a variety of ways.

In the 1640's, Knutsford had the most licensees in all the nine main places in Bucklow Hundred. Lymm had 10 or 11 licensed inn or alehouse-keepers, Altrincham had 12 or 13, Mobberley, Rostherne, Over Tabley and Over Knutsford had just a few each while Knutsford had as many as 39. Out of a population of around 1,000 or less in Knutsford as many as one household in six were running a variety of establishments ranging from good comfortable inns with rooms for visitors and serving French wine, down to rough and dirty alehouses or just a cottage where a jug of ale could be bought. Around a third of licensees in Knutsford were widows. By 1753 there were 21 alehouses in Altrincham and 28 in Knutsford. To keep an alehouse a license was required from Quarter Sessions, granted by JP's and needing two sureties each willing to provide about £10.

Three innkeepers were named for Knutsford in 1639, John Millington, Alice Bentley and John Yarwood, the rest were alehousekeepers. Wine imported from France through Chester or Frodsham was obtainable in large quantities, John Aldcroft of Knutsford was called vintner in 1641. In 1624 the Churchwardens of Wilmslow Parish Church came here to buy 30 quarts of wine at 8d. the quart for their communion services. After Peter Swinton's funeral 20 more gallons of ale were bought in at short notice when the original provisions had been consumed. Obviously Knutsford was catering for people in the neighbourhood, visitors, travellers as well as local inhabitants.

The many dissenters here did not refrain from going to alehouses. Roger Lowe of Ashton in Makerfield (not 30 miles from Knutsford), kept a diary between 1663-1674, was a staunch dissenter but was in an alehouse nearly every day in the neighbourhood including Sundays but as he was living on his own he enjoyed the company, often eating and drinking there with friends. He was an apprentice mercer who often took 'a morning draught' and said that 'I could not trade at times if I did not spend 2d' on ale to potential customers, spending this much daily and up to 3 shillings in company. Clergymen went there often, even after services. They were social meeting places for all, men and women.

The only safe drink was beer of various strengths as water was unsafe and milk was mainly for children. Bread and beer were the very staples of life and children drank small (weak) beer. Ale and beer was consumed in such daily quantities that it was made at home by all who could do so, becoming a livelihood for any who could make enough to sell, a recognised way for a

widow to make an honest living or women to supplement the family income.
Many continued to run their late husband's inn or alehouse often with great
success as we shall see.

Malt Street, site of Knutsford's Malt Kiln

Malted barley was the staple ingredient of ale and Knutsford's malt kiln
was kept busy. One of the maltsters was Thomas Venables who died in
January 1704/5. Among the contents of his kiln were:

one Measure one half measure & peck		5s.10d	
one pikell	5d.	one wiskett	6d.
one old hammer	1d	one hayre cloth	5s
one Tryall (trowel?)	6s.	1 Rake	2d
The Killne grate	2s	4 malt shovels	2s 8d
24 Ribs	18d	Coles Kennill & Turfe	8s

He had 'mault and beanes' valued together at £14 13s 4d, was living in
three rooms and his wearing apparell was worth £2 19s 2d.

The standard of ale and beer was subject to the scrutiny of the Aletasters
appointed by the Manor Court who when approved, hung evergreen by the
door as a sign of good ale. If the standard fell, if they sold short measure,
kept a disorderly house or kept a house without licence the Aletasters and
the constables had the ability to present offenders to JP's. No cases of this
sort appear in Knutsford nor even in the Manor court during the later part

of the 17th century but in 1634 Henry Morton, constable, presented John Hindley at Quarter Sessions in that he

hath set up alehousekeeping without licence as we verily thinke, howsoever so it is that he keepes from time to time much disorder in his house and many of ill condition do frequent his house at unseasonable hours. May it please you to take it into consideration and to deal with him according as the law requires in that case

This alehouse was ordered to be suppressed and 'if he afterwards offends that he shall pay 20s. or be whipped according to law'.

Drunkenness related arguments and fights came to the Quarter Sessions regularly and alcoholism was a problem everywhere. 'Wasting and consuming their means' was the downfall which caused the death of many and could have been the cause of the problems of Peter Antrobus, John Highfield Junior and William Tomlinson and almost certainly that of Rev. Benjamin Crosse. There are Knutsford examples of some who were found drunk on Sunday or even in Church.

The condition of the licenses in the 1640's was

such that whereas the above bounden (name) is admitted to keep a common Alehouse or Tipling house in the place where he now dwelleth and not elsewhere, it is therefore to the said (...) doe not permitt and suffer any misrule or disorder in his said house nor kill nor suffer to be killed, dressed or eaten in his house any flesh upon the several daies prohibited by his Majesty's proclamation; he shall keepe the assize of bread and ale and sell such as shall be wholesome for mens bodies; he shall not permit and suffer any unlawful gameing in his house nor harbour any rogues or vagabonds in his house to the (nuisance?) of the neighbourhood; nor suffer mens sons or servants to sitt drinkinge ... above the space of one hour whereby to waste and consume their means .... And likewise that the said ... shall doe and performe all things accordinge to the said statute in that case dureing the time he continue bound...

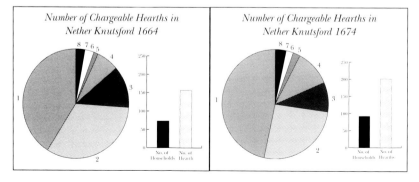

Fig 8. Charts showing the size of houses by the numbers of chargeable hearths in Nether Knutsford in 1664 and 1674

The conditions were changed from time to time, later on alehousekeepers were not to

'permit or suffer or have any playing at dice, cards, tables quoits, loggets, bowls or any other unlawful games in his house, yard, garden or backside; nor to suffer or remain in his house any person or persons not being his ordinary household servant, upon any sabbath day or holy day during the time of divine service or sermon'.

There were also strict instructions about vagrants and the criminal element. There was to be no buying or pawning stolen goods and especially, no one was to drink after nine of the clock in the night time.

From the inventories of the Knutsford inns it is evident that some rooms were given names which could be portrayed by a picture on the door easily recognisable by those who could not read.

Between 1671 and 1674, Nether Knutsford had twenty three inns or alehouses and Over Knutsford had five. In Nether Knutsford, the three largest inns had 8 hearths, three more had 6 hearths, three had 3 hearths, seven had 2 hearths and seven more had 1 hearth. These were licensed by fourteen men and nine women. In Over Knutsford, one alehouse had 2 hearths and the rest had just 1 hearth, the licensees there being four men and one woman.

Between the 17th century and today many inns have come and gone in Knutsford and many names have changed. As inns and alehouses were often referred to in conversation as 'such a person's' house, it is only in occasional documents that an inn was named. In 1664 and 1674 the three inns in Knutsford which each had 8 hearths, were its largest buildings. One was The George, one The Cock and the other the inn owned by the

The George Hotel passageway from King Street

Pollards, father and then son. This may have been The Rose and Crown or The Swan, for that was large by 1720 but may have grown to that size in intervening years.

The George was run by John Aldcroft from 1640 and the following year his license called him Vintner. When he died a raised tombstone which used to be in St. Helena's churchyard bore the inscription: 'Here lyeth the body of John Aldcroft of Nether Knutsford, Vintner who died 13 Oct 1663 aged 56'. He saw much activity and comings and goings during the Civil War. Military leaders, meetings at his inn and around his fire were provided with plenty of food, sack and French wine to cheer them. All of the Knutsford hostelries must have enjoyed the custom of the troops stationed on the heath at times during this war. The George conjures images of the fire and candle light reflecting from the brass, plate and silver. A respected well known figure, he was certainly very well dressed in his £10 worth of apparel, fittingly attired to be host to gentry and all other important customers from throughout the county and on Court days.

On his death his widow Mary took over and continued there for many years, probably until her death in 1689. In 1667 she lived at The George with her three servants and daughter Jane who was the only one of their children still at home. A few years after Mary's death The George Inn was sold. The deeds of sale in 1694 of The George Inn, was with 'the shop, 2 barns, the gardens, signs and signe posts, the pavilions and wainscots, lands etc, in consideration of £211 2s.'

The George was next known in 1697 to be in the hands of Henry Warburton when the second Interrogatory of the Church by the Consistory

The Georgian Assembly Rooms at the Royal George

Court was held there. He was the third generation innkeeper at a smaller inn in Knutsford previously where Sir Thomas Mainwaring sometimes dined with his friends.

The George Inn was chosen by Quarter Sessions as the place to pay money for the new bridges in 1675 and it was the inn where John Aldcroft vintner managed the postal stage as Knutsford's postmaster during the Civil War and Commonwealth, Sir Peter Leycester often paying him 2d. to post a letter. It was called 'The George' long before the Hanoverians came to the throne so it could once have been The George and Dragon. It is likely that an inn has been on this site of old but the present building dates from the 18th century. It is a great loss to Knutsford that it has closed in 2002 having seen so much of Knutsford's history. The Georgian Assembly Rooms there became the venue of special social occasions for a very wide area until recent times.

Another of the three largest inns was **The Cock** which was run by Jeffrey Bentley in 1621 and after his death by his widow Alice who held the license until 1641. We then lose sight of it until 1669 when it was being run by Ellen Shaw. She was a hard working woman, complained of by the Common Moor Lookers in the Manor Court for forcibly breaking open the Common Moor gate to fetch and deliver cattle to the Cock meadow in 1676, 'to the great prejudice of a way both to the Church and Market'. Its location is unknown, but it was central for people paying their mize for the poor and for posting up the election results. Ellen Shaw ran a good plain inn with no frills, no window curtains as some had but she left it in a good state for her son.

It was Ellen's son Richard who had been apprenticed to Benjamin Hobson the feltmaker but after the unfortunate happenings there he went back home and helped his Mother. He learned the trade and took over after she died. He was Knutsford postmaster between 1698 and 1700. In 1686 he had married Judith Aldcroft possibly some relative of the above John and Mary, who when she was widowed in 1709, became the next proprietor of The Cock. How long she remained there is unclear but her husband and brothers-in-law John and Thomas Shaw kept the postmaster business in the family continuously between them from 1698 until 1720. She died in 1734.

We have no name for the inn run by the Pollards but it was large with 15 or 16 rooms. It may have been The Rose and Crown. Thomas (d.1687) had a good cellar of claret and white wine but his son Robert (d.1692) stocked ale, beer and cider although by then the war with France who were supporting the exiled King James's army in Ireland prevented French wine from coming into the country. Thomas also had a large amount of pewter and many cooking vessels, food, fuel and candles. There were virginals in the lower parlour upon which his daughter Sarah may have entertained customers as she inherited them. The wives of both father and son died before them. Thomas Pollard's inventory listed the clear profits of intacks for a term of seven years, valued at £10.

Another large inn, **The Swan** was receiving much custom. It may have been near to The George. In 1687 it was leased to Robert Holland, of the Swan, succeeding his father Thomas. Presumably he was innkeeper here for several more years. The Swan was leased by Sir Thomas Mainwaring who often dined there in the 1680's with his family and friends. After him John Bertles from the tanning family was innkeeper there for possibly twenty years before his death in 1720. When he died, this inn had 17 rooms, large, but the contents were not valued as highly as those of The George or of the Pollard's inn. Like several of the others, there was a jack and two spits in the House, a sign that cooking was being done for company. His wife Mary could sign her name but whether she carried on running the Swan as some widows did is not known.

One of the smaller inns was that run by Samuel Withers (Widder) whose agricultural holding was worth a quarter of his estate. Like many but not all of the inns they were able to supply some of the food as well as drink for their customers and hay for their horses. Some of the inns had no agricultural items at all which was a marked change from the centuries old land-dependant way of life. Margaret Withers was assessed for 4 hearths the year after her husband died but gave up the inn shortly after that and left Knutsford. Samuel had another 6 roomed house with a stable in Dasbury (Daresbury?) where she may have gone to live. Samuel Withers in 1663 is the only one among the alehouse keepers for whom an inventory survives, who had an hour glass with which to time the drinking as the license condition stipulated in the 1640's although this may no longer have been in force after the Restoration.

There is no doubt that there were some alehouses in Knutsford which were disreputable, but in Knutsford everyone knew everyone else and there was always someone quick and ready to inform on any irregular happenings. One Inn which saw the seamy side of life was **The Red Lion**, the landlords of which were the Royles, their fortunes fluctuated from Robert, his son George and then George's widow Elizabeth. The Red Lion stood next to the present White Lion which was itself one of Knutsford's new buildings in the 1690's. Robert Royle was literate and had land, was an overseer of the poor with Robert Thornley in 1668 and appeared as a member of the Manor Court from time to time until the mid 1670's. In 1667 his household consisted of his wife Alice, five children and a servant. He may have begun to develop a drink problem which gradually became worse during the last twenty years of his life which was evidenced by sales of his land, his more frequent court appearances during that time and was not helped by a certain drinking family of Hales who were mostly involved. Ann Hale had been an alehouse keeper in the 1640's and the two Hale brothers, John and George both whitelimers and sister Alice Hale were probably related. There was a love/hate relationship between the families. Robert on one occasion was fined for fornication with Alice Hale. There were drunken quarrels and fights between father and son and between brothers. The Royles took the Hales to Court accusing them of theft of a red serge petticoat and of threatening behaviour, and of attacking Robert Royle who was afraid one of them would do him bodily harm or kill him. In many court appearances they were constantly bound over to keep the peace or to be of good behaviour. Each was as bad as the other. Robert was accused of insulting behaviour and being in a drunken state. One time in an argument he called Mr. Legh of Booths 'a scabb' and another day made very rude comparison between Mr. Legh's estate and 'my Lord Bridgewater's fair place'. John Hale and friends in 1673 were presented by the Chapel wardens for 'prophaning the Lord's Day and abusing the chapel wardens'. Much of the profits if any of the Red Lion were either consumed in drink by the landlord, his son and his friends or went to pay the many court fines and fees. It is a wonder that they kept their license.

Son George was a butcher who inherited his father's inn and sadly his problem, as well as his friends and he carried on where his father had left off which was a poor prospect for the Red Lion. It was held together, one suspects, by George's strong minded second wife Elizabeth. When George died in 1704, the contents of the Red Lion (p.190) were valued at only about £11 excluding a bond owing to him and some debts. The furniture is nearly all stated in the chart, very little but tables, forms and the beds. The bond though, may have been Elizabeth's saving. When as a widow she took over as mistress of her own house she rolled up her sleeves and set about clearing the house of disreputable company and worked to enlarge the Red Lion as well as caring for at least some of her orphaned grandchildren or step-grandchildren. In just over ten years she had transformed the inn to twice its former size, had acquired land and was leasing two other houses

The White Lion built 1687 with the (new) eighteenth century Angel beyond

from John Egerton Esq., one of which may have been another alehouse. The chart shows how much the Inn had grown. She left 'my now dwelling house the Red Lion Inn' and most of its contents to cover her legacies to all her family, especially to her many grandchildren and her widowed daughter Mary Pimlott and to some of them she left property. Elizabeth Royle showed her money consciousness and practicality by not only setting aside the cost of her funeral but the proving of her will and for making an inventory of her goods and chattels when making her own will.

This will was complicated and she requested her 'truly loving friend John Swinton, gentleman' to aid and assist in its execution. John Swinton in the Red Lion! 10 years previously he would not have crossed the threshhold.

The proof of Elizabeth's clean sweep and again, her practicality is shown by the inclusion in her inventory uniquely among all the inns, of chamber pots, seven of them and a close stool.

The Royles and the Hales were by no means the only noisy revellers in Knutsford, who were a constant part of life. Peter Lowndes of Over Knutsford, yeoman and Edward Witter, yeoman, made frequent Court appearances in the early 18th century and countless others spent unrecorded spells in the stocks.

Another existing innkeeper's inventory of this period is that of John Hollingworth whose eight roomed inn contained 10 beds and 33 chairs. The name of his inn is another that is not known.

There was then the **Bowling Green Inn** which stood near to the old Bowling Green on Green Street, near to where the present block of retirement flats now stands. The green survived until the 1980's. It was in this inn in October 1717 that the Court Leet sat down to their 'court dinner', 28 men at a shilling a head, 5 men at 6d a head while the 'Baylefs' supped 2 shillings worth of ale. They repeated this enjoyable event the following May.

The White Lion has the date 1687 over a front window and its landlord soon after it was built was Thomas Birchenough who witnessed Samuel Leadbeater's outburst. **The Golden Lion** used to stand in the Market place in the 18th century which had its beginnings in 1690 when 2 cottages formed part of a Leadbeater/Swinton marriage settlement. In 1739 this was 3 cottages and a brewhouse and by the end of the century, certainly in 1803, it was the Golden Lion. This survived until the 1930's. The buildings of the present Cross Keys, White Bear, the Lord Eldon and the newly built Angel were all in Knutsford in the early 18th century as well as the inns mentioned above.

Jeffrey Aldcroft,
the Post Office and Knutsford Postmasters

Jeffrey Aldcroft was the eldest son of John Aldcroft, the vintner at the George. Before his father died in 1663, he was married and in his own business in a shop as a mercer. He enjoyed the prestige custom of both Sir

Peter Leycester and the Leghs of Norbury Booths. In 1662 John Gandy, a servant of the late Mr. John Legh (d.1660), had been given maintenance for Mistress Ann Legh a sister of young Peter Legh. They shopped several times at Jeffrey Aldcroft's and on one occasion bought materials to make her 'a Pinck collered sarsnett Gowne'

He would seem to have been making a success of his life but in the early 1660's he was already looking for sources of additional income and became involved with helping to gather Rostherne tithes for Ralph Urmston who in his turn was gathering them for a Mr. Wheeler in Chester. Jeffrey Aldcroft though, had a grudge against Ralph Urmston and went about 'devious and malicious ways' to cheat him which ended in a Consistory Court case and Jeffrey was sued for 'tithes of ecclesiastical rights and 20s. costs'. No doubt the fees of the court officials there were added to this and Jeffrey's father probably had to come to the rescue. This may not have been the first time he had got into debt and his father, exasperated and displeased at the trouble, worry and expense, added a clause in his will that Jeffrey was to pay his father's trustees 'the full sum of four score pounds at any time before the end of six months after the death of his (John's) wife Mary'.

June 29			
1662 pd. at the faire in Nether Knottesford for Holland and Cambrick & for pins for her	00	8	2
given then to her in money	0	1	0
pd then for seaven yeards and a halfe of flaxen cloath for smocks for her	0	12	8
pd for three yeards of Allamode for her	0	15	9
pd for a hood for her	0	3	9
July 14 pd to Mr Jeffery Aldcroft for			
1662 five yeards and a halfe of stuff for her as appeares by his note	00	12	10
August pd for Canvas, Bone, Buckram			
1662 ffustian, Callico, silke, Threed and other things to make upp her Pinck collered sarsnett Gowne and for makinge it, as appears by (her) a Bill of the first of August 1662	1	4	6
pd for a wastcoate, 16s. for a paire of Bodies 6s. for a greene Apron and strings 3s. 9d. for a Lase and a Ribon 1s 6d. for mendinge her shooes 0s 10d. for Lase and silke 0s 9d. as appeares by a note of her owne wryteing	1	8	10
pd for dressing a petticoate for her	00	0	6
pd for a lase for her wastcoate	00	1	4

Extracts from the accounts of John Gandy for Mistress Ann Legh of Booths Items bought at Knutsford Fair and from Jeffrey Aldcroft

After his father died, still anxious to earn extra money, he took over his father's job as Postmaster for Knutsford and when the opportunity arose, Postmaster for Manchester as well. Initially he made a success of this earning the praise of the (Deputy?) Postmaster General in London, who said that Aldcroft, 'though living ten miles off has managed it, (the Manchester post) ... very well and with several hours less delay than before'. Jeffrey Aldcroft was nevertheless still financially suspect even in the year after his father died, the manor court requiring him to give security for all the money he had in his hands, of the Church, the school and the poor or to pay it in, which he still had not done in October the following year when he was threatened with a forfeit of 10 shillings.

The postal service had been in public operation since 1635 although there had been postmasters in Manchester from 1625 onwards, so the Aldcrofts were unlikely to have been the first postmasters in Knutsford which was a branch stage on the route from Stone to Manchester, on the main London to Holyhead postal route. A postmaster's duties included keeping at least four good horses or mares and three good strong leather bags lined with baize or cotton. When the buckled and sealed mail bag arrived at the stage, the postmaster took out the bag labelled for that town, sealed the bag again and sent it forward. Post horses were supposed to run at seven miles an hour from 1st April to 30th September and five miles an hour for the rest of the year and could be ridden hard because there was a change of horse waiting at the next stage. Mail was not to be 'staied at any stage above half a quarter of an hour at most' for change of horses. These speeds were rarely achieved due to the bad state of the roads which were quickly affected by bad weather and none too diligent postmasters but their post boys who did the riding were to blow their horns three times a mile or whenever they met anyone on the road. Horses could be hired by the public from postmasters and accompany the post boys to the next stage, (show them the way).

An inn was obviously a convenient place for a postmaster to base his operations, having stabling for the horses. Jeffrey, mercer, was not living at The George, he had no innkeeper's license and it is believed he used the stables of The Rose and Crown, so either lived near to or opposite to that inn. In

ROSE & CROWN   1697   GABLE END

W. R. STRACHAN

1667 he was listed as Agent to the Post Office and earning £4 a year from it, living with his wife Elizabeth, five children and a servant. This was not a great salary and many postmasters at the time complained about their poor pay. Jeffrey soon began to fall behind with his payments to the Post Agents in the neighbouring stages of Stone and Warrington. He became involved in more 'misfortune' and such 'troubles' that he was imprisoned in Chester. From 1672 he was constantly writing to and receiving patient letters from Col. Whitley, Deputy PMG in London. Soon it was Jeffrey's son John who was writing and receiving the letters in Knutsford while trying to keep his father's business going and the post running from stage to stage. Being in prison did not curb Jeffrey's audacity, he wrote from Chester to Col. Whitley to ask for a rise in his salary. When he eventually returned to Knutsford he had not been back long before ill reports about him reached London where he was 'much complayned of, opening letters, detayning them, exactions and many other misdemeanors'. He was dealing with the post and the complaints of Sir Peter Stanley of Alderley in 1676. Colonel Whitley considered replacing him and put forward Henry Warburton's name as a possible successor but in the event that did not prove to be necessary, although he was still very much in debt the next year when Col. Whitley left the Post Office. Jeffrey somehow managed not only to keep his position but to increase his salary four fold before he died in 1689. The postal service was expanding by then and more bags were being collected and delivered to and from the surrounding area during this time. He died three weeks before his mother so he never had to pay the £80 which his father had demanded. The George had to be sold, his father's will being brought to mind by John Aldcroft's old friend William Highfield, then in his 80's, the only surviving trustee of four named in the will who joined with Jeffrey's son John to draw up the sale.

His son John was described as 'Knutsford innholder' in 1682 when he was present at Mere when the Duke of Monmouth came. Alehouse licenses do not exist for every year and there is a long gap at about this time. He may have been helping his grandmother at The George.

Henry Antrobus(4), mercer, not an innkeeper, took over as Postmaster for Knutsford for some years after Aldcroft's death, until 1696. During this time he received and had delivered letters to the Leycester household from Rome, Rotterdam and Venice which had taken about a year to arrive. Just before the turn of the century several tea boxes were delivered in the post to Tabley Hall, a rare luxury for a few.

Being postmaster was not a full time job but its pay which was then £16 pa. was good useful income for the work involved. From 1657 letters were charged at 2d. for not above 20 miles, 4d. for not above 80 miles, etc, and the 2d. post increased to 3d. in 1711 until 1765. These were for single sheets weighing not more than one ounce and more proportionately. A penny post was introduced for London in 1689.

The Old Rose & Crown - Cheshire Image Bank

References:

- *Hearth Tax returns, Wills and inventories etc as before. Alehousekeepers lists in QJF, all in CRO. as before. Alesellers Recognisances, Nether Knutsford, 1639 QDL/2/2/1-3, 1640-1 QDL/2/2/4-7, CRO. Henry Moreton suppression of Alehouse, 1634, Rec. Soc. of Lancs. And Ches. Vol. 94.*
- *John Gandy's accounts: CRO John Legh of Norbury Booths, WC 1663. George Inn sale, 1694, Leigh of High Leigh papers, CRO. The Red Lyon: CRO 1704 EDC No.11-16 and QJF items.*
- *Re Manchester postmaster, 1666-7, Manc'r Central Library, Calendar of State Papers Domestic, p 576. Re The Rose and Crown: information from the late Douglas Markwick.*
- *Post Office records: Col. Roger Whitley was Deputy Postmaster General under Lord Arlington from 1672-1677. He was a friend of Sir Thomas Mainwaring and often visited him at Peover. his letters becoming known as The Peover Papers held in The Post Office, St. Mary Le Grand, London. Col. Whitley's daughter Elizabeth married John, son of Sir Thos. Mainwaring in 1696. JRL Mainwaring manuscripts 5/ No. 19. ROBINSON Howard, Britain's Post Office OUP 1953*
- *JRL Mainwaring manuscripts, 5 Papers No. 19.*

Inventories of Nether Knutsford Innkeepers 1660 - 1720

Names & Dates	Fire places	no. of Rms	Names of Rooms (h) = hearth	no. of Beds	Some of the Contents	Agricultural Items	Total Value
Samuel Withers → (Widder) Feb.1663 (Margaret Withers d.1694)	None in inv. 4 in '64	8	Serpents chamber - 1 bed Star chamber - 1 bed little parlour - 1 bed street parlour the house chamber over shop 3/4beds back chamber sellar - cradle	6 beds 1 cradle	cheese £2.14s fuel 5s. drinking glasses and bottles 2s. pewter £3 5s.6d 4 barrels 6s 8d a case of knives £1. 1s. 9 flaxen sheets £2 8prs. of round sheets 6 chairs, 6 stools, 1 form, (0 tables) looking glass hower glass 2 bibles 1 other book carpet of Citerminster on bed in Star chamber Apparel,saddle,bridle &Armes £3 6s	4 kine & 2 calves £15 2 swine 8 sheep corn £2 10s hay £5 cheese press winnow sheet 7 lbs. flax 5s10d Total : c.£28 4s 4d.	£82.5s
THE GEORGE INN John Aldcroft c.1639 - Oct. 1663 → (Mary Aldcroft 1663 - 1689) grandson John sold The George, Oct.1694	4 in inv. 8 in '64, '73 &'74	16	Street parlour house (h) back parlour (h; - 1 bed new parlour kitchen (h) kitchen chamber - 2 beds new chamber - 2 beds little buttery Green Chamber - 2 beds Red Chamber - 2 beds Blue Chamber (h) - 1 bed chamber over shop (shop?) old brewhouse chamber brewhouse ostlers chamber - 1 bed maids chamber - 2 beds little clossett	13 beds	sacke and French wine £28 beer and ale £4 16s beefe, veale & mutton £4 coal and kennel £3 wood & turf £3 pewter £15. pott & panne brass £4 10s Jack, crowes, dripping pans mortar and pestill plate & silver £15 a case of knives linen £15 26 chairs 24 stools 12 forms 15 tables 18 pictures 1 bible Apparel £10	1 horse, kine, swine and sheep £13 hay £4 carts and other utensil for husbandry £4 for mucke £1 10s Total : £22 10s	£182 3s 10d

Name / Date	inv.	No.	Rooms	beds	Goods	Livestock / Other	Total
Thomas Pollard Senior January 1687/8	4 in inv. 7 in ·73 8 in ·74	16	the Three Tuns - 3 beds; the Sun (h) - 1 bed; the Kings Head - 1bed; Rose and Crown - 4 beds; Redd Lyon - 2 beds; the lower parlour (h) - 1 bed; the Starr; the Bluebell; the Rose - 2 beds; the Wheatesheafe - 1 bed; the Anchor; the Maremaid; the House (h); the kitchen (h); kitchen chamber; sellar; the garner	15 beds	20 gallons of clarret £2 13s; 35 gallons of white wine £2 6s 8d; one hundred 3 qrs &7 pd.of cheese at 20d £1 16s; Beefe, porke and bacon £1 16s; Coals, cannell, wood and turves £2 2s; drinking glasses a brass kettle; 2 iron dripping panns & 4 spitts; 249lb pewter @ $7\frac{1}{2}$ d. £9 7s; A case of knives linen £4 13s; 11 chairs, 26 stools, 3 forms, 11 tables; brewing pan £5 10s cowpery ware £5; 2 doz. glass bottles a salamander; smoothing iron & heaters; 1 pr. virginals £4 9 candlesticks; pictures, window curtains; 2 lanthornes Apparel £2	Two old cows £5; 3 young swine (in the cellar) £1.7s.; In the garner: Rye, oats & barley threshed & unthreshed £4. Hay £3; Sacks & winnow sheets; Horse halter & horse comb etc; Corn shovel, measures, sieves. Cheese press. Total c.£18 2s.	£169 7s.
Robert Pollard (his son) July 1692	5 in inv. 8	15	the house (h); the maremaid; the higher parlour(h) - 1 bed; the Kings Head (h) - 1 bed; the three tuns - 2 beds; the lower parlour(h) - 2 beds; the Rose and Crown - 3 beds; the Redd Lyon - 2 beds; the kitchen chamber; Rose chamber - 3 beds; the Wheatsheaf -1 bed 1cradle; the Starr; the Blewbell; the kitchen (h); sellar	15 beds 1 cradle	Ale & beer £5; 5 doz. & a half bottles of syder £2 15s; fuel £3 linen £10 8s.; much pewter c. £9 10s; much pot and pan brass c.£3; Jack & cord & pulling spits £1 6s 8d; 15+oz. spoons &silver £3 9s 3d; 15 chairs 23 stools 6 forms 20 tables; brewing pan £5 10s 1 boyler; 10 barrels a cheese press; glass bottles cowpery ware; clock and case £1.10s salt chest; window curtains; many pictures & a map; 2 looking glasses & a warming pan; a musket & 3 pistols 15s.; Apparel £1	26 sheep £3 8s; 6 young swine £3; a barren cow £2 13s 4; old hay 10s; hay grass £3; a land of peas 15s.; Total £13 6s 4d	£154 1s 10d desperate debts c.£20

			Rooms	Beds	Inventory	Livestock / Agricultural	Total
THE SWAN (Thomas Holland, then son Robert Holland 1687 "innkeeper of THE SWAN") John Bertles (b.1668 -d.1720)	6 in inv.	17	Lower parlour (h) - 2 beds street parlour (h) Mr.Wallbanks room (h)-1 bed the closet - 1 bed the Starr Room over the cellar - 1 bed Red Lyon chamber - 2 beds Street chamber (h) - 1 bed brewhouse chamber- 1 bed 1cradle room over the house - 1 bed brewhouse (h) granary House (h) cellar Dark buttery Mermaid Drink House Granary	10 beds 1 cradle	pewter £5 linen £8 22 chairs 17stools 6 forms 12 tables large brewing pan & furnace bottom £5 a brass boiler 3s.4d brewing vessels £1 1s 6d barrels & firkins £5 5s kettles glass bottles £1 2s 6d earthenware & glasses 2 dripping pans with Frame a frying pan A Jack & 2 spits ale & wine measures of pewter £1 4s a pendulum clock 12 Roman Empresses in cuts a map of England looking glasses some window curtains	2 pigs (in the cellar) poultry ? malt in the granary £7 4s oats £1 4s Total c.£10	£87 13s 2d
THE COCK (Jeffrey Bentley1620's Alice Bentley - 1640) Ellen Shaw 1669-1683 (Richard Shaw 1683 - 1709) (Judith Shaw 1709 - 1734)	None in inv. 8 in '73 & '74	13	the grate parlour room by the parlour room over the hall - 1 bed room over the old stable1 bed room over the cellar - 1 bed room next - 1 bed Cocke chamber - 1 bed Cocke parlour - 1 bed parlour at cellar head - 1 bed old stable the sellar the kitchen the hall	7 beds	drink in the cellar 7s coals & kennel drink in the cowmpe £1 fuel 10s pewter @ 7d per lb.£4 18 7 a frying pan, a dripping pan, ladles kettles 14 prs. sheets, 28 napkins 5 tablecloths, 2 pillow beares 16 chairs, 12 stools, 2 forms, 3 tables cowmpes, eshens & turnells nine barrels £1 4s, smoothing iron warming pan, looking glass bellows Apparel £1	2 cows 1 calf 5 couples & 5 barren sheep 2 sows & 5 pigs hay £2 5s. oats 7s6d 2 acres of hay 11/4 acres barley a cart & wheels muck cart & wheels plow & 2 harrows wheelbarrow churn Total c.£24 16s 6d	£62 19s 8d

Name / dates		No.	Rooms	Beds	Inventory	Livestock / provisions	Totals
William Bostock d.May 1668	1 in inv. 4 in '64	13	Chamber over the shopp-1bed Morton's Chamber - 1 bed Parradice Chamber - 1 bed Chamber over the house-1bed Chamber over	8 beds	Ale and beere £1 Barrels, cowmpes & all cowperie ware Cheese, beefe, bacon & other provision £1 A beefe tub	1 cowe £3 1 sowe and piggs £1 10s. 4 hennes 1s4d corne 5s. 2 ladders 2s	£275 4s 6d
Sarah Bostock	4 in '73 & '74		the parlour - 3beds Chamber over the Buttery - 1bed Chamber over the Kitchen The Parlour (h) Two out Iles The House (h) Buttery Kitchen (shop)		Turves, coal, kennel, wood & all fewels £1 1 Brewing pann of brass etc pewter dishes, flaggons, spoones, pottingers and all pewter £6 Muggs and earthenware Linen and naperie wares £5 6 8d 12 tables, 10 chairs, 9 stools, 6 forms smoothing iron, back stone, 6 pictures Apparel £5 Ready money £4	Total c. £4 18s 4d	debts creddits & specialties £220 10s.
(Henry Warburton d.Aug.1679)	4 h in 74	10	Flower de luce chamber-1 bed Serpents chamber (h) - 2 beds Bulls Head - 1 bed Street parlour - 1 bed Lower room over sellar-1 bed	9 beds	(damaged inv.) coale, turves, wood an old Jack & five spitts sheets and napkins pewter 6 chairs, 7 stools, 2 tables	none	£117 15s
Ellin Warburton 1679 - 1687 (son Henry in '97 at the sign of The George)	92 in inv.		upper room over sellar -1 bed room over larder - 1 bed chamber over kitchen - 1 bed kitchen (h) the barn (the sellar?)		1 brewing pan & boyler £2 10s flagons & pots £3 smoothing iron much brass, pestles, 2 frying pans warming pan, looking glass, kettle kitterminster table cloth Apparell £3		bond £26
John Hollingworth 1715	4	8	House (h) Little parlour (h) Old parlour. Hall (h) Street parlour (h) Room over Room over hall, Street room	10 beds (rooms not stated)	1 brewing pan & boyler £1 10s barrels 1 Jack, 1 grate & spit & other Iron more £1 15s 33 chairs, 4 forms, 9 tables 1 clock, looking glass	none	£37 13s 2d

			Rooms	beds	Contents	Stock	Total
THE RED LION (Robert Royle d.1687) son George Royle 1704 ?	4 in '64, '73 &'74 2 in inv.	7	Half Moon Chamber Red Lion Chamber - 2 beds Street Parlour House (h) Nags Head Bulls Head kitchen (h)	2 beds	7 forms, 7 tables a screen 1 standing bed, 1 truckle bed boxes 3 and a half yds. of new cloth ready money Apparel £1 10s	1 little horse £1 12 sheep £1 16s Total £2 16s	£35 4s 1d (including bond £20 owing to him and other debts to him £2 15s.)
THE RED LION Elizabeth Royle 1715	2 in inv.	14	the Red Lion House (h) The passage The Buttery the Kitchen (h) the brewhouse the cellar Red Lion Chamber - 2 beds the Green Dragon - 1 bed the Kings Head the Bluebell - 1 bed the New Room - 2 beds the children's Room - 3 beds the Bulls Head the Nags head	9 beds	coals and kennel 10s. 3 dripping pans & three skillets 2 frying pans stock in the cellar £7 12 barrels £2 10s Brewing looms, barrels and brewing pan 10 prs sheets 3 dozen napkins 6 table cloths looking glass pictures 1 copper chamber pot 6 pewter chamber pots 1 close stool and pan warming pan	1 horse 2 cows 2 sows and 8 pigs 2 acres of hay £6 11/4 acres barley £6 cart and wheels a plow and 2 harrows £1 5s a wheelbarrow cheese press, churn, basins	£110 4s 7d including some contents of 2 other houses and (not valued), land worth £32, & 2 houses leased

round sheets = made of thick thread, possibly hemp.   (Samuel Withers' inventory 1663)

Chapter Nine
Work and Leisure

For many centuries Knutsford had been noted for its cloth, yarn and leather, which industries were running side by side.

The Cloth Industry

The cloth industry embraced wool, hemp, flax, in turn linen, and silk. The yarn market in the market hall was already of long standing and continued into the 18th century. Sixteen inventories note 'slippings' and bundles of various types of yarn. This was just before the industrial revolution which was soon to overwhelm and stop these cottage industries.

Of the 123 existing inventories of Knutsford people between 1660 and 1720, a third had in them items relating to the cloth trade, several sorts of spinning wheel, yarn bleached and unbleached, looms, and/or woollen and linen cloth. As only some of all the inventories survive, it is hard to tell what the true proportion of people was, who were involved with textiles. Dyeing was an old Knutsford occupation and there were sharmen here who finished woollen cloth by cropping the nap. There were some silk workers in Knutsford as in Macclesfield and Stockport, well before the main influx of Huguenot refugees to Spitalfields in 1685. Ralph Mourton in 1677, was a silk weaver living in a one hearth cottage with his wife and two daughters, an apprentice and a servant.

The cloth trade was organised by merchants, wholesale and retail, who called themselves by various names such as 'woollen draper' like Henry Burgess and Peter Antrobus and 'mercer' of whom there were many, e.g. John Leigh, Samuel Norbury, Hugh Bertles, Robert Gleave, Thomas Deane, Jeffrey Aldcroft, William Swinton and Henry Antrobus. These merchants organised the supply of raw materials to spinners and weavers and then passed the cloth to the dyers and finishers whose products were then sold by them in their shops. Some was sold in the markets and fairs or sent further afield to London. However, high quality goods were imported here for we know that luxury cloths, fine wool, silks and velvets had been stocked by Sibell Swinton in the 16th century and in the 17th and 18th centuries by Henry Burgess and Henry Antrobus.

Tradesmen and merchants in these times and before did not stick strictly to a trade description and invariably sold a variety of unrelated goods. The Elizabethan Sibell Swinton, glover, sold cloth and playing cards. A hundred years later, Thomas Deane one of the mercers, had £122 worth of 'cloth and stuffe' and £32 worth of grocery and was called grocer in 1672. William Swinton's inventory made no mention of cloth for sale although he had an estate of £1,271, some of which was inherited but it suggests trade, wholesaling and dealing to a considerable extent. Some cloth merchants called themselves yeomen or gentlemen. Richard Sandylands gentleman, had 14 yards of flax and cloth and 40 other yards of cloth (which is not a great deal compared with John Hewitt below), in his estate worth £515. Some of these had warehouses like Henry Burgess and Henry Antrobus and their wealth is proof of their success although there is no documentation of the organisation and extent of their trading in the area and further afield.

John Hewitt clothworker, was running a small 'factory', with spinning, weaving, (three looms), and dyeing all taking place on his premises. He had 47 bolts of cloth, about 650 yards of it, about half described as 'dyed', a linen loom and two other looms with reeds, coats, laths and a warp box, 60 pounds of wool, about 40 pounds of jarsey yarn, 28 pounds of woollen yarn, jarsey combs, 2 pen wheels and a long wheel and a dyeing pan of lead, corb and winch. His inventory amounted to more than £100. On a more domestic scale Thomas Hewitt, although having two linen looms and all materials belonging to them valued at £3, left an estate of only £16 16s 6d. John Norbury was another, with his woollen loom and all that belonged to it worth only 6s 8d. but £9 worth of agricultural items among his goods, altogether worth £29 7s 2d. Some weavers were notoriously poor.

Tailors were allied with the cloth industry, some again working on their own. Others were employed by a woollen draper or a mercer to make clothes for their customers. John Leigh tailor, had estate of £25 but nothing in his inventory to do with tailoring. He may have worked on his master's premises but his own apparel valued at £11 must have been a good advertisement for his skills. Randle Strongitharme who had 'goods in his shop' worth £2, could have worked for himself and travelled to customers on his 'little horse'. His apparel was worth only £2 but he had a wife and two sons to support. His debts came to £106 out of his estate of nearly £200. An impoverished tailor was Edward Owen whose entire estate including his working equipment was £3 16s 3d.

Flax and hemp was imported cheaply from Ireland to Manchester but was also grown in Knutsford and throughout Cheshire. When harvested it was soaked, 'retted' in pits to rot and soften the woody stems, (smelly), dried and then 'broken' with wooden mallets to separate the longer linen fibres and the shorter, courser, rougher tow. Some in Knutsford who had their own ovens were tempted to use these to dry their flax but the manor court stepped in to try to stop the practise: October 1661: 'Ordered ... that noe person within this manor of Knutsford shall hence forward put any hemp or flax in their ovens to be made ready for to breake upon paine of every offence forfeit 12d.' Hemp and tow were made into rope, string, bed cords, canvas and hessian for grain bags, sacks and such like, even for poor people's clothes and sheets, and sailcloth. Hempen as well as flaxen sheets were in use in Knutsford.

Sheep provided wool, meat and leather for many in this neighbourhood but were not kept in great numbers. William Ashton the elder of Over Knutsford butcher, had 115 sheep but in several small flocks kept by others. These helped to stock his butcher's shop and supply the Leycester family regularly with meat. Evidence of clothing work in his home were 2 spinning wheels, 19 lbs yarn and 4 more slippings, 30 lbs hemp, 2 yards of cloth and 7 yards of woollen cloth. John Lockett plasterer, in 1681 had 30 sheep and William Bertles the tanner in 1695 kept 26 sheep.

The inventories of two dyers in this period give detailed descriptions of their dyehouses. Robert Cowpe (died 1677) had numerous assorted vessels including leads, fatts, (vats), 5 casks and some troughs, '2 stone trowes', an iron kettle, great quantities of dye and 'all the stone flaggs and wins (winch) in and about the poole', 'a strong iron weigh beam and boards'. His dyes included

20 pound of logwood, (a good black dye),   5 score pound of copperass,
38 pounds of brasell,   10 pound of indigo, (blue),
brazilwood (imported for red/purple dye),   rustick
four pound of red wood (similar to the brazilwood),   allerin
37 pound of galls,   weediwis
Aleppo galls (from Syria),
200 and a half of the best sort of mather by the short hundred and 540 pound of the worser sort, (imported from the continent, a red dye obtained from the roots, all this madder worth more than £17)
50 pounds of pot ashes,
5 loads of coals and 3 loads of turves (for the heating processes) and some growing hemp.

He had a barn of two bays upon the heath, his books and apparel were worth £1, he kept a fowling gun and a musket, a good horse and saddles valued at £4 10s. He was following a long tradition of dyeing in Knutsford, Hugh Ankers who died in 1574 had also used copperas and galls.

Thomas Gandy, d.1698, lived in a house of similar size to Robert Cowpe's with seven rooms but no dyes were mentioned in his dyehouse or premises. He may have been retired.

In the Dyehouse of utensils thereto	
belonging 2 boyling leads 1 lead ffatt	£08:00:00
1 iron mortar a great tubbs, 1 old ark, 1 iron pott 1 iron bullet	00:13:00
1 lime tubb 3 winches 1 turne and stand belonging to the ffatt	00:08:00
... In the Firehole 1 old grate and cold rake	00:02:00
In coales	04:00:00
in turfe	01:00:00
in kennell	00:10:00
2 saddles 1 packett 1 pillion	00:08:06
1 hatt press Crowe, plancks & pay belonging to itt	02:10:00
40 yards of tentering	03:00:00
the deced.'s wearing apparrell	02:00:00

The valuation of the contents of his house and dyehouse was £39 13s, Robert Cowpe's was £82 12s 2d. Thomas Gandy had been working for well over thirty years because in 1667 his household consisted of his wife, two sons, an apprentice and two servants. Dyers continued in Knutsford throughout the 18th century.

There appears to have been no fulling in Knutsford as there was probably not enough water supply from the brook. This was the process whereby woven woollen cloth was treated, walked or pounded in stocks in urine or potash in a fulling mill to thicken it. This was often carried on near to a tenterfield. Thomas Gandy (above) used Knutsford's tenterfield for his 40 yards of tentering to stretch cloth full length and width on hooks on the frame so that it could dry evenly without shrinking. If raw wool was dyed prior to spinning this was spread and piled on a mesh base raised by wooden frames or trestles. The linen cloth workers having spun their flax into yarn, needed to spread it in rows on the grass to bleach and whiten for six months, woven cloth likewise. The dew (moisture was vital), hot sun and frost were the best whiteners and even moonshine was thought to be beneficial. On Knutsford's well drained field the present Parish Churchyard, on an east-west slope ideal for the purpose, rows were end-on to the prevailing wind to prevent tearing off the tenter hooks and facing south to catch the best of the sun.

In some tenterfields the hand loom weavers both wool and linen, went to lay out their prepared warps side by side prior to fixing to the loom. Cottagers' rooms were small and nearly filled by a loom, so the clean, clear open space of the field was welcome for arranging the long lengths, which when cut could be loosely twisted and tied in a hank for taking back and fixing to the loom. Knutsford had many weavers in its history so it is more than likely that the Tentry Croft was often used for this purpose.

Next to the Tentry Croft on King Street is a row of cottages still standing. Thomas Moreton, sharman, lived here until 1686, his father Raph having lived there before him and Thomas's son and grandson after him until 1741. All generations of the family were connected with the cloth industry.

During the 18th century the wool and linen cloth industry in Knutsford began to decline. Elizabeth Rowley in 1710 had 'yarn and linen cloth at the whiteners' which suggests possibly chemical means of bleaching by then. Some parts of the tentry croft were certainly lying unused because on the north corner a house had been built upon it belonging to John Bradshaw which was to be 'taken down and rebuilt as near as maybe to Henry Morton's' when the field was sold to build the Parish Church.

The industrial revolution in the cloth industry passed Knutsford by because of its lack of water power. The Silk Mill in Silk Mill Street was built c.1754 but was not successful. The mill was used for cotton before the end of the century for a short time.

The Leather Industry

The leather industry was represented in Knutsford from the cow to worked leather and finished products. Some of the main tanners were the Birtles family who have already been mentioned, as well as Samuel Antrobus and Isaac's son John. Isaac was a skinner. Another tanner was Philip Hewitt d.1703 who had the following goods:

five kipp skins	17s	eight veale skins	12s.
six veale skins	9s.	all the bark and other implements	£9s.
eleven Caffling skins	6s		
eight horse skins	£1 12s.		
foure cowe hides	£2 4s.		

John Rylance was another tanner of Over Knutsford where there were several tanyards.

The main customers of the tanners were the shoemakers or cordwainers of whom there were several at any one time in Knutsford. William Gibbon d.1685, had besides his lasts and working tools,

34 tanned hides	£22
kipps, bellies, Butts and hecks	£1 10s.
curried leather at	£1 6s.
Three pairs of men's shoes	8s.6d
Two pairs of women's shoes at	3s.4d.
Six pair of boys and girls shoes at	7s.0d

Another was Thomas Pollard who in 1686 had shoes, tooles, leather and other goods in his shop worth £37 14s 08d and John Aldcroft died that same epidemic year, in a smaller shop with leather 'curried and uncurried', and 'for boots and shoes and for lasts and his working tooles, £6'. There was also a glover and a sadler.

Curriers were leather dressers of whom there were several over this period. In 1667, William Daniel currier, lived with his wife, son, apprentice and servant in a house with two hearths in Crosstown, near to the leather market by the Cross.

It is remarkable that many of these tanners and shoemakers could write their names and regarded education as important.

Women's Work

Among the many tasks which fell to the women, one was to provide food for the winter months with cheese and salted or smoked meat, beef and pork. Some had a salting tub like Mary Antrobus, Isaac's wife who had two flitches of bacon from it. Apple mills and a cider press were in use in some homes in due season, but brewing and bread making were year-round tasks. Women's work in the fields was indispensable but left little documentary evidence in Knutsford. We just have the glimpse of Ellin Shaw driving her cattle.

Yarn making and spinning were also year-long skills as was the dairy work for those with several milk cows, separating cream, churning butter and making cheese. Thirteen inventories have items for cheese making and/or cheese included in them, but there were no full time farmers in Nether Knutsford. One third of Knutsford inventories had no agricultural items at all. Knutsford men were running their shops and trades while some of their women were attending to the cheese making. Mary Antrobus and her household were milking three cows and producing two hundredweight of cheese. Among equipment mentioned in inventories were cheese tubs, chesfords, cheese ladders and cheese presses. Randle Crowther the shoemaker's family, produced two and a half cwt. from two cows and the wife of Thomas Bertles the shoemaker, two cwt. of cheese from three milk cows.

In the more rural surrounding townships where more husbandmen, the farmers lived, Robert Pimlott of Bexton in 1708, had eleven and a half cwt. of cheese from his 13 cows, 6 heifers and 2 calves. Any surplus of cheese for home needs found a ready sale in the market and some grocers' shops. They may have found wider markets.

Women have always undertaken innumerable tasks. Many as we have seen, as widows became innkeepers and some became shopkeepers. Other women brought their produce, livestock and wares to sell at the market. In 1708 a 'Mug woman' was there with her 'crate' of pottery.

Other trades

Grocers and ironmongers sold a variety of goods. John Swinton's two apprentices of 1667, James Johnson and John Brooke set up their own shops in Knutsford. James Johnson (died 1679) had shop goods of more than £90 out of his total estate of £262. He was another of the four in Knutsford who had produced his own trade tokens one of which is in the British Museum dated 1668 which year was very shortly after he had started his own business. His wearing apparel, watch and tobacco box were worth £8, suggesting that he not only smoked tobacco but may have sold it like William Stout, ironmonger and grocer who was trading in Lancaster from the 1690's who said that tobacco was a fourth of what he sold in a year. Knutsford had a tobacconist, Daniel Gill in 1702 (at Peter Wood's house) and another in 1718.

James Johnson's widow Ruhumah, took over her husband's shop after he died and ran it for nine years with some success, her shop had goods worth £98 out of her estate of £260. Thomas Hough may have been another grocer, he had 11 cheeses worth 7s 6d and a cheese press and bills and bonds of £394 out of his estate of £506.

We have no details of the Knutsford grocers' stocks but in Stockport, John Hulme in 1660's, a mercer, sold sugar, almonds, comfits, candied ginger, treacle, honey, currants, raisins, prunes, cinnamon, licorice, brimstone and figs. Some of these may have encroached on the Stockport apothecaries' trade as a grocer there also sold 'drugges and apothecary stuffe'. A Knutsford chapman was selling these in 1666.

This was John Davison who boarded with Ellen Williamson in Over Knutsford. Chapmen were travelling salesmen dealing in a variety of goods. His goods for sale included new cloth, calve skins, books, 'druggs and phisicke stuffe', providing for those not able to travel easily or often into a town. He stocked brown paper bags and kept weights and scales for gold and silver, travelling widely in the neighbourhood and as far as London. He named 25 'Christian friends' and families in his will including John Hatton a smith in Petticoat Lane and Joan Burdd a widow in Spittlefields and nearer home, people in Bramhall, Ashley, Stockport, Mere, Pickmere, Tatton, Dunham Massey as well as in Nether and Over Knutsford. He bequeathed 10s. to poor widows in Knutsford and 20s. to poor people of Over Knutsford out of his estate which was mostly in money and debts owing to him of £230. Cheap print books and news sheets were printed in London and widely sought after from the chapmen or pedlars.

Robert Blacklocke was the chapman from Dumfries who kept up his strong links with Scotland and in Knutsford sold Scotch cloth and holland and other shop goods worth at the end of the century, £56. Sir Peter Leycester bought his shirts and other goods from 'the Scotchman' in August 1678, the Leghs of Norbury Booths were also earlier customers .

There were always a variety of craftsmen in Knutsford one of whom in 1674 was a joiner, Ephraim Broadhurst. He was in Knutsford for only a short time before he died, coming with his wife shortly before a daughter was born to them but soon to die, the cradle and a child's chair still in his house two years later. Broadhurst was in his fifties, at an age when most men were well established in their place of work. His workshop contained his lifetime's collection of tools listed by Peter Wood:

ffour instrum. ts for calculation ec	01: 00: 00
Twenty eight plaines for mouldinge	01: 00: 00
Ninteen of other moulding plains	00: 08: 00
Twenty long plaines for plains and smoothing	00: 10: 00
Three dozen and a halfe of cutting Tooles	00: 07: 06
Nine saws and two paires of Compasses	00: 10: 10
One Auger 6 bitts & a brase 3 gimletts 3 rasps 6 files	00: 03: 08
One paire of pincers 5 bench hooks 3 hold fasts	00: 05: 03
Two hatchetts one Hammer one glue pot	00: 03: 06
Two grinding stones fframe and Troughs	00: 08: 00
Six Benches one Lath & 2 vices 5 turning tooles	00: 17: 08
A pound of glue	00: 00: 06
eight Squares and 2 Rules	00: 03: 00
Three gadges	00: 00: 04
Two stone Chissells	00: 01: 00
In timber and worke unfinished	60: 00: 00

He did not stock nails. He may have been employing others. £4 worth of books may have contained patterns and designs or items from which customers could choose their requirements. He may have come to Knutsford after being engaged by Sir Peter Leycester to work on the interior fittings of his new Chapel, the panelling, the pews and the pulpit, working on a pattern from 'Brazen-Nose-College' Oxford where Sir Peter had been a student. The Chapel begun in June 1675, took three years to complete but Broadhurst died suddenly after two of them, before his work was finished. Although no more is known of Ephraim Broadhurst or his family his tombstone still lies in St. Helena's churchyard giving his age as 55 years. The Tabley Chapel when finished was not consecrated until a year after Sir Peter's death in 1678. It was in continuous use from its consecration until 1929 when severe subsidence caused the building to crack dangerously after which it was carefully removed to its present position near to the newer Tabley House. Some of Ephraim Broadhurst's work must still be evident inside it, as after it was moved only the roof was newly built.

Other Knutsford men had worked on the Tabley Chapel. Peter Wood had provided ironwork, John Worsley, plumber and glazier put in the windows and John Lockett, plasterer, had worked on the ceiling.

John Lockett's estate in 1681 was worth £23 4s, which included the term of 11 years for his dwelling house, £10, and his clothes worth £5 4s. He was a well dressed work or craftsman. John Lockett's family had been in Knutsford since earlier in the century, many of whom had been connected with the construction industry and some of whom were Quakers. Ralph Lockett lived in the first (or last) cottage at the north end of King Street on the east side in 1642, leased from the Earl of Bridgewater. It may have been his son Ralph who leased a property on the other side of the road at that end, from Henry Antrobus later in the century. Edward Lockett in 1665 was one of Knutsford's slaters and a mason.

An earlier plasterer had been Robert Brownfield who in 1662 had goods worth £30 18s. 8d, having a six roomed house with five beds, two ladders, agricultural items of £5 10s. including a cow and six swine and a bond of £14.

There were other craftsmen here in the building trade although evidence of them is scanty. Carpenters like John Holland worked here before 1666 left an estate of £41 9s, had a son John who was also a carpenter. John Shaw of Over Knutsford, was another carpenter with goods of £59 18s which included his four roomed cottage valued at £15.

The estimates for building the proposed Parish Church (1713) reveal Thomas Green another Knutsford plumber and glazier who worked not only for the Leycesters on their gutters and windows in the 1690's but for the Chapel wardens by mending the windows in St. Helena's Church and for '27lb of lead for fastening the stone for the Bull Ring' in 1709 for the Over Knutsford constables. These constables paid others at the same time for making the hole in the stone and fetching it from Booths and Sam Curbishley for the ring and iron in the stone, a major undertaking. The constables were usually more concerned with the repair of the pinfold, the townfield gate and the Shooting Butts and sending boys with urgent messages to neighbouring townships with a Hue and Cry.

They were responsible too for the upkeep of the means of punishment for miscreants, workmen of assorted skills were paid for 'a key, for screws, wedges and studs and plates for the head stocks' and 'for repairing the cookeing stool' on several occasions in the early part of the 18th century which suggests fairly frequent use. The town's musket and sword needed mending sometimes after rough treatment at the shooting butts. The Chapel wardens paid men for repairs to the Church,

Headstocks or pillory

mending the forms, cleaning the Church well, a rope for the 'lich gates', for pulling up nettles and clearing the church yard and found someone to sell or make them a dog whip. They were constantly replacing the leather and laces on the bell clappers for muffling.

The stocks outside Mobberley Church

Another vital group of craftsmen, were the metal workers. There were blacksmiths such as John Stubbs, estate of £53 10s 6d, William Walton, £70 18s 8d, John Allen, £111 15s 9d, John Baguley, £14 9s 6d and Peter Wood, ironworker and gunsmith, £63 16s 3d. Some like Benjamin Blease, nailer had goods of only £15 7s 9d with his bellows and smithy tools worth £2, his horse £1 15s, and wearing apparel 10s. His widow Ellen may have enjoyed the 15 pictures in their three bedded three roomed cottage. Samuel Ryle the cutler, was mending swords and rapiers, perhaps even making them. He had an even smaller estate of £12 17s 3d. Whitesmiths were mentioned occasionally but no details survive for any of them. They were tinsmiths who polished and finished metal goods but did not forge them. Ironmongers like the two Thomas Pooles, father and son, sold metal goods but did not make them. Thomas Poole the elder had provided nails (bought in ready made) for the Leycesters in 1680.

There is no record of any wheelwright or cooper in Knutsford

Two of the millers of Over Knutsford were Jeffrey Aldcroft in 1676 whose wife Frances was a midwife, and Samuel Beighton in 1683. John Foden was the mill wright that year.

A rarer occupation was that of Officer of Excise. From the middle of the seventeenth century there seems always to have been one living in Knutsford, usually a young married man whose babies were baptised at the church. Parliaments after the Civil War introduced duties at ports on imported goods mainly wine and tobacco and inland revenue duties on a great variety of articles and commodities which were sold and used in Knutsford. There were smaller duties on tin, iron, silver, glass, lead, soap, oils and salt with other items added at later dates like malt. In Queen Anne's time, candle making and leather were taxed. These duties were unpopular as might be expected as were the officers who had to collect them. The taxes were frequently changed and the officers often moved to a fresh post after only a few years as becoming too friendly with local people was not thought too advisable. They were required to take the oath of allegiance, affirm the thirty nine articles and to prove that they conformed to the Church of England, like William Hinde of Knutsford in 1680, who needed a certificate from the parson to say that he had received the sacrament of the Lord's Supper which in that year was given to him by Francis Mosely, Rector of Wilmslow when other Gagers of the Office of Excise from the area attended the Parish Church there for that purpose. The permanent presence of such an officer in Knutsford is evidence of the lively state of Knutsford trade.

Many of the workers named above needed to travel in order to buy or order goods, ready made or raw materials. These commodities had then to be either collected from ports or central warehouses or be carted to them. The state of the roads was of concern to them and to others whether on foot, horseback, coach, with a cart or wagon by carrier or carter or by packhorse train. People must have been greatly cheered by the improvement undertaken by the county to build cart bridges in 1675 over the many fords which had previously been the norm over all but the largest rivers in Cheshire. Quarter Sessions reports give graphic descriptions of the hazardous conditions which existed before the bridges were built and the daunting prospects which faced foot travellers. In October 1673...

The Grand Jury of the Quarter Sessions do think it very fitt and convenient that two cart bridges be made over the water called Boothes-Mill-Brooke lying between the townships of Mobberley and of Knutsford there being several great rodes through the water leading from Sheffield and other places that way by Woodhead through this County unto the City of Chester and to Wrexham and Wales and from Knutsford to Stockport and several other towns adjacent without the help of which bridges the said Rode (as it hath formerly been so for the future), will be stopped, and the lives of travellers with the loss of their goods and cattle will be very much hazarded by reason of sudden floods there. We do therefore pray that an order may be speedily made by this Court for the erecting and now making of two such Cart Bridges ...

A bridge over the Birkin between Tatton and Ashley was similarly described as essential, 'for the prevention of the loss of men's lives, goods and carriages' ... and the following year these were both sanctioned, the Booths Mill Bridge at a cost of £182 at the cost of the county, to be levied and paid to John Holland (of Mobberley) and Richard Porter gent. appointed treasurers, and the Birkin Bridge costing £185, Thomas Ashton Esq. the treasurer to receive payment 'at the sign of the George'. This county rate was yet another tax burden on rate payers but the benefits of these bridges and others in the vicinity must have been enormous at the time, stimulating travel and trade and increasing coach and carriage building for gentlemen. The road through Knutsford from Holmes Chapel to Warrington now the A50, was improved and turnpiked in 1752, a further major boost for travel and trade. The cast iron marker on the west Church wall was put up then.

The River Birkin under Booths Mill Bridge, Mobberley Road

Carting could have been a side line for some farmers. Pimlott took a box to London and Robert Wridgway (or Ridgway) from Ollerton, twice went to Cambridge, once to take some books there and three years later to bring back 924lb. weight of books in 1695 for Sir Francis Leycester.

Road accidents were not uncommon, people were thrown from horses and coaches overturned, injuring the occupants. Sir Thomas Mainwaring went to the funeral of a son of 'Goodman Ridgway's of Ollerton who was killed at Congleton with the overturning of a coach which was laden with timber'.

Leisure

Life was not all work and leisure activities and social life were enjoyed by Knutsford people. The popularity of the many inns all day and every day was not entirely due to travellers and visitors. Smoking pipes of tobacco was more prevalent than we might imagine, socially and in private. Peter Swinton, bookseller, was one who sold (clay) pipes.

Dining with friends at home or in the inns was not only popular with the gentry. Around the turn of the 18th century some of Knutsford's homes had dining rooms for the first time, including those of Peter Leigh, clerk, Joseph Hough, apothecary and William Swinton mercer. Music making was a pleasure for Charles Aldcroft of Minshull Lane who owned six instruments of music and some music books. Joseph Hough, apothecary and Thomas Pollard, innkeeper had virginals so it was not only the gentry like Sir Peter Leycester who enjoyed music. Sir Peter thought so highly of his music collection that

Sir Peter Leycester's English Virginals at Tabley House

he stated in his will that, 'none of my heires or Successors shall alienate, Sell, give or Lease out of the house, any of the Bookes, or Instruments of Musicke, so left by this my last will and Testament, to any Person or Persons whomsoever'. His virginals can still be seen in Tabley House.

Families gathered around fire sides, time and energy permitting, for story telling, playing games, reading aloud and singing. From the turn of the 18th century cheese toasting forks appear in several inventories. Many had pets for pleasure although there are no bird cages in Knutsford's inventories as there are in those of Stockport. Joseph Harrison had 'men and dice' for gaming.

Outdoor pursuits were varied. Fowling guns were owned by a joiner, a dyer, a blacksmith, a tailor and a weaver. Gaming laws were strictly enforced by gentry but wild birds and pigeons were obviously welcome trophies for those who could shoot them. Four men had guns and three had pistols. Three men had muskets which were heavy military weapons, with barrels four feet long used by those in the militia or Trained Bands of unpaid part time soldiers for Bucklow and Macclesfield Hundreds in this area. The men who volunteered for this were excused other duties while training. Musters were a fairly common sight on Knutsford Heath, one in September 1674 went on for four days and Sir Thomas Mainwaring went to musters in June and July in 1680 and in June 1683 and '84.

Some went fishing with fishing rods and William Highfield, husbandman, had an eelspear. Sir Thomas Mainwaring stocked his waters with breeding perch. Thomas Hewitt came to a sad end while fishing. He was Over Knutsford constable in 1686 but was found drowned in a marl pit in a field in Peover, thought to have slipped while fishing.

Knutsford's bowling green was the scene of many games. In the inventories Peter Swinton was the only one who had bowls and a jack but he played games there with others.

Mostly for the gentry, communal activities were horse racing on the Heath and on Over Knutsford Heath. The likes of Joseph Harrison, Thomas Delves and their friends were sure to be there. Sir Thomas Mainwaring enjoyed buck shoots in his park each August and September, one year recording that they shot their eleventh buck but occasionally he went otter hunting. Hunting with hounds whether for fox or hare may have been preferred by Peter Legh with his family and friends as most of his leases from 1678 until at least 1707 have clauses which required his tenants to keep a hound or a hound's whelp every hunting quarter, a few with the proviso 'if required'. He charged the tenants an extra 6s. a year if they wished to be discharged from this clause. Hare coursing with greyhounds was popular and earlier in the century in Rostherne some even had a meet on a Sunday.

Public entertainments drew the crowds, cockfighting in particular in the courtyards and 'backsides' of inns where bets were laid to the displeasure of the authorities. Knutsford did not have a cockpit like Congleton and some other market towns but days when rents were due were seized upon as a time to organise a cock fight, word soon getting about to those interested.

Nether Knutsford fairs in May and October and Over Knutsford fair in June were great attractions and colourful events to punctuate the year. Some of Peter Legh's white coated tenants with their halberds did the bidding of his stewards. Principally the function of fairs was for the sales of cloth, cattle and horses and an opportunity for hiring yearly servants but with the increasing growth of well stocked shops and (slightly) better roads in the 18th century, sales at the fairs declined. Travelling people still came nevertheless to offer entertainments for the crowds.

The bear ward with a dancing bear or one for baiting with dogs, ballad singers with happenings in the country turned into songs like travelling newspapers. They moved into alehouses when wet and after dark. Minstrels and fiddlers encouraged dancing to their tunes, strolling players put on shows. Fortune tellers set up their booths along with other side shows and entertainments. Petty chapmen and pedlars sold toys, trinkets and novelties, chap books, laces and ribbons. People climbed onto boxes to speak about their burning passions whether religious or political, or sell patent medicines or cures. Food and drink were available and more in the town. The fair attracted not only working people of all ages but also the gentry. Thomas Mainwarings's guests and family went to the fair at the end of May, only returning home at night and his daughters brought their three young children to the fair for the day in October, both in 1683. The travellers were allowed to move from one fair to another as long as they did not beg, for if they did they were classed as rogues and vagabonds, liable to be whipped and cast out of the town.

May Day was still celebrated in several ways after the Restoration, despite the suppression of such frivolities during the Civil War and Commonwealth. Medieval country traditions still lingered and were being passed on to succeeding generations. In 1669 a woman of uncertain morals and her husband in Allostock woke on May Day to find 'bran dockes and nettles all strewed about the doore besides great store of other weeds and many a cuckoo flower'. Everyone knew the language of flowers. Midsummer day was another day to make merry.

Guy Fawkes night was celebrated with bonfires, fireworks in the form of gunpowder, as much as a pound of it at a time and three dozen of ale were supplied one year at the cost of the constables in Over Knutsford. The Church bells were rung to celebrate coronations, thanksgiving days and victories over the French during Marlborough's campaigns from 1689 into the 1700's. The constables paid for candles for the ringers for two nights ringing on the occasion of Oudenard in July 1708, 'upon the great victory over France in Flanders'. The year before in 1707 on May 8th, the constables 'spent at a Bonfire upon the account of the Union with Scotland in Ale and Gorse, 1s 6d and for gunpowder, 1s.'.

There were countless other ways in which Knutsford people spent their leisure time but they have not been left to us in writing.

Knutsford has grown and changed but the places and some of the buildings of three hundred years ago are still there, being used and lived in. Those people with all their skills and knowledge, a valuable part of Knutsford's history have gone, but deserve to be remembered. Today our expertise is more sophisticated but family life and relationships and human nature remain the same. The social structure of society has altered completely. National and international events still affect us and we still feel strongly about many of them. Domestic life, travel and communication has improved enormously so we can only be thankful in so many ways that we are fortunate enough to be living today.

References:
- *Inventories, Manor Court records, Parish registers, Parish Church records and refs., Highways and bridges accounts, May Day ref. a libel, CRO QJF 97/2 all in Quarter Sessions, Thos. Mainwaring Diary, Hare coursing in Rostherne, Consistory Court, all in C.R.O. as before.*
- *The Silk Mill, LEACH Joan, Knutsford's Textile History, Kn. Hist. and Arch. Asscn. Journal 1978 Vol. 1,1.*
- *Overseers of the Poor and Constables accounts, Cheethams Library as before.*
- *Cheshire Cheese and Farming in the North West: FOSTER, Charles F., Arley Hall Press 1998.*
- *Mugwoman, QJF 136/3/72. Daniel Gill, Cheshire Marriage bonds. Quakers CRO EFC/2/9*
- *GAUTREY A. J, The Excise men at Knutsford, Spring 1982, Journal of Kn. Hist. and Arch. Asscn.*

The cast iron mile marker on the wall of the Parish Church,
put up on completion of the turnpike road 1752

Index